RAILING AT STORMS: AN UPBEAT CHAT WITH TERRY GILLIAM

It was a Pythonesque moment. Terry Gilliam in Great Britain, me in Pennsylvania, both of us visible over Skype, but neither able to hear the other. We were miming frustration. Quickly, we each scrawled our phone numbers onto pads of paper, like drowning scuba divers. One of us instantly discovered his cell phone did not have international calling. Sorry about that phone bill, Terry.

Gilliam was apparently skeptical about my interview request, and I can't say that I blamed him. "The guy from *Exploitation Nation*" doesn't exactly cause the heart to sing. Through his agent, he requested past material. Three volumes of *Movie Outlaw* later, I received word that "Terry would love to speak with you."

The brief technological glitch was just par for the course. It could have been much worse. A monsoon could have formed in my office. Or one of us could have died. When chaos is part of your daily routine, irritations and catastrophe are all the same.

For more than 25 years, Gilliam had been trying to make a movie

Director Gilliam on the set of The Man Who Killed Don Quixote. *(DP Nicola Pecorini in background.) © Alacran Pictures (et al.) All Rights Reserved.*

inspired by Miguel de Cervantes's epic 17th century novel, *The Ingenious Gentleman Don Quixote of La Mancha*, the comedio-tragic story of a Spanish nobleman who, to the chagrin of his well-off and easily embarrassed family, believes himself to be a knight and the champion of chivalry. Quixote's companion is his peasant neighbor, Sancho Panza, who tags along with the knight as a loyal squire on his own futile quest to keep the Don out of trouble. Cervantes's novel has left many readers spellbound, and multiple unsuccessful attempts have been made over the years to adapt it. Its enduring content has been discussed and debated endlessly. By the 19th century, it was considered social commentary, but nobody could ever tell which side Cervantes was on, which seems fitting for this telling as well. It confounded Orson Welles, who died with his adaptation unfinished (Oja Kodar and Jess Franco's existing edit is far removed from Welles's vision) and, while the musical *Man of La Mancha* is a Broadway staple, the film adaptation with Peter O'Toole and Sophia Loren has as many detractors as supporters.

For Gilliam, the manner in which to adapt also proved to be elusive. He and co-writer Tony Grisoni wrote multiple versions of what would ultimately be called *The Man Who Killed Don Quixote*. In some drafts, Quixote was more a concept; in others, he was a living person met through time travel. In 2000, Gilliam began shooting ,with star Johnny Depp as a marketing exec who falls through time to meet Quixote, played by French actor Jean Rochefort. Depp's then-wife, Vanessa Paradis, was to play Aldonza, transformed into Dulcinea, the delusional object of Quixote's chaste love, Dulcinea. Famously, the production became *the* cautionary tale of Hollywood, as catastrophe struck almost immediately. A freak flash flood in Spain destroyed the landscape and rendered a day's work worthless. Rochefort fell too ill to perform and, by the end of the first week, the production was all but canceled. It would take another month before the investors pulled the plug. Gilliam and company returned home.

Other aborted attempts followed. Finally, *The Man Who Killed Don Quixote* found financing, at a lower price tag, and production mounted again. Almost immediately, tragedy struck again, as John Hurt, Gilliam's latest choice for Quixote, died from pancreatic cancer. Ultimately, and appropriately, Gilliam cast long-time collaborator Jonathan Pryce. But because of interference by infamous producer, Paulo Branca, who continues to dispute the rights held by the production, even this success had its price.

"Jonathan wanted to play this role for 15 years. He kept badgering me. It was getting embarrassing," Gilliam says with a laugh. "Because we're friends, I kept avoiding the situation where he would actually press me to be in the movie. Finally, Michael Palin was doing the part, and then, with all the nonsense with Paulo Branca, Michael said, 'I've had enough of this. I'm out,' and Jonathan was there. And he was the right age, finally. He was everything, and I couldn't help but feel that this was meant to be. I get quite—I wouldn't say *spiritual*— but there is a weird feeling I get when I make films. Literally, the film is doing the work and I'm just holding on for dear life. And when everything's right, the film will get itself made. It really is what happened. Adam [Driver] to me is a brilliant Toby. He's just great, and he and Jonathan become this

FROM THE LAW OFFICE OF HAPPY CLOUD MEDIA LLC:

EXPLOITATION NATION

DOWN THE RABBIT HOLE	2
RAILING AT STORMS: AN UPBEAT CHAT WITH TERRY GILLIAM	3
TERRY GILLIAM'S "THE MAN WHO KILLED DON QUIXOTE"	16
THE DEFECTIVE DETECTIVE: THE NEXT WINDMILL	22
SPEAKING FOR THE DEFENSE...	25
SAM RAIMI'S LOST MASTERPIECE, CRIMEWAVE	26
GODZILLA '98	32
I LOVE A GOOD BOMB	44
MOONRAKER	56
SHOCK TREATMENT: WHEN A SEQUEL IS SUPERIOR TO WHAT CAME BEFORE	58
TAKE TWO: SHOCK TREATMENT	63
THE FAN	64
GREASE 2 DESERVES ANOTHER LOOK	67
A HIGHLY OPINIONATED TREATISE AND PAINFUL DEFENSE OF JESS FRANCO'S THE PERVERSE COLLECTION	72
THE CORRUPT ONES	80
1941	83
AN ERNEST ATTEMPT AT ENTERTAINMENT: IN DEFENSE OF ERNEST GOES TO JAIL AND JIM VARNEY	84
SURVIVAL OF THE DEAD	94
TO BE PERFECTLY HONEST, THIS SECTION IS REALLY JUST ONE BIG AD	96
I REFUSE TO DEFEND THE SPLATTER MOVIE	98
KEVIN COSTNER	102
EIGHT FISTS OF "THE DRAGON"	103
BRINGING THE CONVENT (BACK) TO THE SCREEN	112
WHAT OUR FRIENDS ARE UP TO	122
I'D BUY THAT FOR A DOLLAR!	125

Exploitation Nation is published periodically by Happy Cloud Media, LLC, (Amy Lynn Best and Mike Watt, PO Box 1540, McMurray, PA 15317). Exploitation Nation Issue #8 (ISBN 978-1-951036-18-8) is copyright 2020 by Happy Cloud Media LLC. All rights reserved. All featured articles and illustrations are copyright 2020 by their respective writers and artists. Reproductions of any material in whole or in part without its creator's written permission is strictly forbidden. Exploitation Nation accepts no responsibility for unsolicited manuscripts, DVDs, stills, art, or any other materials. Contributions are accepted on an invitational basis only. **Visit Us At Facebook.Com/ExploitationNation and www.happycloudpublishing.com**

Exploitation Nation: Alternate Reality
is published by Happy Cloud Media, LLC
Vol. 1, No. 8 © 2020

Amy Lynn Best:
Publisher
Mike Watt:
Editor
Carolyn Haushalter:
Asst. Editor
Ally Melling & Carol Melling:
Copy Editors

Contributors:
**Amy Lynn Best
Dr. Rhonda Baughman
Justin Channell
Pete Chiarella
Nick Clement
Corey Danna
Mike Haushalter
Jason Lane
Scooter McCrae
Andrew J. Rauch
Terry Thome
Nick Thomson
Doug Waltz**

Cover Illustration, Logo & Layout
Ryan Hose

Special Thanks to:
**Bailey Creamer
Terry Gilliam
Nick Pourgourides
Stefan Ruf
Tom Savini
Thomas Edward Seymour
John Walter Szpunar**

All photographic and artistic content copyright the original holders and is included here for promotional purposes only. No rights are implicit or implied.

DOWN THE RABBIT HOLE

"Every movie is somebody's favorite."

That's an unofficial motto I've tried to keep in mind my entire career. It's not easy. Snark is fun and fun to write, and—boy, howdy—are there some awful movies out there! But on the other hand, negativity is effortless. It's easier to tear something down than to stand your ground and say, "I love this, and I don't care who knows it."

This issue is the "Defend a Film" issue, and it was pitched by ExNat's Jason Lane. His directive was to pick a movie not generally well-regarded by the general public and defend it. The only caveat was that the movie was never intended to be bad. No Ed Wood rip-offs, no cult cheapies, no so-bad-it's-good stuff. Something you feel personally is unfairly maligned. There are some wonderfully odd choices here, as you'll see, and it all proves the declaration above.

Central in this issue is an interview with someone whose films and comedy were essential to many of us. Terry Gilliam, who rose to infamy with his animated segments in Monty Python's Flying Circus, and became one of the most whimsical and satirical directors of our time, agreed to sit down with me (after some convincing from my Movie Outlaw collection—true story!) for a marvelous conversation in 2019, just as The Man Who Killed Don Quixote received its limited run in the United States.

Now, a short word about our sister publication, Grindhouse Purgatory. The latest issue, #15, is on sale now and is a tribute to our late friend, Sid Haig. Best known as "Captain Spaulding" in Rob Zombie's Devils Rejects films, Haig was a veteran of exploitation films, big-budget adventures, and more TV guest appearances than any two other actors combined. He was a wonderful man, a good friend to so many of us, and we were gutted by his passing. GP pays a respectable tribute to the man, and Haig fans of any stripe should check it out.

Oh, as far as the "Favor Repaid" section, you guys know me. If I don't like something, I'd just as soon not review it than dance around it. "Well, the image was usually in focus and the acting seems to be consensual...." I don't do that, and I don't like to trash something. So, if something appears here, you know we're 100 percent behind it. Friends are great, and we'll always support our friends. Fortunately, our friends are all immensely talented motherfu— *ahem.*

Finally, with one more bit of pride, I was humbled to read John Walter Szpunar's review of Exploitation Nation in the newly released Deep Red #2, in which he called our little publication "essential reading." For those of you unfamiliar, Deep Red is the gorgeous relaunch of the late Chas Balun's seminal 'zine. Balun was a critical influence on my early career as well as those of many of my peers, so ExNat's mention in the magazine that bears his name was a marvelous thing to read. I dare say it lends us a certain degree of respectability that I am sure we can easily undercut in future issues.

Issue #9 is in the works as you read this. We have every intention to stay as essential as possible. Thanks for reading!

—*Mike Watt, 2020*

fantastic double act. That wouldn't have happened if events hadn't conspired to get both of them in the movie when they did."

For Gilliam, The Man Who Killed Don Quixote was as much a vendetta as it was a dream project. The tragedy of the ill-fated 2000 production was captured in the documentary, Lost in La Mancha. In it is an image, both haunting and hysterical, of Gilliam standing in the midst of the storm that altered his background (and much of Spain), railing primally at the wind and the rain. And though the film he completed in 2015 is far removed from its original intention, it came with its own terrible storm.

I ask him if he is tired yet of talking about Quixote. "Yes, I'm getting tired of talking about it, but that doesn't matter [laughs]. Anything to keep the fucker alive as far as I'm concerned."

Anyone who's ever seen a documentary about Terry or watched an interview with him knows his amused and sardonic giggle that often hides irritation and is usually rife with fatalism, borne from an innate ability to recognize the cruel jokes lurking within every situation. Twenty-five years is a long time to live with a film. Time, of course, is everyone's enemy, and it was time that altered the premise of Quixote. Gone is the time travel and the marketing exec and, ; in its place is a commercial director whose previous art film adapted Quixote to the detriment of his nonprofessional actors. Director Toby is forced to encounter his past, unable to reconcile a sense of responsibility for his actions, unaware that his dream was toxic. It's a heady stake through the normal whimsy of a Gilliam film. There's a dark and unfamiliar idea here: that dreams can be harmful.

Gilliam has said in the past that all of his films are autobiographical to a degree. The tones of his films correspond to how he feels at that particular stage of life. This Quixote isn't the film Gilliam set out to make 25 years ago because he isn't the same man he was then. "Correct," he tells me. "Trying to stick to the same idea, the same shit, the same take on the subject matter after 30 years, is just ridiculous. That's just stupid. For me, it was trying to keep the thing alive and fresh over each iteration. That's what that was about. And in the end, I think it's a better film than what we set out to make.

"At the beginning, my concern was telling a tale for a modern audience. The 17th century Quixote

A still from "Lost in La Mancha", which chronicled the first disastrous attempt to make "Don Quixote" with Johnny Depp. © IFC Films. All Rights Reserved.

is talking about a 12th century world. The only way to do this would be to get a modern guy in there to walk us through it. It was partly that, but it was also my attack on people who compromise their art by moving into commercials, where the money is good and the work is easy and the talent is betrayed. Even when I've made commercials, I've felt the same way. Whatever little skill or talent I've got is being betrayed just to keep my fingers in some kind of work. That's the only reason I'd take commercials, to keep occupied when everything else is collapsing around me."

So, the commercial director, in this case, is responsible for heartbreak. "Correct," he says again.

"It's an homage to Dr. Frankenstein and his work."

To that end, Gilliam is satisfied that he's finally telling the *right* story. This incarnation is the best way to bring Don Quixote, the man and the concept, into our very troubled modern world. The previous script wouldn't be right today. "There's nothing [from the previous versions] I miss at all. I'm really pleased with it as it is now. I really felt that everything conspired to make this—this was a film that was trying to make itself. I always have this belief that I'm just the hand that writes. The film is trying to come into existence. I'm just trying to help it along. That's how this one felt. Everything about this [production] I feel was better. The cast was better. It was funnier—everything was much better than what we'd started out to do."

Surprisingly, *The Man Who Killed Don Quixote* is more visually restrained than what you might otherwise expect from a Gilliam movie. Even his famed preference for super wide-angle lenses takes a backseat to the story, and longer takes allow things to unfold more gracefully. In many ways, it's his most *introspective* film since *Tideland*, which goes a long way to explain the tone. "I was definitely trying to keep me, the director, out of this. I was trying to make a film—I was using lenses that weren't as wide, I wasn't doing extreme angles, I wasn't doing *any* of that. I was just trying to let the characters live out their lives without me getting in the way. I'm not hiding behind clever visual tricks. I'm really just saying what I wanted to say without working to overimpress the audience with how fucking clever

I am [laughs]."

It's not just that the film has a veneer of sadness. It's far less triumphant than you'd expect a 25-year journey to be; it's rather more resigned, standing before the audience, arms spread, saying, "Well? I'm here." The journey was so personal, the end result reflects that. It's less interested in pleasing you than it is exhausted and expecting you to take it as it is., alt's a movie about madness and disaster in a very matter-of-fact, down-to-earth, actual-size way. It's almost alarming to think that perhaps Gilliam has lost some of his whimsy.

"I'm kind of bored with movies in a strange way," he says early in the conversation, and even now he's indicating that this is a temporary malaise born of exhaustion. "I went to see—and this is not a criticism of Guillermo del Toro's *Shape of Water*—Guillermo is a friend, and I think he's a great film director. But I was watching it when we were in the final stages of editing *Quixote*, and we'd gotten *Quixote* to the point where I was quite happy with it. I went to *Shape of Water* because I'm always amazed to watch Guillermo's skill at work, and I came out kind of 'well, that's a movie,' and I thought *Quixote* was something about reality. It's a very strange thing, but there's a sense that I didn't want the 'movieness' to get in the way of what we were doing. I just wanted to be grounded in what appeared to be reality without any flourishes from the director. As we were shooting it, to me, each day's work was about the actors. I wasn't sure if I knew what I was doing, but I was definitely sure about what the actors were doing. I just wanted to record it, that's all."

This current bout of melancholia is nothing new for Gilliam, as he himself has recounted in past interviews, but the culmination of the past quarter century—the fights, the losses, the grief—you can hear a lot of that in his voice. "My only sense of joy is in the mystery of life and its things, how it all works."

The universe has been kicking a lot of us around, and when you look at the Gilliam output of the last two decades, you see a distinct pattern. *Fear and Loathing in Las Vegas* was not the box office success of 1998, but Gilliam had a distinct glee in his eye when he'd said he hoped it was received with outrage. He welcomed all comers and the reviews did come in, reviling the adaptation of Hunter S. Thompson's surreal satire. Riding that wave of energy, Terry set out to make *The Man Who Killed Don Quixote*, finally and for the first time.

Watch *Lost in La Mancha* to see the man scream back at a storm.

While the storm left behind a wreckage, Rochefort's illness did more so. With the movie cancelled, Gilliam quickly sought new work. He made a veritable deal with the devil and signed with the odious Weinstein brothers to make *The Brothers Grimm*. With stars Heath Ledger and Matt Damon, this should have been a walk in the park, with a script putting Wilhelm and Jacob Grimm in the fantastical center of their darker stories. But the Weinsteins are gangsters at heart—it's nothing shocking or libelous to say, they themselves have admitted it!—and they like a good fight. And if there isn't one, they'll start one. Gilliam has a reputation too. The brothers Weinstein decided that their best tactic would be one of total control. After all, they were the heroes—they'd stepped in at the last minute to "rescue" the film after MGM dropped it from its schedule. Dimension Films was going to gamble on the most expensive film they'd ever made, and they wanted to make damned sure it was a Dimension film, not a goddamned Gilliam one.

Every aspect of the film was micromanaged, down to a prosthetic nose bump Damon was to wear as Will. Damon wasn't even Gilliam's first choice, but the Weinstein brothers weren't convinced of Johnny Depp's star appeal (*Pirates of the Caribbean* would come out during *Grimm*'s production). Every decision was to be run by the even grimmer brothers and every decision was a fight. In this instance, Gilliam couldn't thrive in the chaos.

"I don't know if it's chaos. It's the breaking down of order that I seem to thrive in," he says. "There's something about when things go wrong; it focuses my priorities. Your adrenaline starts working and you no longer have the space or time to do other things. Because I'm always doing and I'm always questioning why I'm doing something. And when catastrophe occurs, you're then just working on instinct. It brings out, time and again, maybe the best of whatever talent I've got. Because, if I'm in a bad corner, I'm pretty good at fighting my way out.

It's how I get into those corners that's the problem."

Except in this case. "[A situation] like the Weinsteins is one moment when I didn't benefit or come up to the plate in the way I'd done on other things. The Weinsteins slowly dredged the enthusiasm out of me. It's the first time and the only time [someone] took the joy of filmmaking out of me. It's just being caught in a situation that you know you shouldn't have gotten into, but it was the only way to salvage the film. And then it was as bad as you thought it would be. The other instances with catastrophes were surprises, they weren't expected, so you've still got a little bit of 'oomph' in you. With the Weinsteins, it was more like Chinese water torture—*drip, drip, drip*. It got to the point where I didn't even want to go in to work, even with my friends— Matt and Heath and the members of the crew who were worth hanging around with—because the whole process was destroyed. It's the one film where I feel I wasn't up to scratch. I feel I could have made a much better film had I had more energy, more willingness to keep the fight going. In

With Jonathan Price. © Alacran Pictures (et al.) All Rights Reserved.

all the other instances, when events crashed and everything is thrown into the air, it's chaos, but we heard 'how do we fix it?' With the Weinsteins, it was never like that. It was always 'what can we do next to try and limit, to try to control, to try to restrict—anything?' It just wore me down, and it's the one film I find difficult to watch because I know I just didn't do as good a job as I should have."

But the Weinsteins didn't even particularly care about the finished film. Once they'd started the fight, that was all they were interested in. "Right. It was about them controlling. They had to be in control, and I was resisting it. But it wasn't that I was just pushing them aside and doing something extraordinary instead. I was just resisting. That's not good. I don't work well that way. I work better when I have a real punch-up I can get involved in."

Tensions got so bad that production was shut down for two weeks, with neither set of antagonists speaking with each other. Gilliam has his detractors, certainly, but even Martin Scorsese has echoed the sentiment (as he said during the production of *Gangs of New York*): The Weinsteins suck the joy out of filmmaking.

It seems that Gilliam could rage against the storm, but a pair of assholes couldn't be judged. I use the word specifically and Gilliam laughs. "There is that [laughs]. There is something fundamental with—I can think of another word one uses for 'assholes.' I've never been in that situation when I was shooting a movie—two people trying to control me. I don't work well under control. And that's it. If two people had said 'do that' and then pushed me over a cliff, I can fly for short periods of time before I hit the ground. I think

that's it. It's not even fighting *order*, it's fighting *control*. Order is a thing I fight, but I respect order. I just don't want to be limited by order all of the time. I like the surprise of chaos and disorder, because things come out of those. It's like Kali, the Hindu goddess of destruction and creation. And I like that kind of volcanic world."

The fight didn't stop when the cameras did. Post-production arguments grew so prolonged that Gilliam was able to shoot *Tideland* in the interim. Of this period, Gilliam has said that *Tideland* was the oasis. Creatively free, beholden to no particular studio, the storm was briefly forgotten.

There was a short period of controversy during *Tideland*'s brief release. *Tideland*, an adaptation of Mitch Cullin's novel, tells the story of a 12-year-old girl, Jeliza-Rose, who lives with the corpse of her drug-addicted father (Jeff Bridges). Gilliam shows her family life without judgment, cooking up fixes for her parents, the slowly rotting corpse of the father, and the odd and disenfranchised characters around her. He does this without judgment, and some audiences were appalled.

Critics, however, particularly Gilliam's directing peers, had nothing but praise for the intensely odd and emotionally generous movie. Around this time, there was talk about Gilliam's penchant for "tilting at the windmills of the establishment," referring to his theme of "madness being the only way of escaping the harsh reality." These would echo throughout history in any discussion of Gilliam's work.

Though I'm hesitant to use the phrase (again), the most "Gilliamesque" film to emerge from this period would be his next, *The Imaginarium of Doctor Parnassus*. Leaving *The Brothers Grimm* behind him, Gilliam reteamed with Heath Ledger, fresh off filming *The Dark Knight* and about to wow the world as the Joker. The script would see a long-awaited reunion with Gilliam's past writing partner, Charles McKeown, and would easily fit alongside *The Adventures of Baron Munchausen* in terms of mad visuals and story. The title character is a semi-holy man in a ramshackle wagon that doubles as a traveling stage for his anachronistic performers. Ledger's character provides the darker nature. Tony has a number of secrets he isn't about to share with Parnassus or the rest of his traveling theater troupe. But at the heart of Parnassus's show is a deal with the devil and a "magic mirror." Pass through and you enter Parnassus's world, your imagination shows your heart's desire, but Mr. Nick shows you something even more tempting….

About two-thirds of the way through production, Ledger suffered an accidental overdose of prescription medicine and died. All that remained to shoot were the three sequences in which Tony himself passes through the mirror and parts of his secrets are revealed. If there was any benefit to Ledger's passing when he did, it was here. Ledger's friends—Johnny Depp, Jude Law, and Colin Farrell—stepped forward to play alternate versions of Tony. Thematically, it worked brilliantly—to the point where it might have worked intentionally, as if Ledger hadn't passed but had yielded his time to his friends. If there is any sense to the universe, it might be grudgingly found there.

"For me, one of the great moments happens when Heath goes through the mirror and it's Johnny on the other side, for the first change," Gilliam says. "People didn't recognize Johnny for maybe the first 10 or 15 seconds of that scene, maybe even longer. They just accepted that it was Heath, only maybe under different makeup. That's extraordinary. Because for me, when that mask comes off, it's Johnny, but not so for a lot of people in the audience. There's something about suspending your disbelief when you go into the cinema. I guess this is what is happening."

But as perfect as the solution to the problem was, there remained the profound absence of the friend. "What bothers me about *Parnassus* is that I'll never get to see the film Heath and I set out to make, and that's sad. But what came out of Heath's exit is absolutely extraordinary, as far as I was concerned. It was also something as simple as the love for another human being. Johnny, Colin, Jude all loved Heath. They came in and did it for nothing. There's something about that—when you're lucky enough to work with really special people, whether it would be Heath, who was an extraordinary person, or Robin [Williams]. It's weird how the forces of life and death and everything conspire to help when there is a kind of purity about what one is doing."

Gilliam's protagonists generally walk the fine line between reality and fantasy, order and chaos, madness and sanity. Madness sometimes takes the form of plausible deniability—is James Cole (Bruce Willis) a genuine time traveler or a genuine schizophrenic? Is Raoul Duke (Depp) really going crashing through the American Dream or are the drugs altering the world around him? For folks like Sam Lowry in *Brazil* and Jeliza-Rose, elaborate fantasy provides the escape hatch from indifferent reality. Sometimes, the madness and the reality have little to do with each other. Perry (Robin Williams) is definitely suffering from a detached personality, but that doesn't mean the concept of the Holy Grail is false. Reality is sometimes the enemy, but Gilliam insists that fantasy and imagination are not things to hold holy either.

"I don't glorify fantasy. I don't glorify *anything* in that sense," he tells me. "I find that it's all a big mystery and either you go with the flow or you fight it. Things just work out. It's a terrible way to go through life, because it's not who I was when I began. I didn't know where I was going, but I was going there with a lot of energy. Now, with age, I kind of float through the whole thing. I'm astonished that I'm still alive and I pretty much get away with murder. That's not bad for a criminal's career. [But] imagination in that sense is about freedom—individual freedom, not necessarily the idea of everyone being free [laughs]. I don't like to think of imagination—as some people would like to think—as always a positive thing. It's not such a positive thing. It just is what it is. Hitler was a very imaginative chap but certainly not one of my favorite people. Imagination is a double- or multiple-edged sword, so it can be anything. I'm really about personal freedom. Everyone being free is just anarchy and chaos, and you can't live in a world like that. It's a terrible, sort of fascistic way of looking at things. 'Only the proper people can be free, but not everybody' [laughs]."

So, who shouldn't be free? "I don't know. I don't want to be the person making that decision in that regard [laughs]. There's a line in *Parnassus*—when Heath and Andrew

Gilliam, Adam Driver, Price, and company in Spain.
© *Alacran Pictures (et al.) All Rights Reserved.*

[Garfield] are talking at night, [saying] Parnassus doesn't want control. He wants the world to control itself. It's kind of like nature makes the choices for us—who gets eaten and who doesn't. I don't want to be the guy making those choices. I'm very selfish. I'm looking after my freedom and that of those I love."

Which is about an honest an answer as anyone could have asked for.

Gilliam moved from the United States to Great Britain in 1967, a period he has referred to as "the worst" of American history. The Vietnam War was all the rage, and Nixon was pulling his dirty tricks. Gilliam left his homeland and set his eye on commercial work in the U.K., which set him on the path to *Monty Python's Flying Circus* and an enduring friendship with five other funny, disenfranchised individuals. From there, he raged against storms and windmills and producers.

The ultimate incarnation of *The Man Who Killed Don Quixote* was planned down to the last detail. I ask Gilliam if there were any surprises once the ball was finally, and unstoppably, rolling. "Maybe the last thing…when we were rehearsing with Jonathan and Adam and Joana and we're just going through reading the script, Adam is doing his last lines when he's become Quixote, 'blah blah blah.' So, I asked him, 'Could you try doing it in a voice more similar to Jonathan's?' And as Adam was reading it, Jonathan suddenly joined in! Two voices floating together, that was my great moment. I felt we'd got the ending. It was so good when you hear that Jonathan is still alive, if only in an aural form. You can't kill the idea that Quixote really cannot die, no matter how many people kill him along the way."

But make no mistake, Quixote still has his enemies. Even with the film completed, the storm had not yet ended. Desperate to find the rest of the budget in 2016, Gilliam made an admitted deal with *a* devil, Portuguese producer Paolo Branca. Branca, who'd helped finance *Cosmopolis* (2012) for David Cronenberg, was deeply distrusted by many around Gilliam, and indeed, his inclusion forced Amazon to back out of a key distribution deal, but the director felt he had little choice. Immediately, Branca demanded full creative control and reduced the budget so significantly that, as mentioned, Michael Palin fled the production. Unwilling to be controlled again, Gilliam fought back against Branca, who ultimately never delivered on the promised funds and suspended the production. Gilliam found new producers and kept working, but Branca insisted he held the necessary rights to the film and has actively fought to keep the film from distribution. A number of European courts have upheld Branca's position, leading to additional court battles that have not yet, as of this writing, been settled.

"What is depressing for me is that *Quixote* was supposed to be a commercial success, and it has not been. And it has not been because Paulo Branco has done his best to frighten away distributors. There is no ordinary way of releasing the movie. It's all been done backwards. It had to be done piecemeal, picking up whatever territories one could, opening the film and hoping there's something there that will help us get to the next stage. It's worked that way because we've had to go with small distributors, who really don't have a lot of money right now to spend. Netflix is wiping out a lot, so they don't have money. They're counting on my or Adam's reputation to bring people in. It's not enough. We do well in big cities but nowhere else. To be a commercial success, you have to hit all the little Podunk towns out there. You've got to reach a large number of people. Cities are not sufficient when you've got a film like this. That's been the most depressing thing of having finished the film, being proud of it, showing it to enough people to know whether the film is working or not. I'd

© *Alacran Pictures (et al.) All Rights Reserved.*

showed it to a *lot* of people—friends, friends of friends, people I have no idea who they are—but I know when something is working. And then I realize it's not making its money back."

The way films are made these days is becoming a mystery for many veteran filmmakers. Look at the outrage sparked by Martin Scorsese's comment than the Marvel films are 'not cinema.' Gilliam was embroiled in a similar controversy, and his humor—and inevitable doubling down—caused more controversy, but controversy is nothing new. When you get down to it, neither Gilliam nor Scorsese is taking this contrary stance to denigrate the filmmakers working with Marvel, but are, in very specific ways, lamenting that the days of films going straight to big-screen theaters are over. We're a bingeing world now, a streaming world. "It's a strange world now," he says. "You work for Netflix—now we all know about *Roma* [the 2018 film written and directed by Alfonso Cuarón], but would we have known about *Roma* had Netflix not been desperate to win an Academy Award and were willing to spend a fortune to do so? We wouldn't. You do something with Netflix and you don't even know how many people have seen the film.

"Talking about me as a filmmaker, I want to know numbers, I want to know *who* is seeing it, who is appreciating it. With Netflix, you don't get any of that information, which is very—I don't know what it means for the future. But I do know it's going to make things very different. I think the fact that's been so successful—in many ways, I think Netflix is fantastic. It's provided so much work for so many writers, directors, actors—and not necessarily needing a bunch of big stars or things. Some of the work has been better than anything I've seen on the big screen in a couple of years. So, it's not a bad thing; it's just changing things in a way I'm not sure I'm going to be happy with in the near future. I like people going into a big black room with a big screen, lots of people watching and experiencing something together. And I think that's something that's going away, except if it's *The Avengers* or *Star Wars*. But that means you have to create a world and continually find ways of replicating that world, keeping it alive with new creatures in it. And once I've created a world, that's it for me. I like to move on to the next one."

As "bored" about filmmaking as Gilliam professes to be, he also admits that he's "desperate" to work again. The problem is, with *Quixote* still in flux and the returns not being great, there is "nothing on my plate," he says. "I've got *The Defective Detective*, which I still think is a good script. I think that would be a fun one to do, because it would be like nothing else out there. It's not a cheap film. My films rely on budgets. If I could spend over $100 million, I might have a better chance of making *The Defective Detective*. I think I only need $70 million. I'm not sure if it's going to ever be made because the script has been sitting around for quite a while. And I've not been able to work out a way of doing it cheaper that I know I can get the money for. I don't see any reason that it's worth doing for over $100 million. I just don't think so. I would probably not be able to say some of the things I want to say in that film for that kind of budget. So, there's always this fine line of having enough money to make the kind of films I want to make, with the kind of visual sense to it and expanse to it. But also, the ideas—you throw too many of the 'wrong kind' of ideas, people run away from that. My stuff is never going to be the kind of 'slam-bang-crash' wonderful adventure with a few moments of insight into humanity [groans]. So, I have nothing to do but wait for the world to end. I'm sort of an Armageddonist myself, but for different reasons. I don't want to end up on the cloud with Jesus. I want the whole thing to be finished with. And the only way for that to happen for me is to die, and then my world disappears. So, I think it's down to individual Armageddons for all of us [laughs].

"Just talking like this, I don't know if it's invigorated me or just tested me more. There's a fine line one treads with these things. A friend of mine [...] had watched *Quixote* three times already. She just got more and more lost in it in a good way, just liking it more and more. And it's a weird thing—I've seen a lot of audiences watching it, and I keep telling people 'you ought to watch it a second time.' If it's too much to process the first time or you don't know what's going on, watch it again. I guarantee it's a better film the second time. It reminds me of a French journalist I was promoting. He was from the south of France and had come out to Paris after many years, we had a long talk and he said [affecting a voice], 'I knew I was going to interview you and before we talked, I watched *Tideland* a second time.' He said the first time he'd seen it, he hated it. He was disgusted by it. He thought it was a piece of shit. And then, when he watched it the second time, he said, 'I think it's the best thing you've ever made, Terry' [laughs]. That's what I like. The fact that there are things that might not have been necessarily apparent the first time. If I can get people to come a second time or a third time, they might find out what the movie is really about!"

Which brings us to today, a period an increasing number of people daily think of as "the worst period," but this time the U.K. is in as much turmoil as the United States. On one shore, we have a corrupt president, on the other Brexit, as controlled by a corrupt prime minister. Like the rest of us, Gilliam is at a loss for what to do. Like any storm, these political forces are things that will not respond to sheer will. He fears the politicians who believe in the Rapture, those in lock-step with religious lunatics who wish to see the end of the world for no other reason than to relish in the suffering of their "enemies." They are, seemingly, in control of our overlords. And while the present is certainly slouching toward Armageddon, the future looks hazier than ever. But is that a bad thing?

"I've always thought that death and the end of things is fascinating. And there's nothing we can do to stop it, ultimately," he says. "Well, I know something will stop us if we can't stop ourselves. We are very good at rebuilding. I think the human race is very good at destroying and then rebuilding. But we live on this little planet here and if we push it too far, there won't be any room left for us I don't think. Maybe we won't destroy it, but we won't make it the nice place it once was."

Since it's increasingly difficult to find joy in a world filled with so much intentional
and avoidable turmoil, where does Gilliam find joy? "I have a two-and-a-half year-old
granddaughter. That little girl makes me laugh, makes me feel young, and makes me feel joyous. And then she wears me out because I don't have the stamina for the kind of long-time joy that I used to have [laughs]. That's literally about it. I do have—I don't know if it's joy, but I do find contentment looking at trees, looking

The Giants bedeviling Quixote. (Javier Iglesias, Manuel Monzón, Ferran Gadea.) © Alacran Films (et al). All Rights Reserved.

at leaves and the sun through them, just looking at the natural world and the magic of it, because it's going to be in trouble pretty soon…. That's why I ended *Quixote* with a happy ending," he says, indicating the inevitable conclusion where, as in *Brazil*, madness prevails. "Let them go out smiling for once. It has the happiest, most romantic ending of any of my plans. These are the things that come out of rehearsals and playing around. It wasn't even written that way in the final script. But you don't always get to do what you'd planned to do."

In *Jabberwocky*, Michael Palin's hapless hero slays the monster and wins the hand of the princess, but it's a peasant woman whom he loves, and now he can never be with her. He wins without getting anything he wants. It's the most Gilliamesque ending of any of his films. "To me, that's a wonderful ending. Nobody gets what they want at the end. I think that's a good way to go through life, just being aware of the likelihood of that and still keep living! Maybe that's all I've got to say to the world. I think the worst thing to happen is to succeed in the way you'd been dreaming of succeeding. It's bound to be bad somehow. It's better to not succeed and to dream that success would be better. I don't know."

Which reminds me of the difference between the Jewish faith and that of Christians: For the Christian, everything is serious, but not hopeless. For the Jew, everything is hopeless, but not serious. I mention this to Terry, who roars with laughter. To make one of the funniest men alive laugh is no small feat. "That's why I've always loved the Jewish sense of humor," he says. "For me, it's always been the cosmic form of humor. It deals with the big ideas, the big thoughts, and doesn't guarantee happiness like we were told as young Americans. It goes on."

FROM THE WINDMILLS OF HIS MIND: TERRY GILLIAM'S THE MAN WHO KILLED DON QUIXOTE

"...and now, after more than 25 years in the making...and unmaking..."

Tobias Grummett (Adam Driver) is a successful American filmmaker. We know this because he's directing a commercial for an energy company, on location in Spain, with massive props necessary to his vision of relating fossil fuels to the great nobleman, Don Quixote de la Mancha. Why would any company put up the money for this if they didn't believe in Toby's vision?

Toby is surrounded by sycophants constantly feeding his ego. While the Boss (Stellan Skarsgård) is a towering menace, the boss's wife (Olga Kurylenko) invites Toby into her bed. As far as the Boss and his company are concerned, Toby is the most important person in Spain.

For whatever reason, everyone believes in Toby except for Toby. The Great Director can't help but believe he's fallen into mediocrity, some malaise of creativity, and his fears are compounded when he stumbles across a gypsy (an enigmatically menacing Óscar Jaenada) selling, among other movies, a DVD of his very first film, *The Man Who Killed Don Quixote*, a black-and-white art movie about Cervantes's very same mad knight.

Fleeing the production, Toby borrows a crewmember's motorcycle and drives into the village. There another discovery awaits him: Javier Sanchez (Jonathan Pryce), the old shoemaker he'd hired to play Don Quixote, remains trapped

in the part—both psychologically and literally, as he is held inside a ramshackle caravan, seemingly doomed to recite his narration behind Toby's film forever. Disaster strikes almost immediately. The caravan burns down, the actor is freed, and Toby, again, flees responsibility.

Things begin to break down further for Toby. The Boss is suspicious, the police want to question him about the fire. Through circumstance, Toby finds himself lost, his only companion the decrepit actor who believes wholeheartedly that he is the one and only undying Don Quixote, the last knight and spokesman for chivalry. Naturally, Quixote needs a Sancho Panza, and thus Toby fulfills this role—reluctantly, resentfully.

This is a madness Toby doesn't want to deal with but can possibly manipulate. However, his connection to the production is not yet severed. The company's investor, Alexei Miiskina (Jordi Mollà), is an oligarch and warlord and has another surprise in store: His mistress is none other than Angelica (Joana Ribeiro), the teenaged barmaid Toby cast in his film as Quixote's Dulcinea. Bewitched by the taste of acting, Angelica chased a dream of fame that led her into the arms of this dangerous man.

With reality becoming as surreal and tenuous as the film worlds he created, Toby is beset on all sides by situations he cannot control and men and women he cannot direct, and his only talents are utterly useless when faced by the chaos around him.

Terry Gilliam has been trying to make a film about Don Quixote since 1989, and the various attempts went through multiple permutations, from straight adaptation to loose inspiration. The version he set out to make in 2000 involved a marketing executive named Toby Grisoni (an inside joke between Gilliam and co-writer Tony Grisoni), who is sent back in time to encounter a very real Quixote. This version, mixing in elements from Mark Twain's *A Connecticut Yankee in King Arthur's Court* (another adaptation Gilliam had worked to bring to screen at more than one point), was to star Johnny Depp as Toby and French actor Jean Rochefort as Quixote. The troubled production got almost as far as a week into shooting before it was shut down by, among other things, military aircraft drills ruining takes, Rochefort becoming too ill to shoot by the fifth day, and a flash flood that destroyed equipment and altered the landscape so completely that matching shots would have been impossible. The weather arrived on day two. By the end of the week, Gilliam had no lead, was about to lose his Hollywood star, and had no usable footage to salvage. This tragedy was relayed in detail in the excellent documentary *Lost in La Mancha* (2002, directed by Keith Fulton and Louis Pepe).

Over successive years, Gilliam mounted two more aborted attempts to revive *Quixote*. As each attempt fell through, other high-profile projects also collapsed around him— his versions of Neil Gaiman's *Good Omens* and Alan Moore's *Watchmen*, as well as his constantly canceled *The Defective Detective* (at one point to star Nicholas Cage). Even the films he did manage to make were not without their catastrophes. Midway through production of *The Imaginarium of*

Doctor Parnassus, his star and close friend Heath Ledger died. Prior to that, the Weinstein brothers seemed to make torture part of their production regimen on *The Brothers Grimm*, resulting in a film satisfying no one. His most personal success, the surreal coming-of-age story *Tideland*, was relatively problem-free during production but arrived with little marketing and critics outraged by the delicate subject matter.

Between 2000 and 2016's final relaunch of *Quixote*, Terry Gilliam became a different man and, therefore, inevitably made a very different film. While the death of actor John Hurt almost killed the project again (although at one point, fellow former-Python Michael Palin was to assume his place in the saddle), Gilliam found his leads in suddenly-hot-thanks-to-*Star Wars* Adam Driver and long-time collaborator Jonathan Pryce, finally old enough to take on the role of the aged nobleman.

Gone were the time travel elements (which didn't really seem to address how Quixote could be alive in the real world). The fancy no longer felt appropriate in a post-9/11 world. The world had become progressively more difficult to live in, and the newer drafts of *The Man Who Killed Don Quixote* reflected that. Rather than a jaded marketing exec, Gilliam and Grisoni eliminated the middleman and made the (for all intents and purposes) directorial head of production the main character. This provided Gilliam a path through the story: a man unaffected by the world around him confronting the people he left behind once his film was done, the people his "vision" irreparably altered.

There is a conceit to this ultimate version of *The Man Who Killed Don Quixote* that is unique even to Gilliam's body of work. While anti-Hollywood Hollywood movies are favorite subjects of big- and small-budget movies alike, the others of this subgenre tend to place the blame on the system and then the people who are crushed within the business' machinery. Bad behavior is cultivated because of the characters' *need* for fame. *Sunset Boulevard*, *The Player*, *The Oscar*, *What Just Happened?*—these are anti-Hollywood morality stories where Hollywood prevails at the end because you can't fight the system, you can't fight the seduction, and it will chew up everyone who comes chasing their dreams.

The Man Who Killed Don Quixote lays the blame on the filmmaker alone. Toby mentions early that his first film was supposed to pave his way to Hollywood, so making him a commercial director removes him from the glitz and glamour of other anti-Hollywood films. He's something else. He's already sold out, but his reputation as a visionary somehow preceded him. Without being told constantly that Toby is a genius, we'd never know for ourselves, and, presumably, neither would Toby. His sense of arrogance and entitlement as he stomps from one situation to another without pausing to understand anyone else's point of view keeps Toby at arm's length from the audience. We are asked constantly to sympathize with him, but Toby seems to resent—and resist—our sympathy.

What we see is Toby refusing

and *The Adventures of Baron Munchausen*. They established a theme that would run throughout the rest of his films in varying strengths, that of the dreamer—the dreamer as a boy (*Time Bandits*), the dreamer as a middle-aged man (*Brazil*), and the dreamer as an elderly man (*Baron Munchausen*). In all three films, the dream was important to cling to. The dream was an escape from the mundane greyness of reality.

In *Don Quixote*, the dream is almost toxic. It has left destruction behind it, brought about madness. The dream is something bad, something to distrust. While Toby isn't as sympathetic as many of Gilliam's past protagonists, we can nonetheless sense the ironic tragedy of *Don Quixote*, a nihilistic sadness greater than even Gilliam's last film, *The Zero Theorem*. Taken with *Zero*, Gilliam seems to be asking, "Why bother? It is all ruined in the end and everyone does what they want anyway."

Because Gilliam is vocal and approachable in interviews, it's tempting to read some of his admitted self-loathing into *Quixote*, which seems rife with guilt and even disgust. The opening sets this up,

responsibility for his direct actions, let alone his indirect influence. It's not his fault that the cobbler is trapped in the role. It was not his fault that Angelica saw the route from films to ersatz prostitution as a straight line either, but neither would have wound up where they are were it not for Toby's desire to make a film. Thus, Toby's own descent into madness seems more fate than escape, a poetic punishment well-earned.

Which brings us to a strange turn when you take Gilliam's entire body of work into consideration. His first three Hollywood films (following *Jabberwocky*) were *Time Bandits*, *Brazil*, beginning with the lead-in to Toby's ridiculous commercial. The arrival of a cartoonish Quixote tilting at the windmill, the classic elements from Cervantes (in reality, the windmill scene that we inextricably associate with Quixote takes up most of one page of the book) is revealed as sham and forced perspective as the camera pulls back and begins a marvelous single-shot unveiling artifice. "It's only a model," Gilliam whispers to us. Visually, this is the least "Gilliamesque" of his work as well. The wide-angle lenses are used sparsely here, because the dream has been dragged down to earth. The madness is both larger-than-life and actual size.

Adam Driver's credit appears when Toby takes the storyboards from the hands of the supervisor and tosses them into the air, the pages fluttering to the ground as if to say, "I'm throwing the script away." It's a subtle moment rife with unsubtlety.

The Man Who Killed Don Quixote is a movie many have been waiting for almost as long as Gilliam has. It has moments of beautiful truth revealed by marvelous performances. While Driver's Toby remains a selfish cypher, likely as empty as his biography implies, he serves well as the audience's guide. Pryce is magnificent as Javier because, of course, he is and was always going to be. Joana Ribeiro rounds out the trio as a bitter and jaded Angelica, no longer the heavenly being implied by her name. Every shot is, to beat a phrase, "worthy of framing," thanks to Gilliam's longtime stalwart cinematographer, Nicola Pecorini. Costumes, sets—all marvelous.

But in keeping with Gilliam's Sisyphean existence, this version

All Photos this section © Alacran Films (et al.) All Rights Reserved.

of *Don Quixote* was also beset, this time by a villainous producer named Paulo Branco, who bullied his way in as an investor and then tried to take over the production wholesale. Failing that, he's been tying up the film in court over script rights issues since 2016, leading to numerous distribution woes and proving once again that the film gods are vicious bastards. As of this writing, *The Man Who Killed Don Quixote* is *only now* opening in the U.K. Fortunately, it is available on DVD and Blu-ray.

It's been well-received by critics and fans, but many reviews have mentioned that the film was not what they'd expected. After 25 years, how could it have been? As far as my perspective goes, this is the movie that Terry Gilliam was always going to make, and the false starts were due to destiny fighting back. On the other hand, I don't believe in destiny. Yet, there you go.

It is obligatory to end with a Quixote/Gilliam comparison. Quixote was mad and dreamed of an earlier, better world. Gilliam is also mad but understands that the idea of a better world is a fantasy. Things are always going to be different. "Better" and "worse" will always be matters of perspective. Gilliam is not the mad knight, nor is he the willing companion, Sancho, caught up in the game. I don't know—maybe in this case he's the Enchanter, revealing the world as the ugly thing it is.

Regardless, *The Man Who Killed Don Quixote* is marvelous, melancholic, and, in keeping with the madness around us these days, very, very appropriate.

THE DEFECTIVE DETECTIVE: THE NEXT WINDMILL

While it's odd to discuss a director in terms of the films he *didn't* make, Terry Gilliam has always been candid about the misfires and the almosts he's made over the years. Yes, the film version of *Good Omens* with Johnny Depp and Robin Williams never came to pass, nor did *Watchmen* with a nude, blue Arnold Schwarzenegger as Dr. Manhattan. *A Tale of Two Cities* collapsed when star Mel Gibson opted for *Braveheart* instead. *A Connecticut Yankee in King Arthur's Court* never really got off the ground. Notoriously, he was J.K. Rowling's first choice to direct *Harry Potter and the Sorcerer's Stone*, but the studios were too afraid of leaving such a cash cow in the iconoclast's hands.

For years, the albatross best associated with Gilliam was *The Man Who Killed Don Quixote*. As discussed, this was *the* cautionary tale in Hollywood. But Gilliam just needed to be in the right place in his own personal history to make the film correctly. If you believe in a "great scheme of things," *Don Quixote* would always have been made; it was just a matter of timing.

But there is another script Gilliam remains passionate about, one that has changed itself over the years but still remains in his sights. It's a story titled *The Defective Detective* that dates back to 1991, about a burnt-out cop whose search for a missing child plunges him into a storybook

Storyboards for The Defective Detective © Terry Gilliam. All Rights Reserved.

world. Gilliam wrote the script with his *The Fisher King* writer, Richard LaGravenese.

Dream editor Phil Stubbs put up a piece about *The Defective Detective* in the magazine, stating: "On June 10, 1993, while working on *The Defective Detective*, Gilliam recorded a diary of the day for the British Film Institute: 'For the last seven months I have been writing and preparing a film called *The Defective Detective*. The whole process is slow and frustrating and has been turning me more and more into a hermit...and a crab. It has been almost three years since I have been behind a camera. I'm not happy and I leave the house less and less. My contact with the outside world is primarily via the telephone and the fax. Richard LaGravenese, my co-writer, is in New York. Margery Simkin, my co-producer, is in Los Angeles....'"[1]

In 1991, while high off his first Hollywood success with *The Fisher King*, Gilliam found each subsequent meeting with executives frustrating beyond belief. He and LaGravenese pitched an idea for adapting Philip K. Dick's *A Scanner Darkly*, and it was rejected, as were a number of other ideas. "I had decided I've got to do something of my own. My ego is so desperate for attention.... This ego, an ugly little thing, has to show it's got a few ideas that are totally its own, and they've got to be shown to be good and earth-shattering and world-changing." Sifting through old notebooks and seeing "nothing good in the world," Gilliam started putting the fantastic alongside the horrific reality. "Suddenly, the idea took the shape of a middle-aged New York cop effectively having a nervous breakdown and being transported back into a kid's fantasy world, where the rules are a child's rules and he has to try to deal with this."[2]

There were images of seedy bars located deep within a foreboding forest; the hero, pursued by villains, escaping through a poster into

---

1 http://www.smart.co.uk/dreams/ddfact.htm

2 *Gilliam on Gilliam*, edited by Ian Christie. 1999 Faber & Faber Ltd., p. 217.

another realm; trees made of old newspaper; a grown man resisting the magic around him because nothing in his life lately has been magical.

At one point, the movie was set to be made with Nick Nolte and Danny DeVito. After *Twelve Monkeys*, Bruce Willis was keen to play the part of the disillusioned cop. Most recently (within the last decade), Nic Cage was set to star. But for whatever reason—the budget, the stars, the studio—the film went back into turnaround.

"I'm so determined to prove to Hollywood that things they don't believe in are possible. In a strange way, I don't think I should still be trying to do *The Defective Detective*, because I've already done it: It's like trying to get *Munchausen* right. Or perhaps it's my *Fanny and Alexander*, a compendium of everything I've ever tried to do on a large scale, so that I can finally get the epic stuff out of my system and go back to doing smaller, more delicate pieces."[3]

But for many artists, the unrealized project, particularly a personal one, is a clarion call. As with *The Man Who Killed Don Quixote*, perhaps *The Defective Detective* will finally find its way to the screen with the Gilliam that was meant to make it.

_____

3   P. 265

"This is a cool idea for a book." — Quentin Tarantino

My Best Friend's Birthday: The Making of a Quentin Tarantino Film is the story of a group of friends who set out to make their own movie in 1983, financing it with Tarantino's minimum wage earnings from his job at a video store. In most biographies and Tarantino histories, this unfinished $5,000 film is mentioned only in passing and is looked upon as little more than a curiosity. But with this oral history, author/editor Andrew J. Rausch details how each of the friends came together, other early film projects they worked on, and how they ended up making (or trying to make) a black-and-white screwball comedy.

He also makes the argument that *My Best Friend's Birthday* is something far more meaningful than a curiosity. Not only did it mark the screenwriting and directorial debut of Quentin Tarantino, one of the greatest filmmakers in history, but it also launched the careers of two other professional filmmakers, Craig Hamann and Roger Avary. **My Best Friend's Birthday: The Making of a Quentin Tarantino Film** provides an in-depth look at the film from its conception to its eventual demise and proves that even at the young age of 20, Tarantino already possessed the talent (in a still rough, unpolished form) that would lead him to make classic films such as *Reservoir Dogs, Pulp Fiction, Kill Bill, Django Unchained,* and *Once Upon a Time in...Hollywood*. The film and screenplay for *My Best Friend's Birthday*, rough as they may be, provide us a glimpse of an artist on the verge of real success, still trying to find and hone his voice.

**Available in paperback, hardback, and Kindle at *Amazon.com*
or order directly from *bearmanormedia.com*.**

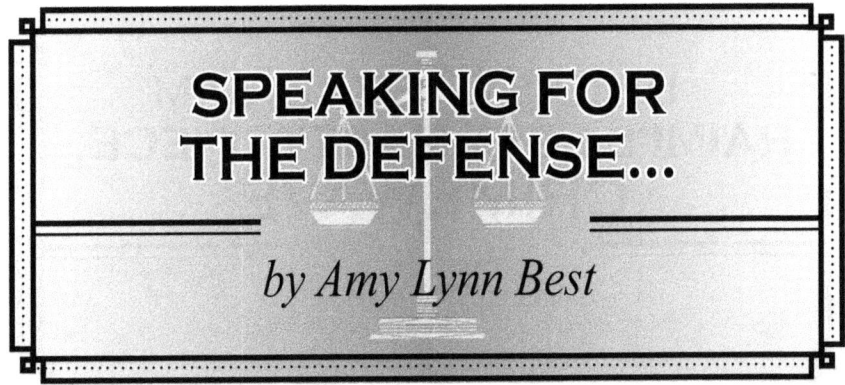

SPEAKING FOR THE DEFENSE...

by Amy Lynn Best

"Every movie is somebody's favorite." And with that in mind, every one of us loves a movie that nobody else seems to love. We try to pass off our loves as "guilty pleasures," but there's nothing to feel guilty about. Love of film—it's what we all have in common, writers and readers of *ExNat*.

With a few rare exceptions, no movie was made specifically to fail. There is too much time and money invested, even for the lowest-budgeted feature. When that rarity comes along—the "One Movie Only I Seem to Love"—we can get defensive. When we come across one of our secret loves being disparaged online or in conversation, we can feel like we're being attacked ourselves or that our love is under attack. But what it comes down to is that there are certain rare movies out there whose audience is in the double digits, and they speak to individuals, rather than groups.

We're not talking about 'so-bad-it's-good' here nor things like *The Room*, which are usually hate-watched. The joy in the viewing comes with the added bonus of ridicule. Those are easy targets and aren't among the films listed here.

What you'll read in the pages that follow are personal pieces aiming to see the best in the easily dismissed. They'll be the most subjective essays you're likely to read, but they were written with love and with the urging to give some of these movies a second chance. Maybe we won't change your opinion, and that's no bad thing.

We're only asking for open minds.

UNEASY AS XYZ: SAM RAIMI'S LOST MASTERPIECE, CRIMEWAVE

By Terry Thome

Crimewave,[1] Sam Raimi's first studio film following the global success of *The Evil Dead*, remains inexplicably unknown to all but the heartiest of Renaissance Pictures fanatics. Even those who have heard of it haven't actively sought it out due to Raimi's and Bruce Campbell's claims that it's a complete misfire and not worth seeing. That's an absolute shame, since not only is *Crimewave* very much worth seeing, it's essential to fully understanding the films Raimi has made since, although, admittedly, his later, more mature films (the romantic baseball movie *For Love of the Game*, the psychic melodrama *The Gift*, and his masterful, if not downright Shakespearean, *A Simple Plan*) don't have the same visceral "Sam-O-cam" swoop and smash as the movies that gave him his cult audience.

When the team of Raimi/Campbell/Speigel was signed by Embassy Pictures, the studio undoubtedly was expecting another *Evil Dead*-type spectacle, with plenty of grue and mayhem. Had they looked at the homemade films that Raimi made with Josh Becker and Scott Speigel, they would have seen that gruesome horror has never been where Raimi's heart is. Raimi has been a lifelong aficionado of the 1930s/1940s film aesthetic. Those movies were the height of slapstick/screwball comedies and dark, romantic detective noir. It was in those films that the Renaissance Pictures crew found an alliance with the Coen Brothers. Joel Coen was an editor on *The Evil Dead* and was writing *Blood Simple* with his brother, Ethan, in the same time period. Their mutual love for those films made it inevitable that they would collaborate on a screenplay that scratched both of their creative itches.

Crimewave began life as *The XYZ Murders*. It was to be a serious, highly stylistic paean to the dark romantic murder mysteries of the mid-20th century. Through rewrites and revisions, *The XYZ Murders* became lighter and broader as Raimi's and the Coens' sense of humor took

---

1 Not to be confused with John Paizs's (*Top of the Food Chain*) identically titled comedy, also from 1985 (aka *The Big Crimewave*)

hold. By the final draft of the screenplay, *The XYZ Murders* became an epic romantic/murder yarn, laced with bursts of slapstick humor and Tex Avery-styled sight gags. What the Renaissance Pictures crew didn't expect was pushback and crackdowns from the studio suits right from the beginning. On *The Evil Dead*, there was no one to answer to. Their investors were professionals—doctors, small business owners, and the like. If Raimi wanted to take a few days to get a certain shot, there was no one there to tell him no. Now, they were in the big leagues and they were being micromanaged every step of the way. To say that they were blindsided by Embassy Pictures' treatment is an understatement. Whole scenes were changed or removed altogether. The lead was written for Bruce Campbell, but the studio had no confidence that he could carry the film. He was relegated to a secondary role. Joe LoDuca, Raimi's choice to write the musical score, was rejected outright. To top all of that, Raimi was not given final cut, and in the end, the film was taken from him.

The film's title was changed from *The XYZ Murders* to *Broken Hearts and Noses* and, finally, *Crimewave*. Unfortunately, the film's release coincided with Embassy Pictures being sold to Columbia Pictures. It was released by Columbia in two U.S. states, Kansas and Alaska, and was

then dumped to cable television. It suffered a similar fate in Europe. In Asian countries, the film retained the title *The XYZ Murders* and was a few minutes longer than the U.S./European cut.

The tangled narrative of *Crimewave* begins with Victor Ajax (Reed Birney, *Four Friends* [1981], *Changeling* [2008]) recounting the story from the electric chair as he awaits his execution. Ernest Trend (producer Edward R. Pressman, producer of *Phantom of the Paradise*, *Das Boot*, *The Crow*, and *The Hand*, among a slew of other films, in his only screen credit) witnesses a backroom deal between his partner, Donald Odegard (Hamid Dana, in his only screen credit), and Ronaldo the Heel (Bruce Campbell, *The Man With The Screaming Brain* [2005], *Bubba Ho-*

Tep [2002]) to sell their security firm, Odegard-Trend Security, and turn it into a strip club. Enraged, Trend calls a pair of exterminators he finds in the Yellow Pages, who just happen to be hitmen as well. The exterminators, Faron Crush (a post-dubbed Paul L. Smith, *Midnight Express* [1978], *Pieces* [1982], *Popeye* [1980]) and Arthur Coddish (Brion James, *Blade Runner* [1982], *Enemy Mine* [1985], *48 Hours* [1982]), are quick and efficient and kill Odegard by electrocution.

Trend thinks he's free of his troubles but immediately runs into two obstacles: Vic, who works for the Odegard-Trend company installing surveillance cameras, and Trend's wife, Helene (the ever reliable Louise Lasser, *Bananas* [1970], *Frankenhooker* [1990], *Mary Hartman, Mary Hartman* [1976-77]). Trend gives Vic the night off to find the woman of his dreams, but Trend's wife, Helene, won't stop snooping and worrying about what's happening across the street, spying on the proceedings with binoculars. Trend, trying to calm his wife, returns to the office, but the exterminators haven't left yet. They end up killing Trend as well as Odegard.

Meanwhile, Vic meets Nancy (Sheree J. Wilson, *Walker, Texas Ranger* [1993–2001]) and falls in love at first sight, but Nancy only has eyes for Ronaldo (of course). They all meet at the Rialto nightclub for an evening of fistfighting, dancing, and dishwashing. It's the worst night of Nancy's life, and Vic takes it upon himself to look after her, whether she likes it or not.

Back at the office, Faron and Arthur realize their error and make an attempt to cover up their crimes, but they can't escape the watchful eyes of Mrs. Trend. Caught red-handed, Faron breaks into the apartment complex to take care of Mrs. Trend, while Arthur has to find a place to dump the bodies. Before long, everyone has descended on the apartment complex and the body count increases.

For all the famous scuttlebutt over Bruce Campbell being replaced as the lead,

Reed Birney (Left) as Victor and Bruce Campbell as Renaldo The Heel. All photos © Embassy Pictures / Renaissance Pictures. All Rights Reserved.

it turns out that Reed Birney (in his first lead) is perfect in the role. His portrayal of Vic is that of a true "aw shucks" nebbish with more heart than brains. Anyone who's seen Campbell do his slick back hair and horn-rimmed glasses nerd character, which he played many times in the Raimi/Becker/Speigel Super 8 mm shorts, knows that it's very broad, with lots of face mugging. It's funny and it works in the right role, but it would have been a total disaster here. Birney's portrayal fits perfectly in the rogue's gallery of classic Coen Brothers characters. Bruce Campbell is really great in his portrayal of Ronaldo the Heel, an oafish cad with thoughts only of himself. His performance in the Rialto restaurant scene is classic Bruce, and it foreshadows the further adventures of Ash Williams in the *Evil Dead* sequels. Sheree J. Wilson acquits herself well as the object of Vic's affection, Nancy. No last name, just Nancy. She plays her role (her feature film debut) with great confidence and fine comic timing. A special shout-out to Ed Pressman, whose portrayal of Ernest Trend is very good. He should've done more movies in front of the camera.

Crimewave is what could be referred to as a slapstick noir. It marries the screwball comedy aesthetic to the dark downbeat romance of Dashiell Hammett detective yarns. There's also a slew of references to Alfred Hitchcock thrillers. In a bonus interview on the 2013 Scream Factory Blu-ray release of *Crimewave*, Reed Birney makes the astute observation that the film is "Alfred Hitchcock directing the Three Stooges." I may be splitting hairs, but I would say it's more like Del Lord directing *Rear Window*.

The story and screenplay are bursting at the seams with Coenisms, even though it was one of their earliest. The characters are drawn from the deep well of quirkiness that defined later Coen Brothers features like *Raising Arizona*, *Fargo*, and, yes,

The Big Lebowski. The good guys are very good, and the bad guys are very bad, but it's done in such a Tex Avery—Droopy versus Spike—slapstick sight-gag style that it's easy for the audience to root for all sides. It's in the dialogue where the Coens prove their worth, even at this early stage in their careers. All the characters speak aloud to themselves, either in a soliloquy fashion, like Vic musing to himself about relationships—"Taking care of yourself, that's important. Taking care of each other, why, that's

romance!"—or general *Popeye*-like asides and non sequiturs that Faron mumbles to himself, Bluto-style, throughout the movie—"Oh, playing hard to get, huh?" Even the bit players have a nobility in their speech and mannerisms, even if for a single line of dialogue. It's the more off-color bits of dialogue that really win the day, even if they aren't socially acceptable anymore…but really, were they ever? Full disclosure, though, the line delivered by a police officer to a young boy found pulling a corpse from an elevator is one of the greatest line deliveries in cinematic history. I won't write it here, but you'll know it when you hear it.

But if it's the Coen Brothers' deadpan delivery that keeps the plot moving, it's Raimi's hyperkinetic style-to-burn direction that keeps the film absolutely fascinating to watch. *The Evil Dead* was Raimi's calling card to the majors, but with *Crimewave*, he was champing at the bit to prove that he was more than a one-trick pony. Indeed, he crafts the entire film as if he might never make one again. Everything in the film has an artifice to it that brings willing viewers into a completely realized world, a world where the technology is modern (for the 1980s: there are video surveillance cameras and the cars are modern), but the architecture and fashions have stalled for a half-century. The Rialto dinner club is all tuxedos and evening gowns lit by neon. The city outside the windows in the Trends' apartment is painted murals. Characters fall from buildings in shots straight out of *Vertigo*. The climax of the film is filmed almost entirely with rear projection process shots. These are all trademark visuals of Raimi, pre-CGI, and these shots would appear in the next two *Evil Dead* movies, as well as his superhero magnum opus, *Darkman*.

The sound design, although once again not exactly what Raimi wanted, is very effective and marries to the visuals well. Music score composer Arlon Ober (*Deep Star Six* [1989], *Child's Play* [1988], Don Dohler's *Nightbeast* [1982], among many others) sometimes overdoes the "wackiness" when punctuating the visuals with comic-sounding music cues but is, at other times, right on target. One particularly memorable part of the score occurs when the rubbing sound of a cuíca underscores (Brion James's) excruciatingly long wait for an elevator car as he awkwardly chews a piece of gum. Fortunately, the sound effects seem to be kept fairly intact. Raimi and Co. recorded the sound effects from Three Stooges shorts audiotape directly from a television broadcast. If the mere sound of a violin string being plucked sends you into giggling fits (as it does me), you'll be in slapstick comedy heaven here.

All in all, this is a film that I find very hard to defend simply because I don't think it needs any defense. *Crimewave* isn't a misfire or a failure or even that dreaded "guilty pleasure." It's a funny, stylish, winning mix of disparate film genres that haven't existed in the mainstream for decades. It might not be what people today are used to, but it is worth your attention.

GODZILLA '98
OR
IMITATION IS THE SINCEREST FORM OF FLATTERY, DAMMIT!
by Jason Lane

Man, this movie gets some hate! And there may be some valid reasons for it. The original *Godzilla* line from Japan was a beloved franchise from Toho Studios that started out much differently than it ended. It began as a social commentary on the responsibilities and overall dangers of a nuclear presence, especially on those who had no association with it, being affected/devastated by its mere vicinity before then overall transforming into a pro wrestling-style romp with cool-looking monsters, cheesy special effects, and an obvious aim toward children. Godzilla's overall themes changed over the years, with the focus shifting more toward action-packed scenes and a tongue-in-cheek feel. With even the sillier films causing some to openly shake their heads, they were still adored by fans of the King of the Monsters.

Until 1998 happened. Then, fans went apeshit.

It seemed like the U.S. version was going to be great. Godzilla was going to be made not only in America, but by the same people (Roland Emmerich and Dean Devlin) who made *Independence Day*, which previously made a ton of money at the box office. And the marketing for *Godzilla* '98 was legendary to the point that there was no escaping it. Ads were everywhere, from street corners, to taxi cabs, to commercials for Taco Bell™, with all of them saying the same thing: This movie is going to be huge and great and cool and awesome!

And then people started hearing concerning things, things like:
- Godzilla wasn't fighting another monster.
- There were constant reshoots and script rewrites.
- They weren't working with reps from Toho in the least.
- They were going to use more CGI than practical effects.
- Godzilla didn't have flame breath.
- Godzilla was being redesigned.

That last one really caused umbrage in some fans, as they loved the classic look and wanted a Hollywood high-cost special effects upgrade and not something radical in design. It didn't help that the hype machine kept saying "size does matter" and even featured a teaser trailer where Godzilla's foot crushed a Tyrannosaurus rex skeleton in a museum (a definite screw-you to the *Jurassic Park* movies). The foot in the shot looked different from the regular Godzilla design, but it was followed by the traditional roar that the character used over the years, which eased some fears. When the full trailer came out, it admittedly looked awesome, showing the aftermath of several attacks and a hint at the monster's size with what looked to be the Big G attacking Manhattan. The tone was dark, more like a throwback to disaster cinema, and focused on none of the actors in the film except for an end shot of Hank Azaria as a cameraman freaking out over some unseen trauma. The audience was promised—and was ready for—a film that had the most famous and dangerous monster of all time destroying anything in its path and finally arriving in NYC. That's what audiences expected.

What they got was...not that.

To say the movie was (and still is) a mess would be an understatement. It wasn't anything like the trailers had promised, feeling less like a Godzilla movie and more like a rip-off of the *Jurassic Park* movies the marketing had made fun of. The forced comedy, the stilted acting by stars (who were obviously mailing it in), the not-that-special-looking special effects, the overall story—all of these were disappointing. But the one thing that was the most unforgiveable to fans was that they simply didn't like the new monster. It was more in line with a hybrid of a Tyrannosaurus and an iguana, with its oversized head and sleek musculature really standing out, plus the fact that he didn't have his radioactive breath, which was sacrilege to any fan. But what really missed the mark was that he didn't have any real personality and certainly wasn't aggressive. Say what you want about any version of Godzilla, but one thing you can't say is that he never showed up ready to fight. In this version more than any other, he was more passive, running away from helicopters and jets, where before, if you attacked Godzilla, he was immediately like, "Oh, want to start some shit? SHIT IS ON!" The added-on plot of the lil' Godzillas, the product placement, the ending (they kill the King of the Monsters with plain old missiles...the hell?), it all led to a curious feeling in which fans not only didn't like the movie, they resented it. And honestly, I was one of those fans.

I watched it that first weekend when it premiered. I was not happy with what I saw, and I had no problem telling my friends the same thing. Back then, we did use them Internets some, but not to the level we do now. Then, there were much different ways to tell if a movie was good or not.

Nowadays:
- Go to a search engine and type the name of the film you're hoping to watch. See how many stars the film has.
- Check out review sites to get a more accurate review.

Back in the day:
- Call up friends who've already seen it and find out if "Hell, yeah, go see this shit!" or "Hell, no, don't see this shit" comes out of their mouths.
- Gene Siskel and Roger Ebert: It sounds cliché, but these two learned colleagues' thumbs and words could add millions to a movie. On a side note, it probably didn't help that Emmerich and Devlin created two characters in the film that lampooned both Siskel and Ebert, since they didn't care for the critics' reviews of their prior films *Independence Day* and *Stargate*. Siskel and Ebert didn't mind being made fun of in film as long as it was (A) funny or (B) a good movie. Since this film accomplished neither, they both tore it apart.
- Another way to tell if a movie

"Here he comes...stomping down the street..."
© *TriStar Pictures / Toho. All rights reserved.*

isn't that great is to see what the second weekend sales are like. If they're comparable to the first weekend's sales, it's prolly a decent flick. If sales drop off quickly, that film prolly sucks. *Godzilla '98*'s first weekend pull was $44 million. The second weekend? $18 million. Sony expected the film to make $100 million that first weekend, so this was a major disappointment.

For a movie that was supposed to surpass *Independence Day*'s blockbuster status, it came nowhere near what was expected and faded away, with its final weekend on the screen during its initial run pulling in a little more than $200,000. Besides the onslaught of VHS and DVD sales later that summer during the film's home release, I honestly mostly forgot about this overbudgeted dreck of a film until it came on HBO late one night while I was at a convention. I was too tired (inebriated) to find the remote to turn the channel, so I just left it on, hoping to doze off.

Imagine my surprise when I watched it completely, thinking to myself, "That wasn't nearly as bad as I remembered."

"Here's news from around the world…"

First, here's some learnin' for ya.

Dragon Con is a yearly convention, held in Atlanta, Georgia, every Labor Day weekend, from Thursday afternoon until the following Monday at 5 p.m. While even the biggest of conventions have six or seven track listings for panels and presentations, Dragon Con boasts an amazing 30+ programming tracks. Also, since this con is put together by nerds for nerds, apart from the regular topics (anime, sci-fi, comics, and movies), Dragon Con features tracks dedicated to costuming, digital media, electronic frontier forums, puppetry, skeptics, and alternate histories. So, with this many options, in addition to the parade, free concerts, demonstrations, battlebots, Filk-singing (spelled correctly), live pro wrestling, *and* various mini bars littered throughout the con, there is no reason you should ever find yourself bored.

I've done panels at Dragon Con for the Silk Road track, which focuses on Asian cinema and culture. But where other people on this track talk about the grace and beauty of the culture (poetry, calligraphy, kimono- and bow-making and folding, etc.), I tend to focus more on pop culture fare, such as kaiju, sci-fi, pro wrestling, mechs, and kung fu, and I always like to have a panel focused on a Godzilla topic or two.

So, I was at Dragon Con 2019 and took a poll. I explained to the fully packed room of people (I brings the crowds, baby!), who were there because the other panels were already full (*sigh*), that I was going to be including their responses in this very selfsame article that you're holding in your hands or e-reading or whatever. That poll was this:

"Raise your hands if you liked *Godzilla '98*."

35

"Raise your hands if you absolutely despised it."

"Raise your hands if you just didn't like it."

I was more interested in that third group of people, as those opinions could be changed. The ones who despised it were going to die on their shields, saying, "Screw that movie!" so there was little hope in changing those minds.

I then asked for reasons why the movie was not liked. I received quotes ranging from "It didn't have the essence of the character that I loved since I was a kid" to "It just sucked." I then stated that I wasn't arguing that this was a good movie. I just didn't think it deserved the hate that it usually got. I also focused on the fact that some of my favorite movies aren't good movies. I love *Friday the 13th Part V: A New Beginning*. It's my favorite of all of them. It's quirky, it's funny, the characters are great, there's (kind of) musical numbers, the kills are fun, and it's directed and shot the most like an exploitation movie. Is it a good movie? Hell, no. It's probably the antidote for a good movie, but it's one of my faves. And that's my point with *Godzilla '98*. There are much worse films out there that don't get the hate that this film gets.

The Giant Gila Monster…

Godzilla fans are some of the friendliest people I've ever met in any fandom, but if they don't agree with you, they'll tell you to go to Hell—in the politest, friendliest way imaginable, of course. The Godzilla fans who don't like *Godzilla '98* refuse to call the monster Godzilla, even though his name is listed, y'know, as the title of the movie. There are actually two other names they call him:

- **GINO**: Gino is an acronym for **G**odzilla **I**n **N**ame **O**nly.
- **Zilla**: This one is a more popular term for him, as it's what Toho Productions named him in their licensing after the movie came out.

Toho has such a dislike of this version of the character that they included him in the movie *Godzilla: Final Wars*, which was a sloppy, overdone battle royale of monsters, all fighting in video game-style sequences. Zilla (his name in the movie) is brought in to fight Godzilla and is killed in approximately 20 seconds, showing a horrible disrespect for the '98 version. You have to give Toho some extra snark points in that *Godzilla '98* is the only monster rendered completely in CGI—poorly done CGI to be honest, and you *know* that was done purposely. When he was destroyed in *Godzilla: Final Wars*, the alien controller (from Planet X!) even yells, "I knew that tuna-eating monster was useless!"

Damn.

On top of all the things listed before, Toho was so offended by the characterization that they refused to even accept any of the profits from the *Godzilla '98* film, sending the money back to Tri-Star with an official protest saying…uh, hold on for just a second. Ah, I see. All right, that last part didn't happen at all, as apparently Toho accepted and cashed all checks regarding *Godzilla* '98. So…yeah.

Toho may not have liked the movie in the least, but hey, they aren't stupid.

Destroy All Monsters

Here's some ready-made items to have on hand if someone throws shade your way on *Godzilla* '98. You know, if you needed them. Whatever.

Statement: "It's the worst of the Godzilla movies." According to a few critic sites, it's actually duking it out with *Godzilla's Revenge* and *Godzilla 1985* for worst-reviewed film. Some other bad movies were rated higher, such as *Godzilla vs. The Sea Monster*, where he fights a giant lobster with a rock (Rawk lawbsta'!), and the less said about "Jet Jaguar" the better.

Statement: "He looks too different from the real Godzilla." Toho's Godzilla was a giant green reptilian biped with a long tail, spinal plates, and arms with opposable thumbs. The Godzilla of 1998 was a giant green reptilian biped with a long tail, spinal plates, and arms with opposable thumbs. It also has a lot more in common with the 1975 American *Godzilla* posters, cartoons, toys, and picture puzzles. But fans were very much against this dramatic change in appearance. Instead of focusing only on the past, try thinking of it in these regards: Bela Lugosi played Dracula in *Dracula*. Did he do a good job? Sure. Gary Oldman played Dracula in *Bram Stoker's Dracula*. Did he do a good job? Sure. Leslie Nielsen played Dracula in *Dracula: Dead and Loving It*. Was he the best one? No, but he was still Dracula. Derek Mears played Jason in the most recent *Friday the 13th*. Not my fave, but he was still a Jason. I myself liked *Godzilla* '98's look, but I would have toned down the Jay Leno chin, though.

The redesign wasn't appreciated by many, but Godzilla has been changed drastically before with no problem from fans. Some changes from the traditional look include:

- The Godzilla artwork for HG Toys' puzzles and related items had him very much in the vein of a Tyrannosaurus rex. By the way, this image is very similar to the 1998 Godzilla upon closer review.
- Marvel Comics had a Godzilla redesign by the great Herb Trimpe, who also designed the King of the Monsters differently from his traditional look, focusing more on the reptilian traits although keeping the Tyrannosaurus rex's tiny arms.
- The NBC Saturday morning Godzilla cartoon also changed his appearance to make him more kid-friendly. The show also added a mutated cancer by the name of Godzookie, but the less said about that the better.

Statement: "The movie was a bomb." Fact: The movie performed well under expectations in the U.S. Its sales were compared to those of Emmerich and Devlin's prior films: 1994's *Stargate* ($55 million budget/$197 million box office) and 1996's *Independence Day* ($78 million budget/$815 million box office). In that sense, *Godzilla '98* did seem to do poorly overall. But then a curious thing happened. The film did well globally. Very, very well, in fact. It actually did so well that *Godzilla '98* was actually the most successful Godzilla movie of all time until Legendary Pictures' 2014 *Godzilla* ($160 million budget/$529 million box office) surpassed it. *Godzilla '98* is pretty much tied right now with Legendary's *Godzilla: King of the Monsters* ($200 million budget/$387 million box office), with *Godzilla '98*'s final tally totaling a $145 million budget and pulling in a combined box office (foreign and domestic) of $379 million. For anyone who doesn't like this movie, consider the fact that at the time, Toho was going through some financial issues—not fatal ones,

"Life comes at you pretty fast..." Matthew Broderick as Ferris Bueller in Godzilla.
© *TriStar Pictures / Toho. All rights reserved.*

but the ones that any studio goes through. Licensing out the Big G to America would have been unheard-of just a few years prior. However, doing so put some much-needed money into Toho accounts. So, like I said, if there are people who despise this movie, ask them if they liked any of the Godzilla films made from '98 until now. If they say yeah, tell them that Toho was able to make more of those films due to having the necessary money, and part of that money came from *Godzilla '98*.

Statement: "The acting sucks ass." No argument here, but I never really expect Lawrence Olivier giving a soliloquy on the unfairness of tortured conscience when there are guys in oversized foam latex suits wrestling around behind him. Don't get me wrong, there are a few Godzilla films where the acting is above par (the original *Godzilla* [*Gojira*] and the much-appreciated *Shin Godzilla*), but most of them have actors reciting dialogue that can be a little tongue-in-cheek.

Statement: "The story sucks ass." Again, no argument here, but there are plenty of Godzilla movies where the film tends to wane a bit plot-wise. Almost as if the writers were merely filling in time and situations to get to the scenes where a giant monster would fight another giant monster. Almost.

Statement: "Godzilla wasn't Godzilla." He definitely lacked a personality in this movie, acting more like a wild animal than a force of nature or a hateful ass or a drunk uncle. Years later, Devlin said that one of the mistakes they made was in not showing him to be either a heroic figure or a villainous one and instead showing him to be more like an endangered animal. You have to wonder how much more this version would have been accepted if he was more aggressive, taking the fight to the military and showing himself to be a giant angel of death rather than an overly large critter that escaped from the zoo and is now being corralled by the local sheriff's department. He is definitely more skittish than in any other version. I have used the argument that in *Monty Python and the Holy Grail*, when the knights come upon the Legendary Black Beast of Arrrgghhhh!, they promptly run away, which is an awesome moment in film, but if something named Godzilla does it in trying to avoid the army, everyone is all "This movie sucks!" This argument is quickly ignored by any Godzilla fan I've tried to use it on. As a matter of fact, just forget that I tried it here. Toho's Godzilla has radioactive fire breath, a rarely used mastery of magnetic fields (?) and an odd aversion to physics. *Godzilla '98* has some scale issues, usually involving CGI, but nothing like the ones listed for Godzilla.

Statement: "It would be an OK movie if they just didn't call it *Godzilla*." Taking into consideration that people actually use *Godzilla '98*'s other nicknames (Gino and Zilla) showcases the very human argument that people are just not going to accept something simply because they're against it. This is completely understandable. I was the exact same way with Van Halen, as I didn't consider them really Van Halen when Sammy Hagar replaced David Lee Roth. Me and my fellow metalheads called this Hager version either Bland Halen or Van Hagar. Since I've gotten older and more mature in my years, I just call them Van Halen now (except for the version fronted by Gary Cherone; fuck that version). You just have to accept the fact that they named this monster Godzilla. That's his name.

Statement: "It ripped off Jurassic Park." Did it rip it off? You betcherass it did, with the velociraptors (I mean baby Godzillas) being the most damning evidence. My only argument is that a lot of Godzilla movies copied a lot of the previous films' same formulas (aliens arrive; bring an attack monster; attack monster attacks; Godzilla shows up; fight, fight, fight; Godzilla wins; roll credits). So, yeah, it ripped off *Jurassic Park*, but there's a fine line between a rip-off (*Godzilla '98*, *Jurassic Park III*) and a film that's an homage (*Cloverfield*).

Statement: "That Puff Daddy song on the soundtrack was just f**king awful." I have absolutely no counter to this. It's just fucking awful.

Statement: "It's the worst of the Godzilla movies." OK now, dammit....

The Year of the Dragon...

If you look at the top ticket sellers in 1998, you might notice that Hollywood was more interested in playing it safe with traditions and standards rather than going for anything too avant-garde. The top movies that year included *Saving Private Ryan*, *There's Something About Mary*, *Rush Hour*, *Armageddon*, and *Lethal Weapon 4*—good movies, but nothing that hadn't been seen before. So, 1998 certainly wasn't a big year for daring films, at least financially, but the few that did try quickly achieved cult status. *The Big Lebowski*, *Pi*, *Run Lola Run* (not to be confused with *Run Fatboy Run*), and *Fear and Loathing in Las Vegas* caught a steady audience that appreciated films of this niche, in heart if not financially. Of note is the movie *Blade*, because not only did it perform amazingly well at the box office ($45 million budget/$131 million box office), but, for good or bad, it was the film that started Marvel Studios into pushing forward on its movie line. How's that going, by the way?

In the top 10 movies that year, *Godzilla '98* was the third best, coming in behind only *Armageddon* and *Saving Private Ryan*, which surprised me upon learning, as I remember hearing from everyone then that it did awfully. It also garnered a few awards nominations as well. The 19th Golden Raspberry Awards nominated the movie in six categories. It ended up winning Worst Supporting Actress (Maria Pitillo) and tied with *The Avengers* and *Psycho* for Worst

Remake or Sequel (TriStar Pictures). Just in case you're curious, the big winner (?) that year for the Razzies was *An Alan Smithee Film: Burn Hollywood Burn*. This sounds pretty damning, but some of my favorite films have been nominated for and won Razzies.

In addition to directing *Godzilla '98*, *Stargate*, and *Independence Day*, Roland Emmerich directed *Universal Soldier*, *The Patriot*, and, most importantly, *10,000 B.C.* From his vision comes *Godzilla '98*, a version they said would be completely different from any version seen before. I think they succeeded here. Dean Devlin produced the aforementioned movies as well, but also, more importantly, *Eight-Legged Freaks*. He also created the show *Leverage*, so take that as you will. *Godzilla '98* starred the following actors:

- Jean Reno as Philippe Roaché, an overly French Secret Service agent who comes to the rescue (!) while trying to cover up his government's hand in creating the giant monster. So, does that count as a rescue when your main mission is a cover-up? Is he trying to be heroic or merely fixing their own shit? On a side note, I think the film would have been more suspenseful if Godzilla fought Léon (the professional) instead of this guy.
- Matthew Broderick as Dr. Nick Tatopoulos, a Nuclear Regulatory Commission scientist tasked with researching the effects of radiation on wildlife. He *juuuuuust* may be onto something here, as apparently nuclear radiation doesn't give you cancer or organ failure, but instead makes you the size of skyscrapers and also provides your own P-Diddy song. Broderick also instantly becomes the object of my hatred, as he appears to have aged three years since '86's *Ferris Bueller's Day Off*. Jackass. On a side note, I think the film would have been more suspenseful if Godzilla fought Ferris Bueller instead of this guy.
- Maria Pitillo as Audrey Timmonds, Dr. Nick's perky ex-girlfriend and spunky reporter who won't take no for an answer unless you ask her politely. It's funny that in a movie where a giant monster threatens the lives of anyone within a five-block radius, she is the most hated thing in this film.
- Hank Azaria as Victor Palotti, Audrey's capable cameraman partner. Palotti is lucky in regard to surviving the dangers around him, but also lucky by being eternally friend-zoned by Audrey, easily making him the luckiest person in this film. He voices several characters on *The Simpsons*, so that means he has more money than God. It may not be politically correct, but I miss Apu. On a side note, I think the film would have been more suspenseful if Godzilla fought the housekeeper from *The Birdcage* instead of this guy.
- Harry Shearer as rating-pandering, story-stealing lead reporter Charles Caiman. He also voices several characters on *The Simpsons*, so he's rich enough to

41

buy everyone in Alaska a Slurpee if he felt like it.

The film went through massive rewrites, story changes, and staff and crew changes from the beginning until Devlin and Emmerich took over. With their track record and coming off uber-blockbuster *Independence Day*, how could they fail?

Uh, don't answer that.

<u>The Beginning of the End…</u>

I've watched and rewatched this film several times over the years and have come to really like it, flaws and all. It wasn't trying to be serious in any measure, and it comes off as how it's supposed to: a dumb, fun summer movie. I think the most unforgiveable thing for Godzilla fans is that they could have made this a decent film with very few changes, but we got what was on the screen instead, which really cries out that the people who made this film didn't know Godzilla at all. *That* is the thing that really sticks in fans' stomachs. If the film had portrayed this Godzilla as a city-destroying threat, had another monster attack, focused less on the characters and more on the battles, or had a reimagining of the first Godzilla, any of these would have been a definite improvement, I concur. But I'm not here to fix this movie or say why the others are superior. I'm just here to say, accept this movie for what it is, nothing more and nothing less.

I have noticed that over the years I've run into several younger people (I'm so old, dammit) who not only

Godzilla is thwarted when he steps on a giant LEGO.
© TriStar Pictures / Toho. All rights reserved.

Jean Reno refuses to apologize for being in Godzilla and doesn't care what you think.
© TriStar Pictures / Toho. All rights reserved.

watched and loved this movie when they were kids, but still love it to this day. And a few Godzilla fans I know have softened their stance on it, if only going from "I hate that piece of #$%# movie!" to "I hate that movie."

Baby steps, I suppose.

Remember that Dragon Con story I mentioned, with the people who raised their hands? I gave them all the facts that I listed above and then asked those same people if any of them had changed their minds. Out of the 21 people who had their hands raised before, five changed their minds, with one guy saying, "I'll give it a chance."

That's all we can ask for. That and Godzilla finally kicking Kong's hairy ass. But more on that in a later article.

Top things fans complain about:
- CGI
- They cast him/her?
- They're remaking it? Dammit.
- Wait, it's a sequel, but just to the first one?
- The director/actor/actress/creator is leaving the franchise?
- They recast him/her?
- Come up with some new ideas, dammit.
- This new idea sucked, dammit.

43

I LOVE A GOOD BOMB

by Dr. Rhonda Baughman

So many reviewers/entertainment journalists in the snark trenches—and who hasn't spent some time there? But the moment has come to rally around your favorite so-called film bombs and expose them for the lovely, unmitigated truth they are! They may not have made box-office bank, but they have shared returns on our hearts, our minds, and the collective consciousness of all our friends, probably because we won't…stop…talking about these films! No matter how much loved ones may plead for mercy, show none! It's more important than ever to stand your ground and defend those bombs—and their music and their fashion and their nuggets of dialogue gold—that made you (and me!) the fantastic little connoisseurs of fine failures we are today.

Wild Orchid (1990):

Panned by critics and poorly received in the U.S., this film was actually a hit in Europe. I consider all of that to be a BIG DAMN compliment.

It's a writer/director Zalman King show right from the opening credits: sexy trumpet synth jazz, a sunset, and Mickey Rourke when…Rourke was rawr. Supermodel Carré Otis gives a hug in the dusty despair of a flyover state before the big-city reign of terror on her innocence begins. There's no Uber in the early '90s,[1] and a bus comes to whisk her away to her fate—which is, apparently, interviewing like Tom Cruise at the beginning of *The Firm*.[2] It was the true era of the vacant supermode,l, and Otis was more appealing than the usual suspects. The shadow woman watching Otis's interview may or may not be Jacqueline Bisset—but it's that quick scene of shadow woman that sets the mood for the whole damn

---

1   And, as of this writing (5.11.19), who knows if there will be an Uber moving forward: https://gizmodo.com/congratulations-to-uber-the-worst-performing-ipo-in-us-1834681882

2   Seriously, an entire scene in each film dedicated to how fucking smart these recent law grads are, and all the cities and firms interviewing and whooing while the rest of us out here with doctorates be like, "Do you want fries with that?"

film. Blink and you might miss it. And I can tell the set designer had a hell of a ball with the budget—all that sleek, minimalist office-rich décor that should have been billed a star too.

A hire-on-the-spot meets business transaction in the lobby, with Bisset as the new boss (so not the same as the old boss) alongside the mystique of a new hotel—which comes before the old hotel—and the international intrigue of going from the Dust Bowl, to New York City, to Rio for a Chinese investment deal—and damn, doesn't all of that just scream one of the true meanings of how to start a film in the early '90s? Yes, it does. Don't argue with me. This shit is epic and in the first eight minutes! Honestly, I thought more of my life would be resemble this film. I've thought this a lot, and it doesn't hurt less any time I say it.

Wild Orchid is part of the "beautiful women wearing unpleasant pantsuits" genre, as well as that true maestro technique of the sweeping vista intertwined with a slo-mo shot of a sweaty, lotion-slapped male volleyball player spiking into the sand. The former was, like, 75 percent of big-budget '80s films well into the '90s (and it's coming around, people; even I have one again). And the latter? Think *Top Gun* and *Side Out*. Should that come around again?

Voyeurism sexcapades on a construction site, at a masquerade ball, and in a limo—the film offers some great business advice for women really looking to get ahead in the patriarchal smackdown of that time period, such as "This guy's a predator...put on some goddamn lipstick!" There's a survival tactic. If I may update that, please? "This guy's a predator...tell him to fuck off and have a flame thrower ready for his ass. Where's my lipstick?" And yes, as a John Wick fan, I did try to pause *Wild Orchid* so I could see what specific type of watch it is that Rourke flashes while the scene plays some stupidly catchy song.[3]

Upon Rourke and Otis's very first

---

3   The band? Ambitious Lovers. The song? "It Only Has to Happen Once." Christ, I might as well fire up my Discogs account. Again. The actual soundtrack is all right, a collection of GREAT and mediocre—there's very little in between that.

45

Mickey Roarke a'smoldering in Wild Orchid.
© *Triumph Releasing. All rights reserved.*

meeting, officially, there's a social norm violation. They just met and he's already creepin' up and whispering into her ear—and they take a walk before dinner, limo and bodyguards in tow, while she parades down a dark alley like it's a fucking runway. *All right, Queen*. Rourke apologizes for being rich, although he's obviously lying and douching around a poverty-stricken area with an unstable government like a typical asshole American. But you can forget all that when Otis gets to the restaurant's hostess station and molests a parrot. Seriously, watch its cute little bird orgasm face when she pets it. It's still better than the cocktail repartee between Rourke and Otis—and I'm not really sure why. The actual dialogue? Rourke's superior acting prowess? That Otis's flawless countenance is actually a distraction? That banter is real fuckin' amateur hour head games and pissing me off? In any event, this is all a precursor to Otis and Rourke attending a post-dinner soiree in fetish/carnival masks and somebody touching somebody and Otis freaking out and running away, tossing her mask down on a rainy street as symbolic of man's pressing need to constantly hide his true self. Or something.

I didn't feel like I was watching the sequel to *9 ½ Weeks* until Rourke is caught smiling at Otis and she calls him out on it. Basinger does the same. Damn. Thing. If anyone smiled at me like Rourke smiles at these women, you'd best note I would be ready to Cynthia Rothrock some faces. And the band playing to a live, dancing crowd (when Rourke and Otis accompany the dysfunctional couple) is also straight outta the *9 ½ Weeks* playbook (the NY street reggae jam).

No one calls hotel security when Otis wakes and Rourke is simply at the foot of her bed (fucking staring again). But not smiling. All right. Then, it's time for motorcycle riding, more psychosexual head games with strangers, and that undercurrent of *Cruel Intentions/Dangerous Liaisons* to flat out become a tidal wave. Everyone survives the debauchery, and we are given *another* masquerade party scene, this time more intimate, and the viewer is reminded again why the saying "Don't shit where you eat" is still relevant in 2019. Don't worry, there's no actual fecal matter. I'm sure someone is saving that idea for *Wild Orchid Ménage à Trois, Bitches: The Lifestyles of Continued Grotesque Depravity by the Ultra-Wealthy* (long title, but I think it still has merit). And I don't hate the limo sex scene. Only Rourke's whispery voyeur narration threatened to ruin it. On spirited limo sex: "Don't cover up. I want to look at you." Only when Rourke points out the reasons for the couple's (Otto and Hanna) inability to communicate does the mad fucking commence. Rourke's brother serves as a body double[4] on the film. Why? I have no idea. Rourke was still fit and still ogled for his pretty face, which I did during the "awkward huggins" scene (Rourke's character is not good at being touched). Literally, perhaps even figuratively. *Wild Orchid* is the literary addition to King's canon. Later, Otis stares at herself naked, literally, and also, we are to presume, figuratively. This is deep shit, folks.

Amid this madness, the little boy Rourke mentors? The boy never speaks, which might be a reference to Rourke as a boy (in some earlier dialogue, Rourke is wooing Otis with tales of his boyhood). Additionally, the taciturn Otto (in the limo) never speaks either. Rourke, in his infinite wisdom, only talks *at* these people, and they don't seem to mind.[5]

He might be annoying in all of his faux-omniscient bullshit, but I do have to note that Rourke interrupts an actual threesome beginning between Bisset, Otis, and a hot man on beach (Jens Peter). Otis is not into this particular sex play and has said so several times. But she's going along, for some trauma reason, I presume. This happens in real life. And Bisset is her fucking boss. Ugh. This scene should make you uncomfortable because not all parties are enthusiastically consenting—and it's not the only one. See below.

The Jerome/Emily scene—we have to discuss this now in the #metoo era. The stereotype continues that, if a man persists long enough, the woman will succumb. Oh, and if she cries and runs, not to worry; she'll eventually really like it. I can't defend this part, but uh, I like the lighting in the scene. Emily was supposed to be perceived as I and

Roark and Carré Otis.
© Triumph Releasing. All rights reserved.

frigid and somehow this deflowering is her entry into womanhood/the real world/Wheeler's world? Oh, who the fuck knows. This is a rape scene.

As the film begins to wind down, I found a special love for the "going as twins"/fireworks moment—Bisset, when she says, "Goodbye, Wheeler. Goodbye, motherfucker," she's really releasing some kind of energy at this point. I wonder what was

---

4   This guy? http://www.miaminewtimes.com/2009-02-26/news/mickey-rourke-s-brother-is-a-homeless-street-artist/ Also, just wow: https://www.nytimes.com/2008/11/30/magazine/30rourke-t.html

5   #smashthepatriarchy

happening on set at the time. Lots of unburdening of the soul going on in this scene, in this sector of corporate America. A PIL song dead-stops the whole shebang, but no matter how you slice it, the energy in this scene is different from the first 70 minutes. It's bizarre. Intentional? Accidental (*shrugs*)?

"Wheeler's Howl" is one of the good songs on the soundtrack, but the character in the film is a superficial jackass, and I think Rourke just really liked bikes at this time—so it's another dead-stop. But *finally*, Otis commands to be touched. Yet more dialogue. Sexy horn blows. Sexcapades ensue. This might be where Rourke's body-doublin' bro is. Bike ride into sunset = full circle. End scene.

The '90s had me believing my future would at least hold more sexy horn than it has. Perhaps I do need more sexy horn in my life. Email me if you can provide sexy horn (think Timmy Cappello in *The Lost Boys* [1987]). I defend this film and all its bullshit because…we need examples like this to wholly show what a gigantic lot of unhealthy relationships look like…and what the job market used to look like and, hopefully, can again.

Angel (1984):

Angel is easy to defend. And maybe I was *way* too young to have watched this film, but I learned valuable lessons early, lessons that some people never learn in their entire bloody lifetime. Rory Calhoun's Kit character taught me the importance of using someone's preferred gender terms. When he walks Angel and her transvestite pal, Mae, home, he calls them "ladies" without a hint of sarcasm or irony. The film taught me sex workers are people too; they have rights, and they're way more interesting than you, Karen. Susan Tyrrell's bull dyke Solly character was not only inspiring, but charming. I am so bummed I didn't have a chance to meet her.

I learned early to be A-OK with transvestites, hookers, misfits, and lesbian artists. Cops still sucked, as do well-meaning guidance counselors. And, if you pay close attention to Angel's conversation with said counselor about Angel's extracurricular activities and straight A's, you have my entire high school career explained succinctly (sans hooker part, which is probably for the best) and, hence, my early corporate America drone training. Holy shit—I

never stood a chance. This realization would make me have a nervous breakdown, but I already had one of those, which I think of like first love (i.e., first, only one). Overall, the acting's not great here, and all of the sequels were technically box office bombs (and I can't defend those—maybe on my blog)[6]. But although the original *Angel* didn't open as well as hoped, the film would go on to be a sleeper hit, cult classic, and synchronistic teaching tool for me.

Cool as Ice (1991):

So, what do we have here? With mostly negative reviews and lots of Razzie noms (and one win), the film barely recouped a fifth of its budget at the box office, and the director later disowned the film. A 2016 *Rolling Stone* article sums up its doomed nature well.[7]

Either this is a romantic musical or there's, like, at last three dead-stops (not counting the film's intro). But who cares? For the love of God, the movie is playful and silly, and I love the damn soundtrack (where models can guest star!). That same soundtrack now goes for a *stupid amount* of money on Discogs, so I'm not the only lover of this mess who knows its value. The fashion is fun, the set is ridiculous, and the whole thing is warmly harmless. A colorful cornucopia of *hygge*[8].

---

6 www.patreon.com/drbaughman
7 https://www.rollingstone.com/movies/movie-news/cool-as-ice-the-story-behind-vanilla-ices-career-killing-movie-114242/
8 The Danish practice of feeling joy in the moment

Although they do ride some damn manly motorcycles here as well, I'm more extreme than Vanilla Ice *ever* was, but that's the point—that's why it's all amusing fun. Good, clean fun, really, and in 2019, who the fuck even knows what that means anymore? But we did know in 1991, only we were too foolish to see it then, to see how good we had it and never would again. I would give anything for a return to the Sugar Shack, and maybe a visit to the eccentric repair shop run by lovable weirdos, so I can eat their food, electric boogaloo all over town, and flirt with Kristen Minter. And, of course, the ice chip scene between Vanilla and Minter as he wakes her: only comparable to Drew Barrymore and Andras Jones in *Far from Home*. What have we learned? Whether in the desert or in the 'burbs, there are other ways to do the ice cube foreplay that *9 ½ Weeks* didn't show you.

But let's be honest: People can

make fun of the film all they want, but it has some of the best wisdom for the ages, then and now. "If you ain't true to yourself, you ain't true to nobody. Live your life for someone else and you ain't livin'. Straight up fact." That line alone is disco bomb swagger and *Cool as Ice*'s highest defense.

Blown Away (1989):

After seeing this movie, who didn't answer the phone or have a voicemail message reflecting: "Who are you and why do I care?" Or maybe that was just me. Oops. I did the same after watching *Hello, Mary Lou: Prom Night II*. My parents' colleagues and friends were only mildly concerned.[9]

At any rate, I am "I was in love with the Two Coreys" years old. Seriously. I saw *License to Drive* in the theater. My mother took me, and although I didn't clap and squeal when Haim's name hit the big screen as others did, I was nonetheless excited and all squee-on-the-inside. I thoroughly dug *Dream a Little Dream* (mostly for Meredith Salenger) and its beautiful soundtrack, and I worshiped *The Lost Boys* on all levels. Of course we all knew the Corey reign would end badly, and if Feldman's current Hollywood assertions[10] are true (and his stories are insane enough to be true), we at least have a reason for Haim's passing—and it's the child actor curse, yes, but not the kind we think. My only regret is that when I met Haim in Indianapolis in 2010, I wish I had asked him something, anything, about *Blown Away*. I was starstruck, sure, but it was a *Lost Boys* reunion and I had to hurry to meet Chance Michael Corbitt. I was there for fun, not as a journalist, so the thought never occurred to me.

I doubt *Blown Away* was ever meant for the big screen; it was a direct-to-video, two-cut (R and Unrated) flick. I've only noticed very minor differences in the cuts, like some exaggerated kissing and moaning noise dubbing and a longer shot of Haim and Eggert's first party sex scene in her bedroom. An old website says they're the same,[11] but I disagree. There are Internet mumblings that it was a made-for-TV movie, but based on the nudity, this makes zero sense. The reviews and

---

9 "Hi, Mary Lou, [Rhonda] speaking. Sorry I can't come to the phone right now, but I'm busy at the prom [cheerleading]. Places to go. People to kill. Don't bother leaving a message. Vicky [my parents] don't live here anymore." I thought it was hilarious. My dad's boss sounded so terrified. Whoops.

---

10 https://www.rollingstone.com/culture/culture-features/corey-feldman-expose-pedophilia-hollywood-darkest-secrets-825375/
11 https://www.dvdtalk.com reviews/8532/blown-away/

blogs and 'net chatter for this film are ancient, with many even on kinda dead-looking, forgotten websites. And those surround other sites and articles that are basically saying peace out/RIP to Corey Haim. It's all depressing, so much so that I just wanna give the net a good scrub.

The film's love triangle tale itself, while clichéd, works here, as it pits brother against brother, although overall the whole scenario is preposterous: The cops and attorneys are played as fools (and I like Gary Farmer), so this is the only way a devious Eggert can get away with her shenanigans (including missing her target that's only five feet in front of her, with two weapons unloading a half dozen shots). The sex scenes are solid, the 'closed for the season' resort atmosphere is perfect for this kind of thriller, and the acting is fine all around. The underrated Kathleen Robertson is on point as always, Jean LeClerc is appropriately intense, the perfectly lit sweat rivulets on Eggert's upper and lower back during a trying-to-be-quiet-and-failing sex scene should have their own sequel, and there's yet another damn manly motorcycle scene just as macho as *Wild Orchid* and way more macho than *Cool as Ice*.

I defend this movie, then and now, for another reason, or actually four beautiful reasons:

*Two obscure songs: Both EP vinyls by John James (goth/club/rap/dance) 1. "She Bought Love" and 2. "(Still) The Beat Goes On."

*Two pieces of Eggert fashion: Her black dress in the sexy predator dance bar scene and that see-through, fluttery, iridescent white cover-up she wears over her bikini at the party scene—and later in a brief coming to get Haim scene, because the cops are at the door. Five stars for all.

Yes, that's it. That black dress is the reason I even have a Patreon (which will expire on 02/02/2020). I do own the two obscure LPs, as well (my Discogs illustrates my eclectic taste). And if you subscribe, you can see the photographic evidence of this rascality.

Far from Home (1989):

Like I give a palpable hoot about critics. That role is up there with guidance counselors, and "If they knew anything about career moves, would they have ended up as guidance counselors?" (Christian Slater, *Pump Up the Volume*). The same holds true for me about critics: They would prefer to talk about art instead of making it. *DVD Talk* and *TV Guide* were both, like, "Blah blah this movie is 'predictable' and Barrymore is young, so she 'must have been exploited.'" If you've read Drew Barrymore's early bio, *Little Girl Lost*, you probably know better. I read the book the year it came out, 1991. *People* magazine archive stories from the early '90s are still on the Web, and I cut out a number of them back in the day because what girl didn't want to be Barrymore at the height of her Guess modeling career? *Far from Home* may have prepped Barrymore for *Guncrazy*, *Poison Ivy*, and *Mad Love*, but I've never heard her speak in disparaging ways about any of these films, nor *Far from Home*. And it's actually not that predictable, frankly, and the all-star cast is so good, even if you are the big deal who can guess the end (and good for you, whatever), it matters so little because they can all *act*. And for her first onscreen kiss with Jones? Barrymore does a great job too, professional. The attempted rape scene is intense (as it should be, because it is) but not remotely exploitive.

This movie went weirdly unnoticed, except as a cult classic to its rabid fans or, as star Andras Jones and I have discussed, a jerk-off film for teen girls. I still say this is correct. It's not just the adorable Anthony Rapp[12] and the irresistible Jones (and frankly, the tempestuous Tyrrell), it's that hot and dirty trailer park sex[13] scene—and...oh, wow...I also *just* realized a sync about trailer park sex that I absolutely cannot fucking print here—with those two hot and dirty....who even were those people again? BRB, I have to actually research this. Ooh, the woman is Teri Weigel and the man, well, was Murrill Maglio (adult film star and Weigel's husband). He passed away in 2015.

Barrymore writes in a journal in the film, and her father *is* a journalist. I'd grow up to write in approximately 15 journals a year (and yes, I still have them), and I *am* an entertainment journalist. Literally, my life was shaped by the films I watched as a young girl. There was no stopping it, there is still no stopping it. Tyrrell pops up again for me in film here (and in *Angel*, of course); she's so confident and unique. I'll go to the afterlife pissed I could never meet her and hoping to God there's some way we can chat on the other side. Jones speaks fondly not only of the era, but also of the area where the film was shot. Now the site of Burning Man but untouched while they were there, the desert holds many syncs for both Jones and me, and to this day, when I chew ice, I never fail to think of the sexy Barrymore/Jones ice cube scene—and I am OK with all of this. Make no mistake, ice is a motif in the film and, apparently, my life.

---

12   Anthony Rapp was a guest on an episode of *The Radio8Ball Show* podcast, hosted by Andras Jones, and I so wanted that visit between the two co-stars of *Far from Home* to go on **forever**. Young Rhonda, in another universe/on another timeline, howled in teen angst delight.

13   I've seen this movie 800 times, and with this last viewing, I only just caught a *major* personal sync for this sex scene. Holy shit. Mind blown. If you see me at a con and you're buying a copy of *Medium Chill*, you can ask me about it.

Fashion in film has always been a huge love of mine, and this film is no different. The watches—Barrymore wears several simultaneously on one arm, and so did I. It's come around again, if it ever left. Just Google the fabulous Billie Eilish and those pics may pop for you. Barrymore wore chains on her black boots, and so did I. And I still remember the *Easy Rider* joke at my expense in 7th grade. The beautiful simplicity of the sweaty, dusty white cotton tee/tank. I'm telling you, between this movie and Linnea Quigley's Spider ensemble in *Sorority Babes in the Slimeball Bowl-O-Rama*, my youthful fashion moments both unnerved a lot of people and provided me, to this day, with many fond memories.

Bearded legend Richard Masur's Duckett character is probably more my speed these days: He told me capitalism sucked before we all knew it really sucked. "Money means nothing to me" and "I no longer worship at the altar of Mammon" make more sense to me now, as an adult, than they did as a teen, but I'm grateful for this early training. I may have been "the man's" bitch for a little while, but the words of Duckett would eventually find me again and stick around. The "You're off your beetle" quote from Dick Miller, whom I would meet at a con (and may he RIP), is another weird line that stuck with me for all my life. I say it from time to time, and at NO point in my 30 years of saying it, has anyone EVER known what the hell it means. And "I'll be right back," Masur's character says before getting shanked, and we know what *that* means from watching *Scream* (1996). The film kinda nailed it.

I don't eat fish sticks but, if I did, you bet I'd ask if they were Aqua Boy. Matt Frewer is a superstar, Jennifer Tilly a muffin. Connie Sawyer (the Viney Hunt character) is a legend who passed away in 2018 at the age of 105. Creepy kid who never stood a chance, played by Stephanie Walski, ditched acting after this film (a net search turned up that she may or may not be a real estate agent). I would love to know her memories of time on this set. Banco, Nevada, the film's fictional town, strangely reminds me of *a lot* of towns I've visited while driving around the U.S.—a formerly fun hobby that was ruined for me, possibly permanently, in 2018. The ending shot of Jones on the tracks as Frewer and Barrymore ride outta town is classic symbolism, literary even.

So, no, maybe *Home* wasn't a big box buzz or worthy of a Criterion Collection release, but I, myself, and a few serious fans, love this little mess of a film with all our hearts and carry it with us, in many ways, wherever we go.

Tuff Turf (1985):

This is the second bomb on my list from producer Donald P. Borchers (see also: *Far from Home*). Whoever the man is, he has some serious taste I can identify with.

While Ebert blasts its structure, this film made $9 million in theaters and frankly has a gaggle of fans out here *still* screaming about how much we love it and how many lovely

memories from childhood it brings back. Don't deny us this one beautiful thing in the bleak hold of 2019. This film IS fashion and cast and music. It's an updated musical Romeo and Juliet and endlessly quotable: "Life isn't a problem to be solved; it's a mystery to be lived. So, live it" and "Just eat it; you'll never see it again." These two poetic lines have served me well for 30 years. And who didn't run out and get a pair of red pumps after seeing this movie, and then go get some cool '80s accessories, crimp some hair, and do that ponytail wraparound thing Kim Richards does at the country club? And allow me to be frank: I still have a similar version of the black-and-white tee dress she slips on before Spader comes to visit through her bedroom window. I bet some of you could have guessed that.

And speaking of Kim Richards, was she or was she not so fucking gorgeous, so unbelievably flawless that even grown-ass manly men just wanted to be her for five minutes? Don't @ me, and don't bother to fight me. Do not Rotten Tomato at me either. I have a consuming minor in soc and know what the fuck I'm talking about. And now you can laugh all you want, but I have *actually seen* a fight handled very closely to the one briefly shown during the choreographed warehouse dance-off. It was as beautiful and ridiculous and amazing in real life as it was in the film's well-crafted scene. You know the one: James Spader goes around in a few partner pirouettes with a gang member before making a break for it. Imagine that in real life. No? Come see me and I'll demonstrate for you. Prepare to get your ass choreographically kicked.

Creepozoids (1988):

The defense for this apocalyptic atmospheric bomb includes the obvious: On my FB (in the Notes section), there's my old MicroShock interview with Ken Abraham (and I leave it up to you to decide whose ass is more perfect in this film, his or Linnea's); Ashlyn Gere[14] is emoting at a Shakespearean level energy here, and her clothed form is that of an arrogant mannequin; the FX of the baby Creepozoid is so ridiculously great that I know I'm not the only one who wishes I had one to do my bidding and pal around with (before *Bad Milo*, we had the baby Creepozoid); and finally, the Guy Moon[15] score is a

---

14 Billed as Kim McKamy. Also, in a weird sync, her IMDB lists a role in *Angel III*, AND she's a body double in *Basic Instinct*.

15 https://en.wikipedia.org/wiki/Guy_Moon

masterpiece. This is how the multiple award-winner got started.[16] This film's soundtrack/score was recently released on vinyl for Record Store Day (RSD) 2019 from Terror Vision Records and limited to 500 copies. After my score, there are only 498 out there now. I called in favors for that bad boy.

All of the lovable bombs above had one thing in common: As a kid, I really thought my life would look more like these films. A LOT more. Not the instances where I deliberately set out to mimic something either. I'm not trying to meme here, and I don't mean to suggest we all dead-stop and start singing and dancing all over the place (though that would be fine), but montage combinations of the film's colors with the music and fashion and all the pretty, pretty people....

---

16 https://www.imdb.com/name/nm0600615/awards

Come to think on it (and in retrospect), my life *does* look like certain parts of these movies, just not the parts I would have chosen first. *Wild Orchid*? I did get out to see the world after spending way too much time in school. *Angel*? I did get the transvestite friend after all and wrote the book about it. *Cool as Ice*? I've been the outsider who moved into a town and made it her own. *Blown Away*? Definitely the part of my life spent having sex with the bad boys and girls. *Far from Home*? Definitely wasted some time journaling in an insane small town in the desert (valley and high plains), and it was a Burning Man connection that got me there. *Tuff Turf*? Oh, who hasn't waged war against nasty school forces and bullies but still managed to catch a warehouse concert? *Creepozoids*? It definitely feels like the apocalypse this year, and while I didn't battle mutant rats, I did battle some mutant spiders. I'm only halfway done, though. I figure I have at least another 50 years on the planet, so there's still time—still more time to address the gap between the unintentional parts of my life that are straight outta those films and the parts that I'm still hopeful about that may still happen. It's all good stuff, though, even the bad, so I'll take it all as it comes and play it as it lies.

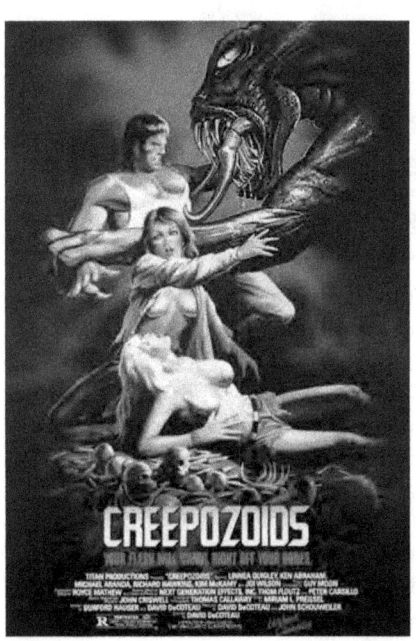

MOONRAKER (1979)

by Mike Haushalter

Moonraker was the 11th entry in the long-running James Bond franchise and the fourth turn for Roger Moore as suave super spy 007. It was the biggest Bond to date, which, looking back, was quite a feat considering it followed *The Spy Who Loved Me*, a film that featured Bond skiing off the side of a mountain, a sleek Lotus Esprit that transformed into a submarine, a ship-swallowing super tanker, Soviet female super spy Maj. Anya Amasova (Barbara Bach) aka Agent XXX, and, of course, the steel-toothed henchman Jaws (Richard Kiel). *The Spy Who Loved Me* not only cemented Moore as the reigning James Bond, it also could have been the biggest film of the 1970s, except that 1977 also saw the release of George Lucas's little space opera *Star Wars*, which changed everything for everyone.

The end credit crawl of *The Spy Who Loved Me* promised that Bond would indeed return....in *For Your Eyes Only*. And return he did, but, as it turned out, *For Your Eyes Only* would have to wait a bit longer. Thanks to *Star Wars* and

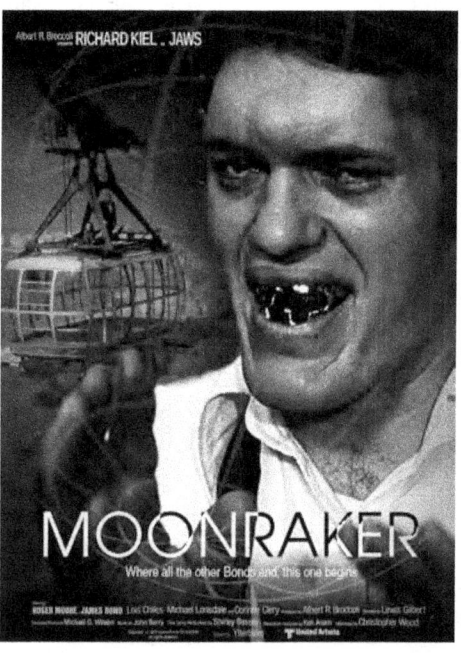

the clamor for every film to now take place in space, such an earthbound James Bond tale would not cut it. In its place came *Moonraker*, a film that, unlike other films that promised the moon, actually delivered it (at least according to the ad hype).

For a time, it was one of the biggest moneymakers of the Bond franchise, but *Moonraker* is not looked upon with much love nowadays. This is a shame, because I think it's one of the best Bond adventures, and it features what is perhaps the pinnacle of all supervillain schemes.

First off, it offers up just about everything *The Spy Who Loved Me* did, only a bit bigger and better. It has fantastic set pieces, including an amazing teaser featuring Bond thrown out of an airplane without a parachute and trying to retrieve one on the way down (done for real by a fantastic stunt team doing over 90 jumps), a great boat chase, a near-deadly turn in a g-force centrifuge device and a fight in a glass museum—all topped off with an epic space battle. It has three great Bond women—Emily Bolton (*Valentino*) as Manuela, Corinne Cléry (*The Story of O*) as Corinne Dufour, and Lois Chiles (*Death on the Nile*) as Holly Goodhead, who excels at putting Bond in his place. It has a return appearance by Richard Kiel as Jaws, who was so beloved by kids that they all wrote letters asking for his return. The film has my favorite Bond villain, Hugo Drax (Michael Lonsdale), a brilliant megalomaniac billionaire with a god complex and a rare, almost-well-thought out plan for world domination. Lonsdale seems to have an almost palpable scorn for Bond, delivering some of the most acerbic dialogue of the franchise and is perhaps the greatest of Bond's adversaries during Moore's tenure as 007.

Another plus for the film is that Moore was on the top of his game in *Moonraker*, offering up all of his famed charm and charisma along with a bit more acting than normal. For once, the unflappable Moore even looks a bit ruffled by some of the danger that comes his way.

I will admit that some of this film has not aged too well. Like almost every Bond film, *Moonraker* is not very politically correct, has a distinct lack of diversity, and, of course, there is a good deal of sexism. Some of its humor is also a bit juvenile even for Bond (even Moore's Bond). But for me, its pluses outweigh the minuses and it's one of my favorites.

Moore as Bond and Lois Chiles as as the classily-named Holly Goodhead.
© United Artists. All Rights Reserved.

SHOCK TREATMENT: WHEN A SEQUEL IS SUPERIOR TO WHAT CAME BEFORE

by Douglas Waltz

I am here to defend the film *Shock Treatment*. Not Sam Fuller's Stuart Whitman film from 1964. And, no, not the film from 1973 starring Alain Delon. Both are fine films that deserve some defense, but not here.

I am talking about the much-maligned sequel to *The Rocky Horror Picture Show*.

Why? Well, because it's a better film than its predecessor, that's why.

As you gasp in horror over this statement, let's run down why *The Rocky Horror Picture Show* holds such a dear place in our collective hearts. It's because it's one of the few films in history that encourages audience participation. People love *The Rocky Horror Picture Show* because of the memories they have of experiencing it in a room of like-minded individuals. Our brains love experiencing things with a large number of like-minded individuals. It's just the way that, for the most part, the human brain functions.

I remember when they had announced the sequel.

Rocky Horror fans lost their shit.

A friend of mine was able to get a copy of the shooting script, and he began poring over it to see how it would be incorporated into the live experience we all loved with *The Rocky Horror Show*. I was one of many who attended the Le Bijou in downtown Kalamazoo for the midnight showing of *Rocky Horror* every week, and I had fun with it. I never went both nights, though. The Le Bijou was a double-screen theater, and the other screen showed things like *Dawn of the Dead*, *Basket Case*, *Repo Man*, and *Liquid Sky*. No way was I missing any of that. But every Saturday, I was there, yelling, dancing, singing, and throwing crap at the screen.

So, yeah, I read the shooting script.

The first thing I recognized was that it wasn't a sequel. It was, well…,it was weird and seemed really obsessed with television.

Then, the day came when it arrived at our local theater, and they played it Friday night instead of the long-running *Rocky Horror*.

It was so quiet in that theater that the ringleaders of the group tried to make snappy patter and stuff, but it fell on its face. I realized, as I watched it, that this was a better movie. You see, *Rocky Horror* started life as a stage production, and it is extremely clever. It skewers the old sci-fi haunted-house movies of the '50s and '60s and adds a healthy dollop of sex and music. What's not to love?

But in the end, the film based on the stage musical plays very much like, well, a stage musical. Tim Curry as Frank N. Furter is so captivating on-screen that he makes the other actors dim in every scene he's in. You look at him. You really have no choice.

So, good movie, fun audience participation.

Now, here's why *Shock Treatment* is a better, smarter movie that demands your attention.

Remember this movie was made in 1981, before the Internet, before streaming services, before smartphones. The biggest movie of the year was *Raiders of the Lost Ark*.

Shock Treatment starts many years later., Brad and Janet have survived their encounter at Dr. Frank N. Furter's—presumably, as nothing in *Rocky Horror* is ever referenced—and have been happily wed, more or less, for quite some time. Denton has morphed into a town set in one giant local television station, DTV.

As the day starts, the station opens its doors and the entire populace of Denton crowds into the huge stadium seating in front of the stage. We then get the Denton Anthem, with Janet's mother and father participating along with Ralph Hapschatt, still played by Jeremy Newson. This leads directly into Denton Dossier, hosted by Betty Hapschatt (Ruby Wax this time around) and Judge Oliver Wright (Charles Gray, who played the narrator in the first film and, in my opinion, is the same character and no one knows it).

After a commercial break for Farley Flavors Fast Food, we head right into Marriage Maze, hosted by Bert Schnick (the amazing Barry Humphries), a blind gameshow host who helps people fix their marriages. And who should they choose for the first round but Brad (Cliff DeYoung) and Janet (Jessica Harper). Everyone assumes that the choice is random, but we know that the new owner of DTV, Farley Flavors, has other plans for the married couple. Soon, Brad has been sent to a rest home (read asylum for this) and Janet is whisked off to

59

L-R Patricia Quinn, Manning Redwood, Jessica Harper, Barry Humphries, Darlene Johnson, Little Nell Campbell. All Photos this section © 20th Century Fox. All Rights Reserved.

be in the local soap opera Dentonvale. Dr. Cosmo McKinley (Richard O'Brien) and Dr. Nation McKinley (Patricia Quinn) want to treat Brad, but Janet puts off signing the forms, after a little advice from Nurse Ansalong (the delightful Nell Campbell, who has a lot of trouble staying in her two-sizes-too-small nurse's outfit throughout the film).

It's interesting to note that, when they are questioning Brad about what is causing their marriage problems, he gets ready to answer, but then Cosmo gives him a hypodermic to the neck and he passes out. It's really the only time we might have had some insight into the whole situation, and it is snubbed out on the spot.

Meanwhile, Janet's parents have won a trip to Dentonvale, where the prize is that you're on a TV show. In 1981, this predates the reality TV glut we all experienced in the '90s and early '00s by quite a few years.

Cosmo and Nation tell Janet that the more famous she becomes, the better Brad will get, so she decides to go along with it. And it isn't long before fame goes right to her head. Meanwhile, Betty and Oliver continue to investigate the goings-on behind the TV station and the new owner, Farley. It's obvious they are getting close to something when their show is cancelled. Ralph delivers the news along with the revelation that he and Betty have been divorced for quite some time, their happy wedding day from the first film nothing more than a dim memory. It's also when Betty gives us one of the oddest, harshest lines in the film when she opens an envelope Ralph gives her, thinking it's her alimony check, and snarls, "Alimony is just another word for rape."

The movie does this throughout. Janet's father feels like he jumped right off the Trump campaign bandwagon when he sings his song while mowing the lawn. The entire song is filled with manly things that men do and ends with the last line "Faggots are maggots. Thank God I'm a man."

Like I said, harsh; probably harsher now than 1981, but still pretty harsh, especially when you consider that is the same year the AIDS virus was identified. The acid is pure Richard O'Brien.

As the film hurtles towards its climax with the nationwide broadcast of Farley Flavors Faith Factory, Betty and Oliver discover some horrifying facts—that Brad and Farley are twin brothers and the McKinleys are nothing more than…character actors? Farley has been manipulating the couple to get what he wants more than anything, the supposed happiness of the wedded bliss of Brad and Janet Majors.

Every one of the principle actors in this film is just on point: Charles Gray as stodgy Judge Oliver Wright, Ruby Wax as Betty Hapschatt, who has eyes for Oliver and can do anything with a hairpin—pick a lock? Start a car? You name it and one of her endless supply of hairpins is there to save the day. Richard O'Brien and Patricia Quinn as the doctors who, while working for Farley, are actually pursuing a bizarre agenda of their own, are slightly reminiscent of Riff Raff and Magenta—enough so that the revelation of their actually being character actors is a clever wink at the audience. Barry Humphries as the ultimate gameshow host, who,, we slowly realize, is a Nazi who escaped from Germany before the fall of the Third Reich, is a delight to watch on the screen. We figure out pretty quickly that the blindness bit is a sham, but when he encounters Janet in her new black dress, his comment that he loves the color is beyond witty. Jessica Harper is, well, I love Jessica Harper and everything she has been in. And her throaty, deep singing voice adds a dimension

Quinn, Rik Mayall, Little Nell, Richard O'Brien, and Cliff DeYoung (on TV).

"Trust me...I'm a doctor."

to her previously one-dimensional character. We have no idea what has happened in the years since the first film, but it's obvious who wears the pants in that marriage. Assertive and funny, she knows it, and when fame comes along, she dives in headfirst, not for Brad, but for herself. She feels she deserves it.

I saved the best for last with Cliff DeYoung. Playing the part of the clueless, disheveled Brad Majors is one thing, but then he becomes the slick snake oil salesman Farley Flavors, and to be honest, the first time I watched it I didn't realize it was the same actor. His movements, his mannerisms…hell, he even sings in a different key, depending on which part he's playing. Just genius to watch on-screen, and, when it culminates into the final showdown during the Faith Factory broadcast, you can see that something happened to Farley that broke him for good. Whether it has anything to do with that facial scar that is never mentioned in the film or not, we will never know. All we know is that Farley has everything and all he wants is what his twin brother has: happiness. After all, isn't that what Denton is all about?

Finally, since this is a musical, let's run down the tunes that move the action along. The obvious winners are the anthem "Denton, U.S.A.," which sets the tone of the film, and "Bitchin' in the Kitchen," which outlines what is going wrong in Brad and Janet's marriage. "Little Black Dress" is just a cute tune that helps break up the fact that they are trying to destroy a marriage from nothing more than pure jealousy. The title song is probably one of the best and a great spotlight for O'Brien's vocal talents, although I worry about that huge vein in his head as he shrieks in Brad's face during the song. "Look What I Did to My Id" might be the strangest song in the film and shows the lengths that people will go to just for a small taste of fame. Finally, the "Duel Duet" between Brad and Farley at the end.

I do want to mention the song "Lullaby," for no other reason than the song itself, taken out of the context of the film, is just sweet. I used to sing it to my children when they were little.

So, *Shock Treatment*—that sequel you've heard of but never watched, the film that flopped when it was first released, which takes the core of Brad and Janet from the first film and firmly deposits them into the insanity of local television, skewering it in the process—,might be one of the best musical comedies, with such a dark edge to it that you have to experience it firsthand.

But I will warn you, the movie has many more layers than you experience with the first viewing, and the more you watch it, the more you will want to watch it.

It gets right into your brain and refuses to leave.

TAKE TWO: SHOCK TREATMENT

by Scooter McCrae

I'm still surprised by the number of *Rocky Horror Picture Show* devotees I encounter who—although they have seen *RHPS* hundreds of times and participated in the floor show and know every single lyric and moment by heart—have either never heard of or never seen its much underappreciated and relatively unknown sequel (or is it an equal, as the poster art contends?), *Shock Treatment*.

It truly grieves me, as I love both films so much—each for very different reasons. *RHPS* is a toe-tapping, don't-dream-it-be-it free-for-all that loves everybody no matter what their sexual orientation or kink, while also having a blast addressing and turning 1950s-genre-film clichés on their heads. *Shock Treatment*, on the other hand, is a bit more of a kick in the teeth, as it confronts rampant consumerism and how the desire to achieve fame at all costs strangles the soul and hurts everybody trapped in its wake. And like its sunnier predecessor, it's also a toe-tapping musical of an entirely different sort.

In this film, the further adventures of Brad and Janet (played this time by Cliff DeYoung and Jessica Harper, respectively), they find themselves trapped inside a large TV studio that constantly broadcasts their live exploits 24 hours a day as they bounce between various game shows and soap operas in an early version of what we are now inured to as "reality television"—although, back in 1981, it all seemed more like a ridiculously twisted sci-fi vision of a world too silly to ever actually happen (if only). In fact, 13 years earlier, Nigel Kneale, legendary creator of the Quatermass character and TV serials, similarly predicted the "reality television" phenomenon is his prescient *The Year of the Sex Olympics*, a TV production that must at some point have been seen by and impacted Richard O'Brien. If ever there was a musical to be made out of a Kneale program, *Shock Treatment* is most certainly it. And that is why I love *Shock Treatment*.

THE FAN (1996)

by Nick Clement

Pulverized by critics and essentially ignored by theatrical audiences, Tony Scott's *The Fan* is an angry, mean, and scathing portrait of a psychopathic knife salesman (a deranged Robert De Niro) who stalks a Barry Bonds-esque baseball superstar (cocky and perfectly cast Wesley Snipes), and it served as Scott's attempt at a straight-ahead thriller. He definitely got the pulse racing, with the wild narrative becoming a tad overblown, turning it into a fun, overheated guilty pleasure, as well as a major stylistic bridge for the action auteur. Its frequent sense of over-the-topness doesn't stop it from being extremely entertaining every step of the way, all the way up to the asinine climax that literally makes zero sense with that torrential rainstorm.

It's also got some glossier-than-glossy cinematography courtesy of Dariusz Wolski, and, as per usual, a throbbing Hans Zimmer musical score that pounds away on the soundtrack. Scott even got some select tracks from The Rolling Stones for this film, and, make no mistake, the famously energetic director definitely put his rock-and-roll spin on America's pastime. Christian Wagner's and Claire

De Niro meets Snipes. © Tri-Star Pictures. All Rights Reserved.

Simpson's aggressive editing patterns help to maintain a wicked-fast pace, with purposefully jagged edges that keep the viewer alert and anxious. Aesthetically, *The Fan* glistens with top-flight professionalism.

But *The Fan* made one thing clear: Never hire a Brit to shoot a baseball movie, because Scott didn't know what he was doing with the game-time scenes in this dark, bombastic thriller. There are numerous mismatched shots, continuity errors between games and teams and players and uniforms, and the climactic moments seem to be set during a hurricane rather than a simple rainstorm. I've heard that Scott objected to some studio-imposed cuts and wanted more scenes with Benicio Del Toro, which, I believe, were shot but then axed. Working with De Niro had to have been a huge incentive for Scott, and it marked a second collaboration, after the previous year's *Crimson Tide*, with cameraman Wolski, who would then be drafted by Ridley Scott for future efforts including *Prometheus* and *The Counselor*.

There's a Nine Inch Nails quality to much of this feverish thriller, which was adapted by screenwriter Phoef Sutton from the original novel by Peter Abrahams, and it paints a nasty portrait of an unhinged man hell-bent on self-destruction in nearly every scene and instance. It's also frequently rather hysterical, even if the laughs are of the darker variety. De Niro essentially does a riff on the various nutballs he'd previously played for the cinema, so, as such, you see bits and pieces of characters from other films peppered throughout. Snipes is effectively cast as the ego-driven superstar, John Leguizamo is

65

aces as the sleazy agent, and Ellen Barkin has a chance to do some nice ball-busting as an in-your-face radio show host who is always looking to egg everyone on. So much of this movie kicks so much ass that it's a shame that the finale goes haywire, but before that, The Fan operates as a blunt and enjoyable smack to the face, made with supreme widescreen style by Scott, who never met an image he couldn't goose for maximum impact.

The Fan is available on a U.S. DVD release (still no American Blu-ray is available) and on German release Blu-ray, the latter of which retains the full 2.35:1 anamorphic widescreen aspect ratio. And trust me, you want that extra room, because this is one of the widest-looking films that Scott ever shot, and, when viewed in pan-and-scan, it can literally be responsible for inducing vomit, as the herky-jerky shifting within the frame is some of the most egregious ever put out on disc or broadcast by cable movie channels. Along with the theatrical cut of Scott's underrated neo-noir thriller Revenge, The Fan is the only other feature from this visual auteur that's not available in the premium home video format. The German special edition contains a snippet of 35mm film stock from the movie laminated into a collectible card (mine features Snipes looking super paranoid in close-up!), as well as a collectible booklet (written in German, so I need to take some classes) and an assortment of interviews, trailers, and an old-school featurette that hints at some scenes that never made the final cut! "Now do you care?"

GREASE 2 DESERVES ANOTHER LOOK
DO IT FOR YOUR COUNTRY

After horror, I don't know of any other genre more unfairly maligned than the musical. This may be why a good number of horror fans are also die-hard musical nerds (don't believe me, ask *Ultra Violent* magazine's Art Ettinger the next time you see him). For some reason, folks who have no trouble with space opera, aliens, uber-macho machine-gun freaks, [add your own trope here] just can't buy random strangers bursting into song. "How do they all know the words? How do they know the same dance?"

Coming up against such lack of imagination can be a real tragedy.

While the musical as a genre seems to have virtually died away (granted, it's been on the downslide since the 1960s), we don't get a full-blown musical on the big screen all that often. When we do, it's something overblown like *Les Misérables* or... *Cats*. It's understandable. They're expensive. They're complicated. Sometimes they become *La Land* and still make money. It's baffling.

Of the classics, I can't think of that many *bad* musicals. There are ones I like and ones I don't, but I can appreciate the care and pomp and circumstance that went into them. Of the non-classics (I'm looking at you, oddly shaped *The Pirate Movie*), some of the "minor" musicals were often dismissed as pop oddities. But there's one that I feel has been unfairly maligned since its release—and failure—in 1982. Scoffed at because it was a unnecessary sequel, dismissed as a series of "music videos" (already an insult in those nascent days of

MTV), it launched as many careers as it killed, but it has an inherently better message than that of its original. I'd even go as far as to say that it has a better score and is better shot, but then I'm straying too far astray. This isn't about *Grease*. It's about *Grease 2*.

Set in 1961, when John F. Kennedy is the shining hope for the future, but bomb shelters are still very much a reality, it's another first-day-of-school for Rydell High. As the entire student body dances its way through "Back to School Again," new-kid Michael Carrington (Maxwell Caulfield) arrives (English cousin to the Australian Sandy Olsson, last seen flying off into space in a convertible driven by the similarly missing Danny Zuko). Though his cousin's friend Frenchie (Didi Conn) is there to be his Virgil during this descent into the First Circle, Michael has to learn about the various rules of Rydell. First: The T-Birds run the school. Second: Pink Ladies don't date anyone but T-Birds. So, his instant infatuation with Stephanie Zinone (Michelle Pfeiffer) is already doomed.

On the other hand, Steph has decided that line about Pink Ladies' narrow dating pool doesn't work for her. For one thing, the T-Birds are the least intimidating gang ever. Their leader is her clingy, insecure ex-boyfriend, Johnny Nogerelli (the inexplicably appealing Adrian Zmed), who really should be paying more attention to Paulette (Lorna Luft) than worrying about who Stephanie is or isn't dating. Steph dreams of a "Cool Rider"—"Gimme a black motorcycle/with a man growing out of the seat"—and isn't shy about saying so. Which gives meek Michael an idea, namely to restore a motorcycle and teach himself how to be the greatest rider ever. He achieves this before Thanksgiving break.

Meanwhile, everyone else in the school is in heat. Louis DiMucci (Peter Frechette) cons Sharon (Maureen

Michelle Pfeiffer's secret to hitting high notes in Grease 2. All photos this section © 20th Century Fox. All Rights Reserved.

L-R: Adrian Zmed, Christopher McDonald, Peter Frechette, Leif Green as the world's least intimidating biker gang, The T-Birds.

Teefy) into a bomb shelter in the hopes she'll give it up before he ships off to war, and the pair sing the patriotically horny "Let's Do It for Our Country." New uber-whitebread substitute teacher Mr. Stewart (Tab Hunter) gets a little flustered by bubbly Ms. Mason (Connie Stevens) and channels that frustration towards getting his bio students' attention, singing about the "debauchery" of the bees and flowers in "Reproduction"—and I defy anyone to resist dancing to this film's "Greased Lightning."

Returning to Stephanie, the incognito Michael arrives on the scene in "Who's That Guy," the impossibly mysterious Cool Rider of her dreams. He attracts the ire of the T-Birds and the slightly scuzzier Scorpions. Motorcycle chases happen. At one point, the Rider is believed to be dead. I mean, nobody could've made that jump! Stephanie has a minor breakdown during the talent show, scuttling Sharon's "Girl for All Seasons" choreography, forcing the entire audience to enter her mind as she switches to a minor key and sings a duet with her imaginary Cool Rider in "Turn Back the Hands of Time."

Rather than help a student through an emotional metastasis, the student body elects Stephanie Queen of the Luau. Johnny is King, of course, because he's also top-billed. During the luau, the Scorpions tear things up but are chased off by the miraculous reappearance of the Cool Rider, who reveals himself to the gang. As a reward, he gets a membership jacket into the T-Birds, which means he can now date Stephanie—even though she's already made it clear that this rule doesn't work for her! Anyway, everyone sings "We'll Be Together" as they all fail to contemplate a future outside of Rydell High.

Grease 2 had cynical origins. *Grease* producer Alan Carr rushed the film into production to claim an expiring $5 million bonus from his

The smoldering intensity of Maxwell Caulfield and Pfeiffer.

original contract. He approached the first film's choreographer, Patricia Birch, to direct. Birch had been associated as choreographer with *Grease* since its '72 off-Broadway opening. Initially hesitant—none of the first film's creative team was returning, and there was no finished script from Ken Finkleman, as he was writing and directing *Airplane II* at the same time. Still, Birch threw caution to the wind and took on the challenge. Cinematography would be courtesy Frank Stanley, who prior had shot four tough-guy action movies for Clint Eastwood. Louis St. Louis, who had written new music for *Grease*, was coming aboard for the sequel, and that is one of the film's chief benefits. Michael Linde would be responsible for the movie's two best songs: "Reproduction" and "Cool Rider."

Also not returning were the two leads from *Grease*—Travolta and Newton-John were doing other things (at one point, the idea was floated that they'd have a cameo as owners of a gas station in town, but that was jettisoned for being, among other things, depressing). The new cast members were primarily unknowns. Caulfield was a British pretty boy Carr had seen on Broadway. Pfeiffer had done a couple of minor TV roles and was cast as a "wild card" by Birch. Luft was then best-known as Liza Minelli's half-sister. Zmed had just played Danny Zuko on stage and was taller than the role's runner-up, Tom Cruise.

What makes *Grease 2* work is the absolute sincerity of the cast and crew. However you feel about the first film, it was meant to be a nostalgia piece. The majority of the cast members are far too old to be believed as high schoolers (a problem *Grease 2* shares to a lesser degree), and there's a lot of winking at the camera going on. In *Grease 2*, everyone is committed to the reality they're in. Birch keeps the camera wide-open during the larger group numbers, and everyone looks like they're having fun.

My personal favorite parts of the film are the more surreal moments. I've never been able to work out if some of these things are intentional or just inevitable by-products of the genre. "Cool Rider" starts with Stephanie explaining to Michael why he isn't good enough for her, but midway through, Michael is no longer relevant to her thought processes. He watches as she continues to sing about her ideal…and then she leaves, taking the song with her. Michael has a brief conversation with Frenchie, and we can still hear the song continuing, presumably as Stephanie makes her way home.

The film's talent show climax is another favorite moment. We never do get the entirety of "Girl for All Seasons." The performance is cut off twice in rehearsals, and, during the actual show, Stephanie, overcome by her grief for the presumed-dead Rider, goes into her imagination and has a duet with him. But she's also still on stage in front of the entire school—many of whom look appropriately freaked out that their friend is having some sort of episode—and she comes out of her trance singing the song that played in her head…and the talent show band has somehow followed the key change!

But when you get down to it, my hands-down favorite bit is the delivery of its message. In the original, Danny and Sandy Magi-Gift each other's personalities—he becomes a jock and she becomes a leather girl, changing themselves to be what they think the other person wants. In *Grease 2*, Stephanie isn't going to change for anyone. She wants what she wants and doesn't see why she should compromise. Moreover, she's "tired of being someone's chick." Her Cool Rider would be her partner.

If Michael wants to be with her, he'd better start taking her interests into consideration. Michael doesn't seem to compromise who he is, but he puts the Rider on as a role to see if it fits him. Stephanie is his goal, but he intends to earn her, not win her.

The music is lively and contagious ("Reproduction" and "Cool Rider" have become staples at horror con after-parties…OK, it's a staple at Pittsburgh's Horror Realm), and it should have been better-received than it was. For my money, it deserves a second chance and a little more respect than it's gotten in the past. At the very least, could we get a Blu-ray, Shout Factory?

As the Pink Ladies: Maureen Teefy, Lorna Luft, Alison Price, and Pfeiffer.

A HIGHLY OPINIONATED TREATISE AND PAINFUL DEFENSE OF JESS FRANCO'S THE PERVERSE COLLECTION

by Dr. Rhonda Baughman

Anything good can happen. Defending bombs for *ExNat*, I can defend JF for *GP*. All truth—I worked on one JF film, *the lost film*, as those of us who were in it call it (or maybe just me). It's the one JF film you may never see. Our producer is dead. Lina Romay is dead. Jess Franco is dead. My director is still alive, but, frankly, if I were this guy, I'd be distancing myself from this *Poltergeist*-set curse meets *Final Destination* shit too. And don't tell me otherwise! It's just like that, but with, you know, lots of nudity and high creep sex factors (the two things those movies certainly do not have).

I could probably spend a good chunk of the rest of my time on this planet watching Franco films (heaven only knows how many movies he really has;, sources differ on the number). The guy had more pseudonyms than...well, than me and JT LeRoy combined. But that's not the point. And love him or hate him, Franco and his canon won't disappear anytime soon, and that's really saying something about the current state of cinema—which often feels like those sad, greasy kernels at the bottom of the soggy cup, and I want to suck on them but don't want to get my hands salty and dirty. I'm not really sure where the fuck I was going with that analogy, but here we are, and I feel the need to wash my hands. Actually, I was just demonstrating what it feels like watching a Franco film: It starts one way, gets weird, we have no idea what's happening, and then it's time to wash hands. Am I right or am I right?

What kind of energy will I unleash with defending this cinematic madness? I wondered. I just want to have *fun* on my own terms with the time I have left, and this, defending a genius madman's collection, seemed like a good way to do that very thing. I think Franco would have approved. I'd pull out a Ouija board and ask, but that really is how a horror film begins and, while I'm not paranoid, I am cautious.

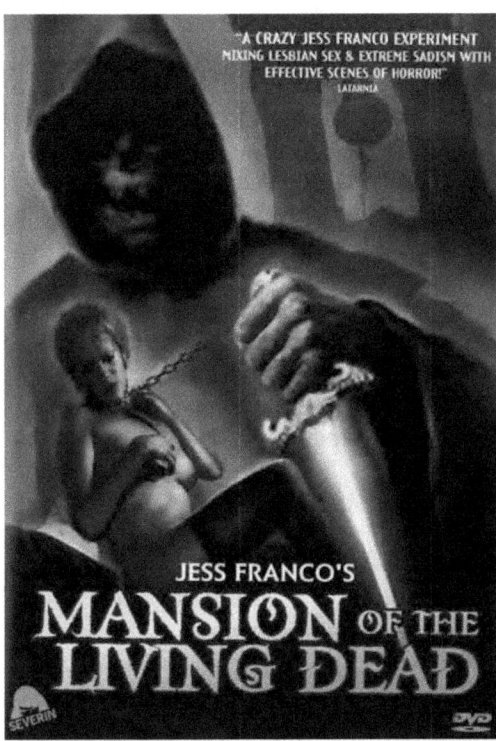

The Mansion of the Living Dead (1982) or (1985) (No one seems to agree.)

Candy Coster IS Lina Romay. Well, she's certainly the only actress who can legitimately pull off Franco's dialogue here with anything resembling finesse or authenticity. The sets are beautiful, the naked women are beautiful, the atmosphere is creepy-beautiful—and this is the type of film on which one can easily perform witchcraft, so really the movie defends itself. Oh, the plot! Right! Good vacation idea turned bad. Minor lesbian hijinks. Terrible living dudes and terrible dead dudes doing terrible dude things: for example, worshiping Satan, leaving a girl hanging (literally and figuratively), and rape. Trigger warning about 45 minutes in for an extended rape scene (and there's another one later). So, men behaving badly and subjugating women and making terrible excuses for their terrible behavior. I'm not being critical, just trying to be honest. The death cult eventually finds its salvation in (ironically?) a woman. The particular Severin release I watched had a GREAT interview with Franco (*The Mansion That Jess Built*) that explained a LOT. One thing I will also say about Franco films (not just this one): Some of them make me uncomfortable. I'm not referring to just the rape scenes either, but *other* things: Maybe it's a consensual sex scene, maybe it's just some dialogue, maybe it's something sensual sans nudity, or maybe it's something weird—and I'm hoping you know what I mean without giving a specific example—but *something* in the film (pick whatever you want) makes me uncomfortable. And I appreciate Franco's movie for that reason: I am forced to self-reflect and examine exactly why I am uncomfortable. Not easy to do, but totally necessary for growth.

***Macumba Sexual* (1983) AKA #yuppiesbeware AKA #weirdshitafoot AKA #hellovagina**

Like just about all Franco movies—damn, are his locations gorgeous! And from the get-go, Romay is naked. Like, the film doesn't even start with her clothed. She was definitely not shy about the human form, and she does put clothes on at approximately the 20-minute mark. Just kidding, they're back off two minutes later. Clothes runtime: two2 minutes. Her unclothed runtime: 78 minutes. Credits: 0 minutes. And full disclosure, I only know what "macumba" means because of *Dawn of the Dead* (1978).

This flick clocks in at 80 minutes, and I think my preferred Franco length is 45-50 minutes. His story ideas themselves are phenomenal, even literary. He's mentioned various authors in his interviews—ones I've been meaning to check out—and it shows (example: Gustavo Adolfo Bécquer)! But literary or not, the actual visually coherent execution of said ideas is hit-or-miss. I doubt Franco would even mind if I said that I can *see* the literary genius potential, if not the actual executed genius. It has to do with character development, and this film is a prime example of it—as in, there is none. I had a watch party at my house and everyone, at one point or another, asked, "Who the hell is this person now?" Halfway through, we decided it didn't matter, since we assumed the whole damn film was a dream. I zoned out at one point, only to zone back in and ask if those people were making out on a Snuggie, but alas, no, it was just a fluffy cape. Lots of moaning and screaming audio, and sometimes it syncs with what's on-screen and sometimes it doesn't. But I think that's the point: One can never really tell the fine line between pleasurable vocalization and displeasured utterance. Or I might just be giving too much credit to incomprehensible plot and terrible sound dubbing.

Also like a lot of Franco films, the kissing is awkward here. It rarely fails in his films—there's always some kissing scene where I can't help thinking, "Uh, I don't think these people even like each other." But then, with the sex scenes themselves and this flick in particular, I just...I don't think they're acting. And speaking of awkward, one of the sex scenes wasn't so much the sex (—or even awkward) —as it was kinda terrifying. I'm pretty sure someone should have put the camera down to see if the actress was all right—and seizure-free. I'm actually not trying to be funny either, because the scene in question wasn't funny nor sensual, it was damn creepy. I think Jess and Lina probably had a crush on Ajita Wilson and brought her onto the film for that reason (she laughs and reminds me of the hooker Rourke picks up in *9 ½ Weeks*). Sadly, Wilson would actually die from a brain hemorrhage lessonly a few than years after this film was made, and somehow, after seeing the movie, I'm not even a little bit surprised. I wound up liking *Mansion of the Living Dead* more: Now *that* was surprising to me. Unsurprising, my favorite part of this disc was the 22-minute interview *Voodoo Jess*. I loved hearing how Jess and Lina met and how they spoke of one another. It's understandable that, after one passed away, the other quickly followed. And, based on their love and light in general, and not just for one another, I can see why Kevin Collins (director of the unreleased *Take-Away Spirit*) lost the passion to finish the film once his friends died: They were a force of nature.

Some final notes after watching the interview and recalling the tiny plot about buying the island house: I think Zalman King used this tale of Jess's to make *Wild Orchid*. Also, Franco acts in this one, and if you watch the interview, his part makes sense, AS DOES some of the more intense and inexplicable behavior. What happened to these people on this set is what happened to those on the set of *The Attic Expeditions* (2001). Some energy was opened, and it's impossible to close once committed to film. The picture used for this blog is from this film and its use is intentional.

The Inconfessable Orgies of Emmanuelle (1982)
AKA *Emmanuelle Exposed* and one of the who-even-knows-how-many in the *Emmanuelle* series

This one, correctly, is listed as a pornographic drama, and I don't think I saw Lina Romay (or a pseudonym) in this one. Loved the opening title artwork—very weirdly Spanish. And I might run the risk of sounding like a prude here, which I certainly am not, but I don't like old pornography, and I don't like new pornography either. Not because it's vulgar per se, but I find myself bored. Is that weird? I feel like that's weird. And speaking of vulgar, the character of Tony hilariously states: "I moved to this place to escape the mob and vulgarity of the people of Spain."

At the beginning of the movie, characters are visiting a wax museum, which is both terrifying and phenomenal! I bet this will be the highlight of the movie for me. I hope not, but I have a feeling. (Seriously!

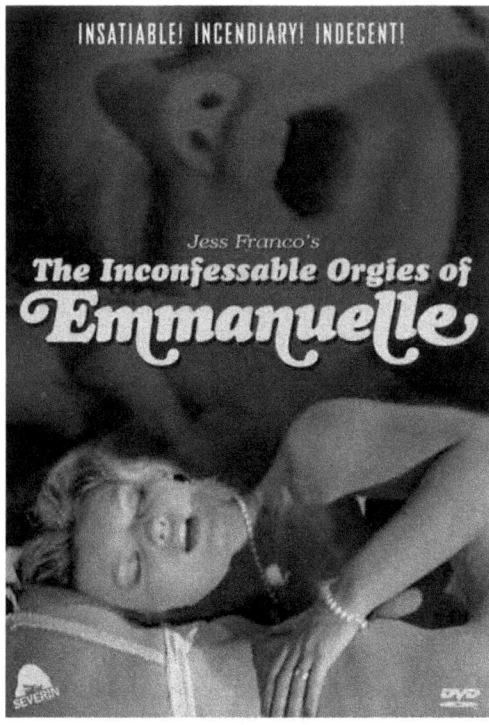

hanging off dangerously.

The world's longest stripper scene goes on for at least 10 minutes——the camera zoom factor had me shouting, "*Vagina*, we get it!"—intercut with the creepy laughing yuppies, and I was already checking my watch on this one. At least when a member of the crowd left the spectator seat to become a participant, it was consensual—that is, in no way shamed or coerced or peer-pressured to get on stage with the stripper. However, the participant was behaving as a drunken asshole tourist, so that kinda ruined any attractive factor. Franco mentioned that he himself enjoys his cameos where he plays the fool, and I am wondering now if he doesn't have someone playing one in every on of his films. Also, if there is a plot in this one, I couldn't suss it out. I think everyone's just…on vacation? Bummer this couldn't have been a National Lampoon. That might have been more fun.

I checked how far we were in at the 40-minute mark and all I thought was "Shit, 45 more minutes of this one." It's actually not all that pornographic—much less so, *much* less so, than other Franco films—so I wonder why this one got that category online and some others in this set did not. The dialogue is juicier than the visuals in this one—I mean, this entry is all late-night HBO naughtiness. And the dialogue definitely made me feel some way, and it's the emotion

If Chuck Connors came out, I would have thought *Tourist Trap 2*!) Tied for best thing in this film will be locations. It's been shot on the Mediterranean, and it is gorgeous. If you get as bored as I do during some films, there's nothing wrong with hitting mute and then speaking your own dialogue or even reading the subtitles aloud. That made me laugh; in the Franco interviews, I mean, he's speaking English, and there are still English subtitles because he is so hard to understand. Kevin Collins verified that was just a thing, because Jess knew so many languages and mumbled and spoke in stream-of-consciousness much of the time. It's at this point that I am sorry he never came to our film set OR I got to go to one of his. I feel like I was on the last car of the era train with no luggage and one foot heading toward sad. *Totally* not what was intended, I suspect. I think Franco wanted racy, and it came out close to maudlin instead. Whoops.

But wait! I think part of that is that for all this film's rush to be edgy and sexual, it comes out more hopes and dreams, really, and this film couldn't be made today, not in any more of an interesting way. The repeated up-close shots of flowers with dew are what I refer to in class as heavy-handed symbolism. No matter the shot or subject matter, Franco knew how to light a scene (or choose the crew that did).

Damn, it gets rapey at the 54-minute mark. I wish that wasn't an endless theme in this series. However, there really isn't much of a true porn element in this one, and, out of all of them, I would have really expected it here, so don't be fooled by the category. Strangely, during the few consensual scenes there are, everyone looks so bored. Was that intentional? When I get down to it, who *was* more bored with this movie, me or the actors? However, the end of this one? Holy shit, I wanted to hurt someone. The dialogue ending is mean, *really* mean, like the end of a Hemingway story IF he was even more a drunken misogynist with a cruel streak for the sake of it. Unbelievable! I never saw it coming. I don't ever want to see it again. But I knew it, *knew* something was up with the dialogue halfway through. The dialogue had more attention paid to it than anything else. Now I know why. Hell, *Requiem for a Dream* had a nicer ending.

I did manage to watch the interview on this disc. *Now* the film makes more sense. In fact, the interview is *essential* to this film (say, if it were shown for a film class). I wish I had watched it before the movie—it may have been less strenuous on my brain. The interview itself is so timely, so synchronous to our political days, as to be almost scary. Additionally, the interview is essential viewing because you can see the message Franco intends and not confuse him (the person in real life) with the aforementioned, much crueler Hemingway-esque ego.

One thing I will say for this box set: Jess Franco is way more literary than I would have guessed. I bet that dude was very well-read in real life.

The Sexual Story of O (1984)

Now, the title is already confusing to me. I've read *Story of O* (1954), the Pauline Réage classic story, and I have seen the film adaptation (1975) of title. (I snoozed out during part 2 (1984,), and the *other* one, with Klaus Kinski on the cover, scares me—I don't know if I will ever be ready for that one, which is loosely based on the Anne Desclos novel *Retour à Roissy* and called *The Fruits of Passion*).

Like *Mansion*, in this *O*, we have scenes of women peeing, which they all do, yes, but I'm just used to not doing it with the door wide-open nor seeing it repeatedly on film, although it's a thing of Franco's to normalize and not fetishize such a thing, I think.

In better news, at least everyone looks like they're having a good time here. Great exterior shots in this one, because, again, they have a beautiful location. The clothes—when anyone is wearing any—are fantastico! And the dialogue? Are those prayers? Is that book dialogue? This one is the most literary of all of them. Although there is no order to these films, I feel like I watched them in the right way.

The lead male in this is energetic, let me tell you! I guess voyeurism, which is much like a spectator sport in my own mind, must look like tryouts all the time for all parties. Both women have cute hair, the kind I wish I could pull off (yes, this again, Dear Reader), although the more dominant of the two wanders around with a stylish scarf (which you know will be a prop at some point) that I have not seen on Kerri Green in *Three for the Road* (1987). And the lead women—not quite twins, but damn, they so look almost the same! Looks like I'll also be watching the final of the Franco interviews on this disc afterward. And, for the *first* time in *any* of the films in this boxed set, the initial sex scenes didn't gross or creep me out. Hallelujah! Although—and don't quote me on this one—I think I saw improper threesome etiquette at one point, which DID strike me as strange. I laughed, though, when Franco called Americans close-minded in another of his interviews, because he was right. Sex and nudity have always weirded out Americans, and the series *True Blood* would have us believe it is our culture's tendency toward Puritanism. That show was probably right.

Also, this movie could never be made again. These people just wander in and out of each other's condos—no knocking or calling out names, no matter where you are now. This would most likely get you shot. (I am already reminded of Ice-T's last tweet, the one where he suggested Amazon delivery workers wear vests identifying themselves, because he "caught someone creepin' up to [his]

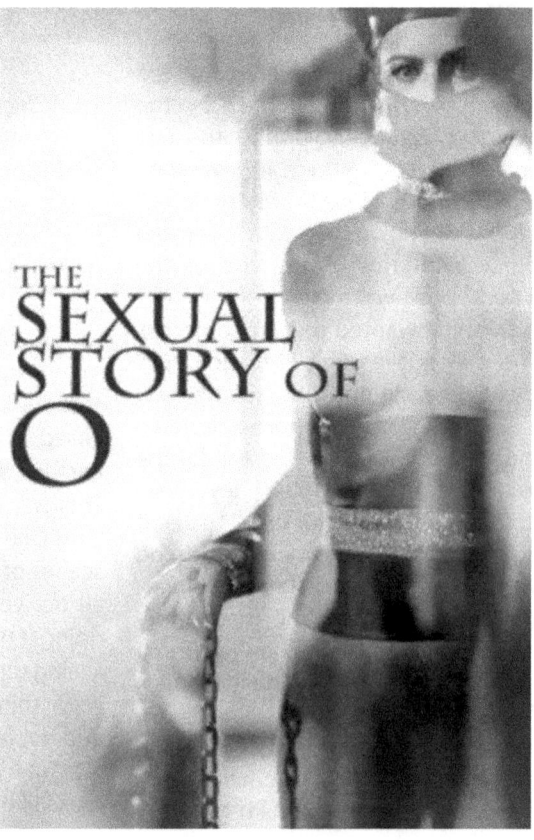

crib" and "almost shot him." I laughed because that is so Ice-T.)

Hell and damnation—at 50 minutes in, the film gets all "rich people doing creepy rich people things," and on an island, no less. Ugh. Dammit. And they get so nasty and spiteful. You know the dialogue is for real too. Why am I even surprised? God, the whole "rich people at lunch" scene made me wish for a meteor strike right into their table. Gotta tell ya, if I were in the young "victim" spot, rich folks would have been cut, maimed, and gutted. The "go down swinging" mentality is a NE Ohio trait of mine and, frankly, why I'm no sub. I take orders not at all well unless it's consensual. It's one of two reasons I didn't go into the military. Also, in the film, the goofy rich asshole in the bow tie would have been the first to taste my wrath. It's a despicable rape scene (the victim is unconscious), and bow tie man develops half a faux conscience midway through, but then not really. You find out the worst reason why he can't perform, and this is all so fucking Weinstein-era that I doubt any of this film is fiction. I think Franco had something against this class of people and set out to make them look bad. Yes, but, as I said, I think his choice of class subjects was such fertile ground for awful behavior that he didn't have to go far or try too hard. And when you, the viewer, see rich people not even remotely giving a shit about their lush surroundings and privilege, if you're like me, you'll really howl then. But the good news is that Bow Tie's foil, Exuberant Guy (from the beginning), at the very least does us all proud by doing *exactly* what I would have done in his place (although I wouldn't have done this to begin with, but whatever). Team Vengeance is the order of the day. The final shot is *so literary,* that *Dexter* (the series) stole it, and I bet you I will think of more as time goes on.

The last interview is interesting. It shows Franco being so direct that he's almost mean. I'm not sure if we would have gotten along at all on set. I got on well with Kevin, very well, but his personality is radically different from what I see Franco's as, and overall, I think I learned the most from that set. At any rate, the final interview has the reason Franco never shot again with my favorite three actors (they were his least favorite actors) and has Franco being honest about people who talk books and authors but don't necessarily read those books and authors, so the talk is just talk. He's right and, frankly, he synchronistically and posthumously hit the nail on the head on another reason why I took a break from social media: Damn, did I just get sick reading others' stupid opinions about nothing! This film, for Franco, was about escapism, his obsession with the sea (which will eventually consume everything— seems he knew it even back then), and getting out of his comfort zone. Again, I can wholly relate, and this film and its interview prove I'm not late to the party. We just find things when we're supposed to find them.

THE CORRUPT ONES (1967)

by Pete Chiarella

So, what would make a film with an international cast, an exotic location, and a lot of action just vanish? Even better, why would this film, after being seen only once by a 15-year-old 42P, stay with him until its VHS release more than 20 years down the road? There is no answer. People who have seen this film have agreed that it is almost a template for films such as *Raiders of the Lost Ark*.

The film was a French/Spanish/West German co-production, released by Warner Brothers, filmed in Hong Kong (substituting for Macau, the most dangerous city in the world). I was in my first year of high school; I hated it and would cut class often, walk to my local grindhouse, the Embassy Theater, and catch the matinee. I cut school a lot, and at times, I was the only person in the theater. It was a whole 75 cents to get in. Weekday matinees didn't draw many people, but the projectionists union had something to do with the theater staying open at this time. Usually there were some winos there, as 75 cents gave them a safe, warm place to sleep for a couple of hours.

This new film, *The Corrupt Ones*, was playing with a cheesy British James Bond knockoff, *The 2nd Best Secret Agent in the Whole Wide World*, so I settled in as the film began to run.

It starts with a fight in a boxcar of a moving train. Men are fighting over a medallion one guy is wearing. That guy pulls a knife but is choked to death by the cord on the medallion. The winner yanks the medallion off the corpse and holds it up as the credits roll. Dusty Springfield sings the title song (that song, "The Corrupt Ones," also stayed with me). The medallion is the infamous "Peking Medallion" (the film's alternate title) that has been lost for over 1,000 years and is the important goal for the others to follow.

Photographer Cliff Wilder (Robert Stack) has snuck over the border into Red China. He is taking pictures when he gets spotted by soldiers. Abandoning his equipment, he is chased to a boat owned by Danny Mancini (Italian actor Maurizio Arena), who is also running from something. They elude the soldiers and are back in Macau. Danny slips Cliff a small package and asks him to hold it for him. Cliff goes back to his hotel and has a visitor, Lilly Mancini (Elke

Sommer), who claims to be Danny's wife and wants the package. Cliff pleads ignorance until Lilly pulls a gun on him. He throws her out.

Cliff gets a message that Danny wants to meet him and to go to the House of Fans. Jasmine, a prostitute, tells Cliff where to meet Danny. Jasmine also has an idea that something is going on that will be worth a lot of money. Danny is waiting at a warehouse but is ambushed by a large Asian man and taken away. We see Danny getting tortured with a blowtorch. Cliff is attacked by two Asian guys, but they get shot by some American guys. Cliff, no dummy, steals their car.

Back at his hotel, Cliff is visited by local magistrate Pinto (Werner Peters from *The Bird with the Crystal Plumage*). Pinto informs Cliff that two factions control the crime in this city: the Tong, led by Tina (Nancy Kwan), and the American mob, led by Joe Brandon (Christian Marquand). Cliff snickers that Pinto forgot to include himself. Pinto takes Cliff back to where he was ambushed. Cliff denies everything, telling Pinto that Jasmine sent him there. Pinto knows the woman, so they go back to the House of Fans, where they find Jasmine dead. Cliff says that Danny Mancini can clear it all up, and Pinto takes him to a funeral parlor, where Lilly is paying her respects to her dead husband. When Pinto tells Cliff he is going to be taken to the station and searched, Cliff puts the medallion in the casket. Pinto isn't convinced that Cliff is truthful, telling him that the medallion is the key to a treasure worth millions.

Brandon and his henchman torture Cliff, who is soon "rescued" by the

Tong. Brandon's men arrive and it's a huge fight. Bloodied, Cliff goes to Lilly's place and tells her the medallion is in Danny's coffin and they can get it in the morning.

Morning comes and Lilly is gone. Cliff goes to the graveyard and sees the coffin has been dug up. The Tong and the gangsters converge on Cliff, but Pinto shows up again. Cliff tracks down Lilly, who tells him she hid the medallion behind a headstone. Cliff retrieves the medallion and holds it over a map. After making some calculations, he finds the real location of the treasure.

Pinto, however, has run out of patience. He sets up a meeting with Tina and Brandon, proposing a three-way split. They set Lilly up for the acid face-bath. Cliff shows up with the medallion, offering a trade for Lilly. Tina and Brandon cut Pinto out and Tina gets an ancient scholar to go over the medallion.

Cliff offers Pinto a deal since they need him to do something "official" to get to the treasure. The treasure is under the Temple of the Bells. When one of Brandon's men finds out that Pinto had the temple closed for "repairs," Brandon and Tina take out Pinto's officers and follow the three to a booby-trapped underground vault.

They find a huge chamber, with a solid gold figure on a horse and a huge jewel-encrusted crown. When Tina and Brandon bust in with guns drawn, Pinto tells them that there is enough for all of them, but Brandon disagrees. Cliff rushes Brandon and a random gunshot hits the decaying ropes holding the door to the chamber open. The door caves in, trapping them all.

There is air coming in from somewhere, and they use a torch to find a way out. Tina is ready to double-cross Brandon, but they then hear Chinese voices and realize they're in Red China. Tina is gunned down in a hail of machinegun fire. Brandon trades shots with the soldiers as he drags the treasure chest back into the chamber. A grenade causes a cave-in and Brandon is buried with the treasure.

Cliff, Lilly, and Pinto make it to the border and over the fence. They bemoan that they have lost the treasure. Pinto, however, takes off his shoe and shakes out three large gemstones. "I couldn't resist taking a souvenir," he says as he gives each of them a stone. The three head back to Macau as the title song plays over the credits.

The Corrupt Ones never showed up on late night TV, even though, back in the early '70s, they used all kinds of obscure films to fill the after-midnight slots. The film never surfaced there. When home video hit in the '80s, AVCO Embassy released it in a bland box that wouldn't make anyone want to see it.

I felt in this era of manufactured-on-demand DVD-Rs, maybe Warner Brothers would put it out. No such luck. I found a Blu-ray from Germany on eBay and bought that one. Why this film hasn't had a decent release is a mystery to me. It's never dull and has a great plot, a great cast, and some over-the-top violence for its time. Watching it once again to write this article took me back to a better time when I just loved sitting in decrepit theaters watching films like this.

The Corrupt Ones is truly a lost film, especially in the states. Full of plot twists, double-crosses, brutal violence, and more, it needs to be seen by fans. Take it from me, it is worth searching out and having in any fan's collection.

L-R: Robert Stack, Werner Peters, Nancy Kwan. © Constantin Film/Warner Brothers. All Rights Reserved.

1941

by Andrew J. Rausch

Steven Spielberg's World War II comedy *1941* was a bomb theatrically and is widely considered a "bad" movie. Whether it made money or not, claims of the film being a bad movie are categorically false. Any film with a scene featuring Slim Pickens facing off against Toshiro Mifune and Christopher Lee inside a Japanese submarine can't help but be entertaining. The film, about a thwarted Japanese attack on California, was helmed by Spielberg, fresh off the mega-successful *Jaws*, and was conceived by John Milius, super-fresh off the mega-successful *Apocalypse Now*. (They were released just three months apart). Because of the talent involved, including a who's-who cast of high-profile comic actors and film icons, audiences and critics went into theaters in 1979 with insanely high (and unreachable) expectations. I would assert that this is the primary reason the film is considered a "bad" movie. But I believe it's high time *1941* was reappraised. Yes, it has its problems—much of its humor is lowbrow (but who cares?) and John Belushi is criminally underused—but this film is fantastic.

I believe in the future, after everyone in this film—it includes legends like Robert Stack, Warren Oates, Dan Ackroyd, Belushi, John Candy, Elisha Cook, Jr., Mickey Rourke, and Ned Beatty, just to name a few—are dead, *1941* will be looked upon favorably. Spielberg's entire catalog will endure and when film historians re-examine it, this undervalued gem's bevy of stars alone will provide reason enough to be remembered. But beyond that, it's funny and entertaining. What more could you ask for? If you need more, the film also features cameos by the likes of Penny Marshall, James Caan, and directors Samuel Fuller and John Landis.

AN ERNEST ATTEMPT AT ENTERTAINMENT: IN DEFENSE OF ERNEST GOES TO JAIL AND JIM VARNEY

by Justin Channell

The late '80s and early '90s created an odd mix of comedic cinematic punching bags. From the braindead comedic stylings of Pauly Shore to the "late-career seasoned professional taking a paycheck" work of Leslie Nielsen and Rodney Dangerfield, the end of the 20th century created a surprising amount of "bad" comedies. Add in a lot of bad post-*Wayne's World* SNL features, strangely beloved flash-in-the-pans (like the Rik Mayall vehicle *Drop Dead Fred* and the obnoxious oeuvre of Australia's Yahoo Serious), and countless direct-to-video one-off indie flicks from standups trying to break into film, and you have a odd goulash of scatalogical goofs that seem to cater only to idiots.

Yet, you'll still find intelligent Millennials and Gen-X'ers who are die-hard fans of this kind of trash. They grew up on the lowest of the low-brow to get a laugh at their local cineplex or video store. I'm not knocking them, because I'm one of them. But of the comedy stars that graced both silver and cathode-ray screens in our time, one stands above all the others.

Exploiting the specific market intersection of children and the children-at-heart of Appalachia, Jim Varney's Ernest P. Worrell character made an unexpected leap from the king of regional commercials to a notable box office draw. Of all of the faces that graced dollar theaters and drive-ins in the '80s and '90s, Jim Varney seemed to come the closest to hitting the classic clowns of television. Varney's portrayal should be lauded in the same way Charlie Chaplin, Soupy Sales, and even Marcel Marceau were clowns for their respective generations and reach. But despite the financial success and enjoyability of the "Ernest" film and television franchise, the character embodied by Shakespearean-trained character actor Jim Varney has long been the subject of ridicule both by ironic "bad movie" fans and highbrow film fans who seemingly don't understand the purpose of a dumb comedy made to entertain young mountain children and their kin for about 90 minutes.

But cop that attitude near the target audience—a film fan of a certain age from the hills of West

Virginia all the way down to the most southern tip of Florida—and be prepared for a fight. Not only are you out of your element in terms of Appalachian artistic appreciation, but you may not know the background of Varney's ne'er-do-well character or how it touched the hill-children who came of age during the Reagan/Bush and Clinton administrations.

Of the ten feature films starring Varney as the famed manchild, none represent the beautifully odd craft that director John Cherry III and writer Coke Sams brought to these unexpectedly beloved goofball features more than 1990's *Ernest Goes to Jail*. While the follow-up, the Halloween-themed *Ernest Scared Stupid*, usually takes the top spot of Ernest film rankings, *Jail* is an entry that deserves defense. While *Scared Stupid* is admirable for the craft of the Chiodo Brothers and Fantasy II Effects repurposing and perfecting their best work from *Killer Klowns From Outer Space, Jail*'s stylistic choices and performances elevate it as an unsung gem in an unfairly derided American cinematic staple. A part of the only-in-America subgenre of goofball prison comedies with a strong theatrical and surprisingly subversive style, *Jail* represents the usual Ernest crew at the top of their game. Plus, a dual role allows Varney to finally show his full chops as an actor.

Cashing in with a catchphrase and a Khaki cap

To truly understand the appeal of Ernest, you must start from the beginning. Varney's khaki-hat and denim-vested dimwit first appeared in the early '80s in the most Reagan-era way possible: a television commercial. But it wasn't just a single ad break that made Ernest P. Worrell and his "KnowhutImean, Vern?" catchphrase a household name with obnoxiously pervasive quotability. Ernest infiltrated the airwaves like a virus that spread and sucked cash from regional advertising clients across the United States.

Varney developed the character for the Nashville-based ad agency Carden and Cherry. While there has been some debate over whether Cherry or Varney created the Ernest character, what is

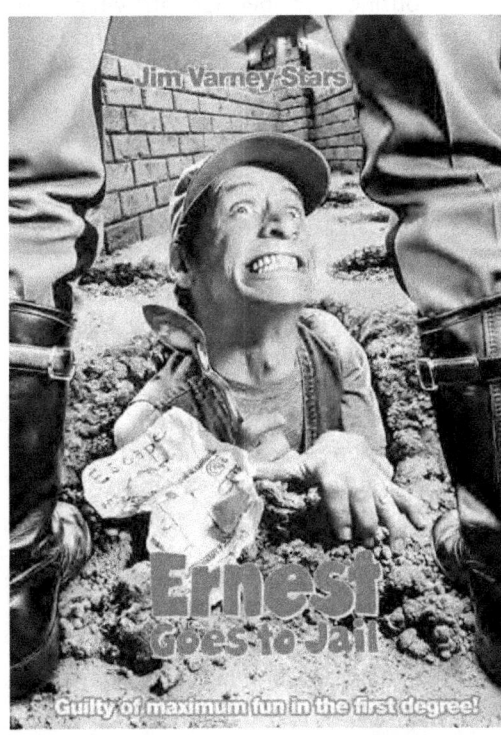
Guilty of maximum fun in the first degree!

clear is that his initial appearances in local TV spots were a huge hit. The ads followed the general premise of Varney's Ernest character wanting to give tips and advice to his neighbor, "Vern." We never saw Vern—instead, *we* were Vern. The camera gave a point-of-view of this long-suffering neighbor who has to constantly deal with his childlike neighbor's antics and promotion of local businesses.

And Ernest promoted a lot of businesses. As the character's popularity grew, Varney began performing the character in bulk shoots where he would cover multiple products for multiple regions across the United States. Whether it was car dealerships, dairy farms, or local news affiliates, Ernest would be there to tell Vern about it—and likely destroy his body or Vern's home in a ludicrous live-action cartoon fashion.

Soon, national brands took attention and Ernest began hawking things like big sodas to Vern. Cherry took his ambitions to the big screen. He knew the "Hey Vern!" shtick wasn't going to hold an audience's attention for 90 minutes, so he instead concocted a bizarre family-friendly sci-fi flick, *Dr. Otto and the Riddle of the Gloom Beam*. A regionally released bait-and-switch that used Ernest's good standing to drag fans of the commercials to the theater to see Varney only appear as the beloved character for a few minutes, it's no surprise it was quickly forgotten. It didn't even wind up on VHS until well into the '90s. However, VHS compilations of the ads and new sketches with Varney as Ernest and his family were a surprise hit in the time where anything on a rental tape could turn a profit.

What really broke Ernest into Hollywood was a stroke of luck at a promotional event at a Florida NASCAR track. Disney executives brought costumed mascots from their theme park and saw a lackluster response from the crowd. But when Varney came out as his trademark disheveled goofball and gained huge cheers from the crowd, they saw dollar signs. Cherry, Varney, and Sams got to work on Ernest's first proper cinematic venture.

With distribution from Disney's live-action Touchstone Pictures arm and a sizable cash injection from the Silver Screen Partners financing group—whose board included future president George W. Bush—Cherry and *Ernest Goes to Camp* and *Ernest Saves Christmas*. Both did significant business on low budgets, which led to Cherry's biggest budget and box-office success to date, *Ernest Goes to Jail*.

Mistaken identities

Apart from Varney, Cherry's other moneymaker in the commercial business was the duo act "Me and My Brother Bobby" played by *Hee Haw* regular Gailard Sartain and Nashville character actor Bill Byrge. A classic silent-man-foil gag with Sartain's Chuck as a heavyset loudmouth and Byrge as the deadpan brother with a face that could only come from the south, the series was an attempt to have a franchisable character like Ernest. It was never a huge success; but Cherry and Varney brought Startain and Byrge along in their Disney deal, with most of the early *Ernest* pictures featuring lengthy scenes of the duo yucking it up, usually with some elaborate prop comedy involved.

There is one thing no one can take away from *Ernest Goes to Jail*, and that is the honesty of the title. It certainly is a movie about Ernest going to jail—and to get there, Ernest and the audience have to go through a series of outlandish set pieces. As with most Ernest films, we open with the character with a completely new home and a new job. The closest thing we get to canon is that Ernest's old comedic foils Chuck and Bobby have followed him to help terrorize another town.

This time around, Ernest is a night janitor at a small-town bank, while Chuck and Bobby are a ragtag security team with the latest "state-of-the-art" equipment. Of course, this just leads to a lot of wacky prop comedy that often endangers the bank's manager, Mr. Pendlesmythe (Dan Leegant). Their clear ineptitude to protect the bank is obvious from the first frame of the film.

While Ernest dreams of making it to the next level of his career as a bank teller, he can barely cut it as a janitor. At the start of the film, Ernest's nightly task of running the floor polisher turns into an intense sequence where the device literally drags our embattled hero across the room and onto the ceiling. The scene features some truly impressive art direction and Steadicam work. The entire sequence just oozes with fun. It continues to build as Ernest receives an electric shock that turns him into a human electromagnet. After attracting every single tiny piece of metal in the bank lobby, he is chased by a set of filing cabinets and locks himself in a safe, where two safety deposit boxes knock him

unconscious. This seemingly stops his new troublesome superpower.

It's worth noting that the logic behind Ernest's electromagnetism will leave you with more questions than answers. It's best not to think too much about it beyond it being fun to watch, because I'm pretty sure that's all the filmmakers did.

The next morning, Charlotte, a bank teller with a heart of gold (played by Barbara Bush —no relation to the film's financier), discovers Ernest's mess. She wants him to get it cleaned up before Mr. Pendlesmythe arrives. Ernest opens up to her about his trouble learning the material required to become a bank teller. Plus, Mr. Pendlesmythe has it out for him— mostly because of the fact he's a terrible janitor who causes elaborate messes that can only be properly conveyed with a Steadicam and thousands of dollars in special effects.

Feeling pity on a man who wants to go from a thankless minimum wage job to an even-more thankless barely above-minimum wage job, Charlotte offers to take Ernest to discuss his options for moving up the corporate ladder over dinner. Ernest gets ready for the day the way any live-action animated character in a post-Pee-Wee Herman world would: putting on one of his many identical denim vest outfits and getting into a gigantic washing machine large enough to clean both clothes and people. He narrates the process to his dog, Rimshot, a Jack Russell terrier that stands as one of the few recurring elements of the Ernest Cinematic Universe (ECU, from here on out).

Unfortunately, a jury-rigged industrial-sized drying machine has a short in the wire that again turns Ernest electromagnetic right before the date! Is all of this dumb distraction from the plot? Absolutely, but watching Jim Varney do his own nonsensical riff on Chaplin's dinnertable comedy from *The Gold Rush* is an absolute delight.

In terms of actual story development, we also learn about a local Death Row inmate named Felix Nash (Varney in a dual role). In the nearby Dracup Maximum Security Prison, one of Nash's associates, Bartlett (Barry Scott) has murdered another inmate and is facing trial. Meanwhile, Nash has the warden (Charles Napier) breathing down his neck, because he's days away from the electric chair.

Ernest winds up on the jury. Despite having much pride in his call for jury duty, Ernest is an expectedly terrible juror. During proceedings, he stops paying attention to the trial and instead draws attention to himself by busting an ink pen in his mouth. It is a bit of physical comedy that is equally entertaining and repulsive.

As Ernest tries to rid himself of the ludicrous amount of ink in his mouth, Bartlett and his lawyer notice that he is the spitting image of Nash. They concoct a scheme to convince the jury to visit the prison to see the scene of the crime. Surprisingly, the plan works and Ernest thinks he's part of an incredibly unorthodox jury field trip until he gets locked up in Nash's cell. Bartlett also gets off on the murder rap when Nash helps convince the jury through unseen conniving. (I think it's safe to assume he threatened to murder each and every one of his eleven colleagues.)

With Ernest in his place, Nash is excited to learn he's traded places with a guy that works the night shift at a bank with two clueless morons running security. But despite Bobby's trademark silence, he's the only one who notices that something is off with Ernest.

One of the film's best scenes involves Bobby following Nash as he stakes out his plan, with Byrge's naturally humorous look and rail-thin body making for a lot of inspired physical comedy and optically enhanced jokes. It's hard not to crack a genuine smile at the sight of Byrge peering and disappearing from behind an empty coat rack. The visual effects, despite their and long-in-the-tooth optically printed appearance, still manage to hold up. You can see the seams, but considering it's a goofball live-action cartoon, it actually works to the film's favor.

Also, in a clever bit, everyone notices that the bank is actually clean, but barely notes the changes in Ernest's personality. At least not until Nash makes a pass at Charlotte, redecorates Ernest's rube goldberg of a home into a sleazy love den, and tosses Rimshot out the door.

Meanwhile, Ernest is struggling to break out of prison. Nash's other henchman, Lyle (Randall "Tex" Cobb) is charmed by his new cellmate's antics. Standing in his way is Bartlett, who reminds him that he has to keep up appearances as Nash. With the help of some intimidation techniques, Ernest finally looks the part—just in time for the warden to inform him that Nash's is set to go to the electric chair.

Will Nash get away with his schemes? Can Chuck and Bobby's security system protect the bank instead of just kill their boss? Speaking of death, will Ernest die in the electric chair? Will the common thread of Ernest gaining powers from electricity come into play? Will you be left with more questions about what happens when Ernest is electrocuted? Well, you'll just have to watch *Ernest Goes to Jail* to find out!

Not convinced by the convoluted plot synopsis? Well, read on to learn why this flick deserves your respect.

Admission of bias

The reason I couldn't pass up defending *Ernest Goes to Jail* in this edition of *Exploitation Nation* is that it's been present for my entire love of film—nay, it's literally part of my entire being. Jim Varney being chased by a floor polisher is my first conscious memory.

In 1990, my mother was chaperoning a school trip for one of my siblings. It was a reward day at a local movie house in Fairmont, WV, that was split into three screens to compete with multiplexes. My mother in her infinite wisdom brought me along, because who doesn't love 3-year-olds in movie theater? The movie selections for my sibling's classes that day were *Ernest Goes to Jail* or *Teenage Mutant Ninja Turtles*. Assuming that the goofball antics of Jim Varney would be more nurturing to a developing child's brain than a dark, violent Jim Henson foam and animatronic demo reel, she took me to see the former.

As the film unreeled and the opening led to the opening zinger of whip-pans, slapstick violence, and Varney mugging, I squealed in horror. The moment must have been enough to trigger my hippocampus to begin storing memories, as I can distinctly visualize all of this. My mother took me from the theater with tears flowing from my eyes and quickly negotiated a move into the other screening room. I had no problem with *Ninja Turtles* and my mother said I "didn't make a peep."

After hearing the story for years as a kid, I became irritated as any young boy would be by any reminder of having his masculinity questioned by crying at something as mundane as a Jim Varney scene. After a short bit of demand, I brought *Ernest Goes to Jail* home on VHS where it became a long-time favorite.

As a crazy end to that story, I found myself in the basement of that theater about twenty years later. Turns out, the owners never threw out any posters. Long story short, I now have the poster that was on display at the first time I was at a movie theater—which also happens to also be my first memory ever.

Motion for the defense

The Ernest films have no pretension. John Cherry, Coke Sams, and Jim Varney knew just what they were making every time they stepped on set. Cherry and Sams were ad men. They weren't making high art; they were making a product. They just needed enough dumb humor to entertain people for 90 minutes—and there is nothing wrong with that at all.

They knew their target market was easily amused. They catered to that and made the most entertaining films they could while getting to show off their skill as visual artists. *Jail* shows them at the top of their game. It's remarkable how an unexpectedly dark turn was chosen for such a goofball franchise. What's more remarkable is that a talented—and clearly enthusiastic—crew of artists got a sizable budget from Disney to realize this insanity.

The opening titles and most of the optical effects are incredibly impressive from a technical standpoint. Personally, I'm a sucker for a good opening title sequence and *Jail* has one that would make Saul Bass proud. Featuring silhouettes of Ernest trying to thwart corrections officers on bright color backdrops—similar to the popular iPod commercials of the early 2000s—and topped with Warholian photocopied animations of Varney's trademark expressions, it's worth the cost of admission alone.

But the true unsung hero of the film is cinematographer Peter Stein. The film is gorgeously shot with a generous amount of camera movement and Steadicam. It feels like the collaborations between Sam Raimi and Bill Pope at times—especially the aforementioned floor buffer opening sequence.

Stein's choice to light the prison scenes in a stark theatrical style with heavy pinks and blues similar to *Suspiria*'s color palette makes for some of the film's most stylish moments. On the note of the pinks, the art department deserves credit for outfitting the prison's entire guards with bright pink Nazi-esque uniforms. It's quite surreal and oddly subversive for a '90s Disney-released family film. It's hard to deny that the choice was stylistic, as earlier scenes with Nash in the prison do not feature this stylized lighting and guards dressed in black. These touches are what makes Cherry deserve much more credit as a director than he will ever get, thanks to the undeservedly poor reputation of Ernest films.

Above all of the choices made behind the camera, the crucial ingredient to any Ernest film is obviously Varney's performance. But *Jail* also marks a rare dramatic role from Varney as the criminal doppelganger Nash. It's certainly no rarity to see a dual-role from Varney, as the entire series has scenes of Ernest "transforming" or imagining himself as different characters. This is a carryover from the commercials, *Dr. Otto*, and the TV series, *Hey Vern! It's Ernest*.

But there is a different flair to Varney's multiple performances in *Jail*: as far-fetched as the plot may be at times, it marks a rare moment in the series where all of Varney's characters are diegetic to the story. In other entries, it seems Ernest breaks into schizophrenic monologues that may or may not be in his head in order to fit Varney's multiple characters. In *Jail*, when you see Varney in drag as the elderly nagging Auntie Nelda, it's because Ernest is using a disguise. In the other films, it's seemingly because Ernest is suffering from dissociative identity disorder. It's an oddly grounded aspect in an otherwise haywire film.

Varney's multiple characters and dialects also harken back to his days as a touring stand-up comedian. His forte was impersonations and

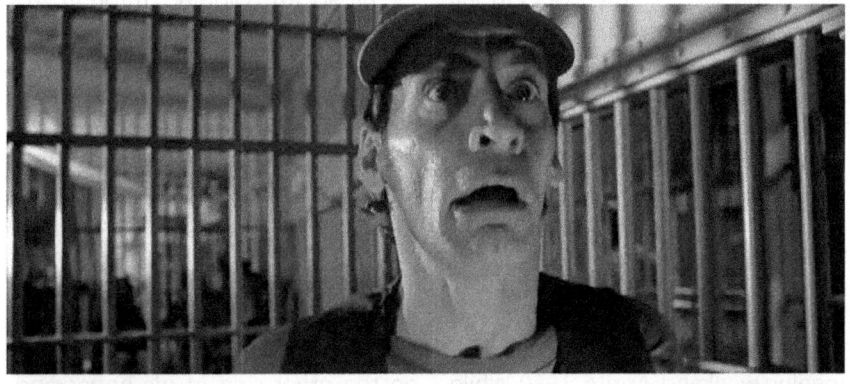

All photos this section © Buena Vista Pictures. All Rights Reserved.

character work. But this is likely just Varney's way of finding another stage on which to perform. In the early '70s, Varney studied Shakespeare at the Barter Theatre in Abingdon, VA—the longest-running equity theatre in the U.S. By the end of the decade, he had a stint in television with appearances on *Fernwood 2 Night* and *Pink Lady and Jeff*. As the '80s hit, Varney crossed paths with Cherry and found his true fame—albeit with tragedy of typecasting.

This is why Varney's serious tone in *Jail* makes it an important piece. We get to see a side of Jim Varney, the actor, that only audiences at the Barter or Pioneer Playhouse in Danville, KY, got to see. Varney never got the chance to showcase his dramatic chops more than he did here. At the time of his lung cancer death in 2000, it was reported he had written a screenplay about West Virginia's infamous Hatfield-McCoy family feud. This—along with the aborted final Ernest film, *Ernest the Pirate*—remain dreams in the hearts of Varney fans.

Thanks to the talent and charm of Varney and the skill of the workers behind the scenes, *Ernest Goes to Jail* succeeds in all of its artistic goals. Granted, those goals are to allow anyone to have a mindless laugh at a redneck clown and hopefully not analyze the plot as much as I have here.

Regardless, the film is also a success in the eye of the most objective judge in Hollywood: money. Debuting at #3 on April 6, 1990, *Ernest Goes to Jail* brought in $6 million on opening weekend, April 6, 1990. While it couldn't take down the titans of *Ninja Turtles* and *Pretty Woman*, it beat out every other film that debuted that weekend. In comparison, John Waters' *Cry-Baby* opened on nearly the same number of screens that weekend, but only hit #8 with a $3 million take.

While it was by no means a runaway smash, the little film brought in a grand total of $25 million over the course of seven weeks. Adding on to the built-in popularity of Ernest films on video and TV, and *Jail* was one in another of the low-risk, reasonable-profit investments for Disney and Silver Screen Partners.

Even if you read this piece and don't agree with my assessment on the artistic merits of *Ernest Goes to Jail*, you have to admit one thing: it didn't lose anyone any money—not even a future president.

Introducing new evidence

Something felt off about a few recent rewatches of *Ernest Goes to Jail*. The ending felt incomplete. Something told me that there was an extended ending, but I found no sign of it existing. Well, it turns out I did remember that scene from a TV broadcast. Digging through my sources before writing this article, I discovered that the TV edit of the film has an extra coda, along with some cuts for a rather tame PG movie.

The extended TV ending finds Ernest finally working as a bank teller, but typing on his new computer leads to another bout with becoming magnetized and getting chased by filing cabinets. Is it necessary? No, but it does feel nice to get to see Ernest on the other side of his hopes and dreams for a change.

But at least one of the scenes

added to make up for time is truly perplexing. Before his escape, Nash had planned a conjugal visit. Because he took his place in prison, Ernest gets to also take Nash's place in having sex with his wife. Yes, the TV-censor-approved cut of *Ernest Goes to Jail* shockingly tries to answer the age-old question of, "Does Ernest P. Worrell fuck?"

The answer is still unclear, but he certainly does get raped. Because Ernest is somewhere between a child and a living cartoon, he has to ask the guards what a conjugal visit is. He isn't given an answer. He's just led into a cell with a bed with Nash's wife who tells him, "It's been such a long time." Ernest cries out for help before she pounces on him, and the prison guards just laugh. Later, the guards drag him from the cell with his clothes tattered and skin covered in lipstick and hickeys. In a daze, he laughs and says, "Let's hear it for the criminal justice system."

This is really a scene that was cut from the film's PG-rated theatrical run and reinserted for sponsor-approved TV broadcasts. I can't make this shit up. To be fair, if there was going to be a rape scene in *Ernest Goes to Jail*, this is a surprising route for them to take.

Other deleted scenes are more fun in nature and stress Ernest's cartoon abilities. In one failed jailbreak, Ernest becomes distracted by making elaborate shadow puppets in the guard's search light. This is much more in line with what you'd expect from an Ernest movie, as opposed to a rape scene.

Another jailbreak scene bridges the scene where Ernest is put in two balls-and-chains for the Auntie Nelda scene. In the cut scene, the guards initially only add the shackle and weight to one leg. But Ernest attempts to escape by pole vaulting over the prison wall. The weight on his leg causes the pole to stick to an upright position. The weight then stretches his leg to about thrice its normal size. These two inspired bits could have been left in the final edit—though their inclusion here shows a rougher audio mix than the main feature scenes.

Someone call Criterion or Arrow. If they want to do a 4K remaster with these scenes reinserted as a director's cut, I can help with the edit and write the scholarly essay for this should-be cultural milestone.

I'll see you in October with a tall glass of milk for my yearly *Ernest Scared Stupid* viewing.

SURVIVAL OF THE DEAD

by Nick Thomson

In 2009, George A. Romero released what was to become his final film: *Survival of the Dead*. Commonly derided as Romero's "worst" film by far, it came in the wake of 2007's patchy but intriguing *Diary of the Dead*, which struggled to overcome the strictures of the "found footage" format and a generational gap that prematurely tackled its subject (subjective reportage in 21st century media). However, the flack *Survival* has received is unfair, because the film's message has become only more potent in recent years, proving it to be a prescient piece of filmmaking that expressed one of Romero's strongest recurring themes.

It's hard for any new entry in a long-established film franchise to be accepted with open arms, which Romero's last three outings with the dead all endured. However, 2005's *Land of the Dead* has since "bedded in" as a time capsule of the war on terror, to join historical snapshots of civil rights (*Night*), consumerism (*Dawn*), and militarism (*Day*). In turn, *Survival* has proven in the last decade that its skewering of political division is needed more than ever.

In the warring families of Plum Island—the O'Flynns and the Muldoons—at each other's throats for generations, we see the entrenched squadrons of not only America's but the world's political Left and Right. Clashing over whether to put the dead "to sleep" or "keep them with us," the bitterly opposed clans are equally brutish in their thinking, with calls for peace from the center ground (O'Flynn's daughter, Janet) frustratingly left unheard.

The pair are positively grotesque. Muldoon is a proud chauvinist whose almost-fetishistic obsession with his lineage walks hand in hand with his murderous treatment of Plum Island's "refugee immigrants," later found rotting by the shore. And who sent them? O'Flynn. Before turning to human trafficking in the apocalypse (as much to annoy Muldoon as to line his own pockets), this habitual liar and his posse is invading a family's home based on hearsay regarding their children. The only result is more death and destruction.

The need to "put down" the dead is undoubtedly correct, but O'Flynn's unyielding methodology wouldn't

rationality, their petty human arrogance infecting everyone, while their common enemy doggedly plagues them all. Each has something valid to say, but neither is listening—and certainly not learning. Indeed, themes like this are something that Romero explored throughout his career, not only in the *Dead* films, but also in *The Crazies*, *Martin*, and *Knightriders*. Though sometimes blunt, *Survival* is as much a Romero film as any other.

Despite a few awkward and disjointed *Loony Tunes*-style gags (the primary focus of critics' ire), Romero's zombie western saw a committed and principled filmmaker still proving he had something to teach society, while also indulging in a little fun in his twilight years. The final image of *Survival* may be the perfect summation of his life's work, as potent, prescient, and pertinent as ever: O'Flynn and Muldoon—"bound and determined" to "stick it to" each other—failing to fire empty weapons at one another while a giant moonrise of inevitability and absolute truth looms in the background. Perhaps some folks will never learn, in life or in death, with the common people left to pick their way through the detritus littering the path of least resistance.

look out of place under the gaze of Stalin, while Muldoon's coveting of "what's ours" smacks of the worst the 1 percent has to offer. It's safe to say that, through Bush/Obama/Trump, we've found ourselves in a quagmire of social, political, and cultural upheaval. What else are O'Flynn and Muldoon but a mirror of the current landscape, where the virtual war on speech, thought, and language would render Orwell stunned with disbelief at the absurdity of it all. Fundamentalist Muldoon's desperate need for O'Flynn to admit who was "right" and who was "wrong" stabs directly into the heart of these fractious times.

O'Flynn and Muldoon's raging egos devolve into browbeating and chest-thumping at the expense of

Nick is the writer of the multi-award-winning film For Want of a Nail, *the author of the horror novellas* Dug Deep *and* How Mr. Snuffles III and Others Met Their Maker, *and a staff writer for SleazeFiend Magazine. www.deadshed.com*

TO BE PERFECTLY HONEST, THIS SECTION IS REALLY JUST ONE BIG AD

At the tail end of the '80s, George Romero decided it was time to revamp his seminal 1968 classic, *Night of the Living Dead*. The low-budget black-and-white horror film had an immense impact on the filmgoing culture and revitalized the fading genre. A hit on the drive-in circuit, *NOTLD* spawned two sequels, including the hit *Dawn of the Dead*, and cemented Romero's reputation as a master of terror. Since the two sequels were in color and reflected the times they were made (the budding consumerism and mall culture of the late '70s and the economic excess of the '80s, all hidden behind a gory conceit of the walking dead overrunning the world), Romero felt that a new *Night of the Living Dead* would be appropriate to celebrate the dying of the '80s and the coming of the '90s. If nothing else, a remake would go a long way toward correcting the fact that none of the original filmmakers saw a dime from the original. A key copyright notice had been left off the finished film, effectively placing *NOTLD '68* in the public domain.

To direct the new version, Romero handpicked his protégé, Tom Savini, who had come through the '80s as a special effects legend. Savini sat down with artist Brad Hunter and planned out the film on paper. "Hitchcock said you make the movie twice," Savini explained. "You make it in the storyboards first. Then, you film it." Savini's vision, *NOTLD '90*, was filled with imaginative set pieces, unique gore scenes, and a brand-new take on the character of Barbara. No longer the near-comatose victim of the original (as played by Judith O'Dea), this new Barbara was a hero cut from the same cloth as Ellen Ripley and Sarah Conner—a badass, rifle-toting survivor, played by actress and stunt woman Patricia Tallman.

For one reason or another, many of Savini's planned sequences fell by the wayside. Producers told him things couldn't be shot because of time constraints, budgetary concerns, etc. A director's vision denied.

While the resulting film was not initially well-received by critics or the public, it has been reassessed by film lovers and scholars over the years, and many have determined it to be as good as its predecessor and, in many aspects, even better. While the original will always remain at the top of the lists of classic horror, Savini's remake is respectable, accomplished, and a marvelous film on its own.

In 2019, we at Happy Cloud Media, LLC, were proud to bring the public Savini's original storyboards for NOTLD '90 in a volume titled *Night of the Living Dead '90: The Version You've Never Seen*, by Tom Savini[1], and for the first time, fans could see every bit of the director's intent, including his lost set pieces and ideas to make "zombies scary again." The unique book was called "a real treat for fans of the film and the zombie genre. [...]

---

1 Cover art by Christian Stavrakis;, layout and design by *ExNat*'s own Ryan Hose!

This is a book that deserves a place on your bookshelf right next to Paul R. Gagne's classic tome *The Zombies That Ate Pittsburgh: The Films of George A. Romero*. [...]. This is one of the coolest, most fun horror film-related books you will ever see."—*Diabolique* magazine. "It's an essential that horror buffs of all kinds should have in their library."—*Cinema Crazed*

So, yeah, this is an ad but also a celebration about a movie that thousands have come around to love and cherish. If you're a fan of the *Dead* films, if you grew up on Savini's effects, or if you love unique bits of film history, check it out.

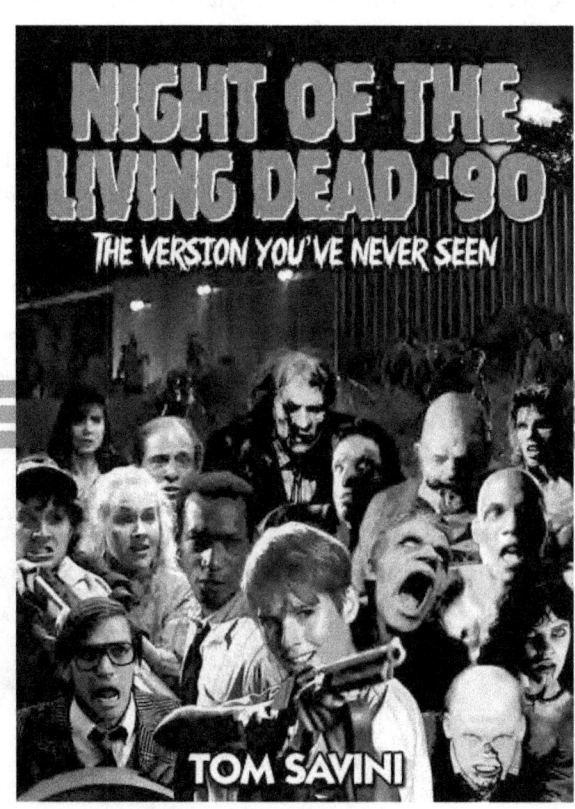

WE WATCHED THEM FOR THE KILLS: I REFUSE TO DEFEND THE SPLATTER MOVIE

Outside of pornography, is there any other genre more maligned than horror?[1] In my years in the genre as both a journalist and filmmaker, I've been accused on more than one occasion of both producing and supporting filth, misogyny, and immorality, for the simple acts of making and loving horror films. Every horror fan at some point or another has found him- or herself in a losing argument over horror, forced to defend something we love, for the simple reason that our love—and the genre—are misunderstood.

I could easily recycle the arguments: Horror serves as a visual release for aggressive thoughts, the violent fantasies satiate a primal need that dates back to the oral tradition, it's a simple progression of the *fantastiqué*, it's *grande guignol* writ large for the screen, they're morality lessons drenched in blood, etc. They're tired arguments, and we're all tired of making them. Violent movies are no more a cause of violence than video games, comic books, skipping

---

1   Yes, I mentioned the musical a few pages back. I think it goes: musical, horror, porn, movies based on "Baby Shark."

Fisher Stevens gives you all the fingers in The Burning. © Miramax Films. All Rights Reserved.

church, or not eating your vegetables. Horror is an easy scapegoat, a simple answer to a complicated question. The Columbine murderers would have committed the same crimes whether they'd been horror fans or die-hard musical nerds.

Where horror fans do themselves a disservice is in trying to argue at all. With most circular arguments, the ones leveling the accusation aren't necessarily interested in debate more than they just want to be right. Because, when you get right down to it, most horror geeks—particularly if you grew up in the slasher heyday of the '80s—were drawn to the movies *because* of the gore; or, rather, because we knew how the effects were done and wanted to see it.

So many of us had subscriptions to *Fangoria* and *Starlog*. And every issue of *Fangoria* in those early days had how-to sections—how to make scars, how to build oozing wounds, how this effect or that was accomplished. On the covers were the likes of Tom Savini and Rick Baker and Rob Bottin and Stan Winston and Steven Johnson, the special effects rock stars. From those issues were born thousands of budding basement effects champs, many of whom have gone on to work in the film industry, myself included—though I learned early on that I lack the necessary skills and patience for effects work.

But we absorbed these images and regurgitated them into our own art. We knew how to make bullet-hits; we knew how much of a fake body we needed to make to pull off an effect (a Savini dictum: "What do I need to see to believe?"); whatever our budgets couldn't pull off, our imagination made up for. Hell, so many of us learned editing from these films. They taught us how long is *too long* to linger on an effect; conversely, they taught us sometimes you need to let the effect linger a few frames longer to *really* resonate.

In short, when we saw the guts oozing out of the TV set from *Videodrome* on the *Fangoria* cover, we *needed* to see that for ourselves.

We *needed* to see a defeated Jason Voorhees, his partially bisected

And here we spoil the end of Friday the 13th: The Final Chapter.
© Paramount Pictures. All Rights Reserved.

head sliding down the blade of a machete.

We *needed* to see that shish kebab skewer the unlucky victim in *Happy Birthday to Me*, even if none of us can remember that actor's name.

We *needed* to see Max Renn reduce Barry Convex to a mass of twitching tumors in *Videodrome*, just as we needed to see Michael Ironside explode in *Scanners*.

The gore was our *fantastiqué*. We knew it was safe because we knew it was fake. But we had to see it for ourselves. We needed to let our own bloodlust come out in whoops as we metaphorically danced around the flashing campfire shadows of the silver screen.

We watched these things for the kills. *The Prowler, Prom Night, Terror Train, The Mutilator, The Howling, Re-Animator, From Beyond*—we wanted the monsters, we wanted the sharp ow-y weapons, we wanted the blood. They weren't guilty pleasures either. For the preteen *Fango* reader, these movies were highly sought. How many of us delighted in finding that one mom-and-pop video store that didn't care how old

Matt Craven demonstrates the wrong way to eat a shish-ka-bob in Happy Birthday to Me. © Columbia Pictures. All Rights Reserved.

you were and would rent anything short of *Girls Gone Wild* to us eager kids? How many of us left that store with armloads of slashers? How many of these were watched surreptitiously at sleepovers, with the TV turned down low, lest the screaming alert the parental units who would otherwise deny us the access to these forbidden entertainments?

The slashers were our rites of passage. Our parents had *I Was a Teenage Werewolf* and the Corman Poe cycle—all of which were criticized for violence and pushing the envelope.

Think how shocking something like H.G. Lewis's *Blood Feast* was to see, 40 feet tall on the drive-in screen! That horrifying, redder-than-red blood spilling everywhere, undercutting the film's tongue-in-cheek tone—is that where the hysteria renewed?

Ultimately, it doesn't matter. We '80s kids who grew up on the gore went on to be stellar pillars of society, and we're the ones fueling the current nostalgia trend. We're the reason Scream Factory invests in remastering things like *The Burning*. And since we're the adults now, we won't be shamed into denying our love for the grotesque and depraved. Hell, we might be better people for it. Gore films prepared us for just about any ridiculous emergency, short of a decapitation, and maybe even that as well.

From those of us who came through the '80s unscathed, to watch the cycle repeat throughout the '90s and beyond, to the gore film: We salute you.

Tom Savini's "How to Get a Headache" with David Sederholm in The Prowler.
© Graduation Films. All Rights Reserved

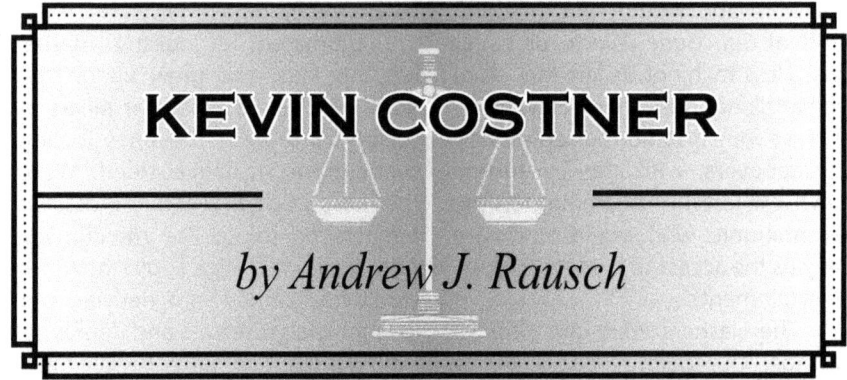

KEVIN COSTNER

by Andrew J. Rausch

I was asked to defend a film that was widely perceived as being a "bad" film. I decided instead to defend an actor who is (falsely) perceived as being a "bad" actor. That man is Kevin Costner. When I think of bad actors, I think of William Shatner hamming it up with his staccato start and stop delivery. I think of just about every performer in *Plan 9 from Outer Space*. I think of Chuck Norris, showing all the emotion of a brick. Or Steven Seagal, always, in anything. Tommy Wiseau... But Kevin Costner does not fit alongside those people.

Granted, Kevin Costner isn't a Daniel Day Lewis or Meryl Streep, but he isn't a *bad* actor. Have you seen *Perfect World*, *The Untouchables*, *Open Range*, or *Field of Dreams*? The man does marvelous work in each of these and receives zero credit. Yes, he's been in some stinkers (*Waterworld* and *Robin Hood: Prince of Thieves* come to mind). Yes, he seems smug and some of his collaborators say he is a dick. Yes, *Dances with Wolves* won a Best Picture Oscar it didn't deserve (although it's not a bad film either). Yes, Costner should give up doing those spotty, here and there accents. *Robin Hood*, anyone? But...for every misstep, there are multiple truly great entries on his filmography. Few actors have enjoyed a run of solid films like Costner had from 1987 to 1992 (*The Untouchables*, *No Way Out*, *Bull Durham*, *Field of Dreams*, *Revenge*, *Dances with Wolves*, *Robin Hood*, *JFK*, and *The Bodyguard*).

I would contend that *Wyatt Earp*, while too long, is an extremely underrated film that lost much of its luster when *Tombstone* beat it to the box office by six months. I also believe Clint Eastwood's *Perfect World* is an insanely undervalued picture (and that Costner gives a really fine turn in it). And for the record, I believe Costner's finest performance was in *Open Range*. The truth of the matter is, Kevin Costner has become the cinematic equivalent of Nickelback; everyone says he sucks because, well, everyone else says it. It's the cool thing to think and say. But if you ask people what sucks about him, they don't generally have a response. And the reason for this is simple—because it's horse—*ahem*.

EIGHT FISTS OF "THE DRAGON"

by Mike Haushalter

You may be asking yourself why someone would review eight *Bloodfist* films (I know my editor was asking that very question), or perhaps why were eight of them made? As to why I reviewed them, that's simple enough: I was looking to cleanse my palate, so to speak, after reviewing a frightful amount of lesbian vampire movies for the first issue of *Exploitation Nation*. I was looking to switch gears and remembered that in the late '90s or early 2000s, I had read about the *Bloodfist* films in a video guide (which one, I can't recall). In the review of film four or five, the reviewer joked about the amount of extra film stock Roger Corman must have had on hand to be making all these sequels, and it just kind of stuck with me. Why so many *Bloodfist* films were made is not so much of a surprise when you dig a bit deeper and realize how big a direct-to-video star Don "The Dragon" Wilson was in the 1990s. The man was a small-screen action superstar who, at his height of popularity, made five films in 13 months, with his own titles competing with each other at video rental stores across the nation.

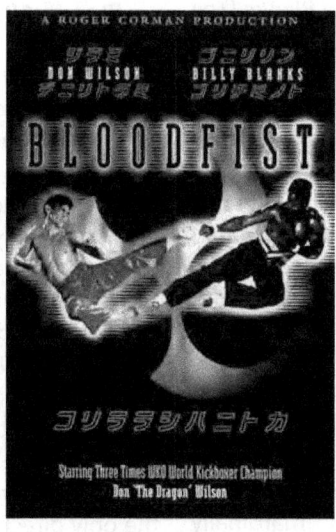

Bloodfist (1989)

Retired kickboxer Jake Raye (Don Wilson) travels to Manila after learning his brother was murdered following a kickboxing bout. Once there, Jake enters the same tournament his brother was part of in hopes of discovering who murdered his brother.

Bloodfist was Roger Corman's low-budget answer to the success of the Jean-Claude Van Damme efforts *Bloodsport* and

Kickboxer (kind of surprised they didn't call this film *Kicksport* or *Bloodboxer*), and, in all honesty, it's a better film than *Bloodsport* (I have not seen *Kickboxer* in years, so I won't speculate on whether it's better or worse than that film at this time). How good is it? Well, it's good enough that Corman had the film remade another four times (in fact, *Bloodfist* is a loose remake of *TNT Jackson*). While *Bloodsport* may feature some bigger-name actors, *Bloodfist* has a slightly more interesting and coherent story and has better staged fights.

The cast includes Don "The Dragon" Wilson (*Batman Forever* and countless more *Bloodfist* films), who may not have Van Damme's coke-fueled charm or charisma but is a hell of an onscreen fighter and, at very least, a decent actor. Joe Mari Avellana (*Demons of Paradise*, *Bloodfist II*, and *Wheels of Fire*) makes a very fine Mr. Miyagi with a secret past. Michael Shaner (*Lethal Weapon*, *Crime Zone*, and *Angelfist*) plays the charming comedy relief buddy, plus there are cameos by Billy Blanks (*The Last Boy Scout* and the inventor of Tae Bo), Vic Diaz (*The Big Bird House*, *Raw Force*, and *Beyond Atlantis*) and Cris Aguilar (*McBain* and *Delta Force 2: The Colombian Connection*).

Bloodfist was directed by Terence H. Winkless (*The Nest*, *Rage and Honor*, and a ton of Power Rangers films and episodes), and he fills the film with wall-to-wall kick boxing action, training montages, and even a little bit of T&A.

Is *Bloodfist* a lost action classic? No, it's not; it's a fair time-waster at best, and, while having superior fight sequences and being marginally

better story-wise than the Van Damme films, it lacks the showmanship and energy that the Van Damme efforts had, which is probably why you can get the Van Damme films at Walmart and most of the *Bloodfist* films are out of print.

Bloodfist II (1990)

Kickboxing champion Jake Raye (Don "The Dragon" Wilson) gives up his title after killing a man in the ring. Just as Jake begins to enjoy his retirement, he gets a call from an old friend who needs help out of a jam in Manila, only to be caught up in a mad scheme to gather top-rated fighters from around the world for an underground deathmatch.

Bloodfist II is a halfwit and threadbare *Enter the Dragon* retread with a say-no-to-drugs message that, if nothing else, proves that Don "The Dragon" Wilson is no Bruce Lee. It is the only direct sequel in the *Bloodfist* franchise, but the only thing it seems to have in common with the first film is some of the same cast and the fact that Wilson is playing the same character (well, has the same name as he did in the first film anyhow). It starts out promisingly with some good street fighting and car stunts before stalling out in the middle of the film as it turns into shanghaied fighters forced into a game of death on an island paradise (the evil villain owns the island and named it Paradise—true story).

It is the first and only directing effort from Andy Blumenthal (his only other credits are for second unit work on *Time Trackers* and *Dance of the Damned*), and it looks like it may have been the point at which he decided to call it quits—and who can blame him?

While I can give the film high marks for its many bouts of martial arts action, that is all that it has going for it, as, story-wise, this is just a stinker.

Bloodfist III: Forced to Fight (1992)

Jimmy Boland (Don "The Dragon" Wilson), a half-Asian kickboxer doing time for a murder he didn't commit, is caught in the middle of a race war in a maximum-security prison after he kills a black gang leader for sodomizing one of his friends.

Third time's a charm, as they say, and it really seems that way here with *Bloodfist III: Forced to Fight* (the last film in the series to be released theatrically). It's a fierce prison drama that has more on its mind than simply just the bloodsport death matches that fueled the first two *Bloodfist* flicks. It's a much smarter film than its predecessors, intent on telling a weighty narrative about racism and friendship where fighting is just part of the story, not the reason for the story. While this outing of the franchise is not as focused on fighting as the first two films (or even those that would come after it), what fights it has are still hard-hitting and contain a gritty realism missing from the previous films (and most that come after). Don's character's life feels like it is really on the line rather than just showy punch-ups. The fights between Wilson and Gregory McKinney are particularly well-matched and brutal. The best ingredient in the film is probably screen veteran Richard Roundtree, who adds some class and respectability.

This is not my favorite in the series, but it's probably one of the best films that Wilson has been part of. When I started down the path of reviewing all the *Bloodfist* films, I assumed they would all be pretty much xeroxed rehashes featuring the same kickboxing hero. Seems like I was wrong. After the first two, they throw away the idea of recurring characters and just seem to have slapped *Bloodfist* on every third or so film Wilson made in the '90s. And after seeing *Bloodfist III: Forced To Fight*, I am ayOK with that.

Bloodfist IV: Die Trying (1992)

Danny Holt (Don "The Dragon" Wilson) accidently repossesses a powerful arms merchant's car containing a very important box of chocolates. It's a mistake that comes with a horrible price—his friends are killed, his daughter is kidnapped, and the police think he may be to blame. On the run with no one to turn to, Danny takes matters into his own hands in a race against arms dealers, the CIA, and the FBI to save his daughter and clear his name.

Don "The Dragon" Wilson shows off his acting chops and karate chops in this action-packed entry in the *Bloodfist* series. In this film, he's a repo man on the run, trying to save his kid and clear his name. It's a pretty top-tier effort that is much better than you would expect from the fourth film in a series that doesn't even have recurring characters beyond the second film.

It has some great fights, a hard-hitting opening fight with "Judo" Gene LeBell (the "Godfather of Grappling") that has some great headbutts, a two-on-one match in a restaurant, two fights with a lion-maned Gary Daniels, and two fights with the very sexy Catya Sassoon. It has a great cast, with knockout performances from Liz Torres as Lt. Garcia, James Tolkan as FBI agent Sterling, and Amanda Wyss as Shannon. Finally, it's got a good script and a story with some good twists and turns that keep you guessing who the real villains are for a good part of the film.

It's not exactly *Universal Soldier* or *Under Siege* (the Van Damme and Seagal vehicles of the same year), but it's a great direct-to-video effort just the same and the third of four that year for Don.

***Angelfist* (1993)**

Kristie Lang is murdered after she snaps some photos of an assassination in the Philippines, where she is taking part in a kickboxing tournament. Hearing the news of her death, a cop from Los Angeles, Kat Lang (Catya Sassoon), flies to Manila to sort things out and bring justice to those responsible for her sister's death.

Angelfist is an action-packed remake of *Bloodfist* (and *TNT Jackson*—now that I think about it, *Bloodfist* is also a gender-switched remake of *TNT*

Jackson) from legendary filmmaker Cirio H. Santiago.

The film seems to be an attempt at turning Sassoon into some sort of female version of Don "The Dragon" Wilson (which didn't seem to work out as well as planned, I am guessing, since she only made one more film after this).

Sassoon gets ample opportunity to show off her stuff and was a decent-enough onscreen fighter. She looked good doing kicks and took hits well. She is backed up with some good performances, with Michael Shaner (*Bloodfist*) as her love interest/comedic relief and Melissa Moore (*Samurai Cop*) as a fellow kickboxer who gets into a memorable icehouse fight.

Santiago structures *Angelfist* much more like a straight-out action film than a martial arts tournament film like *Bloodfist* or *Bloodsport*. As such, most of the ring bouts are presented as fast-cut montages instead of full-fledged tournament fight scenes. He also adds some firefights and two shower scenes and reuses the topless hotel room brawl scene that made his early films *TNT Jackson* and *Firecracker* so memorable (giving Sassoon a chance to show off more than her kicks).

I have seen many of Santiago's films over the years and I have to say this is one of his best outings. It is well-paced, has a decent story, and is chock-full of stunts, fights, and T&A. And it even has some dialogue that earns the film a passing grade on the Bechdel test; a real winner all the way around.

***Bloodfist V: Human Target* (1994)**

W.K.A. World Kickboxing Champion Don "The Dragon" Wilson is Jimmy Stanton, an amnesia victim struggling to regain his memory after taking a bullet to the head. He is on the run from Asian arms dealers and the NSA, with no idea of whom to trust as he races to find out who he was and why everyone seems to want him dead.

Bloodfist V: Human Target is a decent 1994 direct-to-video martial arts thriller directed by first-timer Jeff Yonis for Roger Corman's New Concorde. It stars Don "The Dragon" Wilson, Denice Duff (*Bloodstone: Subspecies II*), Yuji Okumoto (*Brain Smasher*), Don Stark (*That '70s Show*), and Steve James (*American Ninja 1-3*).

In most cases, when you're reviewing the fourth sequel in a film franchise, you will, at some point, probably make a joke or two about how they must have written the script with a xerox machine or just whited out the 3 on the title and wrote in 4 or 5 (you know the films I mean). Because most of the time, when filmmakers get to this point in a film series, if they are not just outright remaking one of the previous entries, they are either scraping the bottom of the barrel for ideas or sending everyone into space. But after the single misstep that was Part 2, the *Bloodfist* films started to come together. This may be because after the second film there are no continuing characters, the only consistent thing in each film being Wilson. Of course, considering Wilson's lack of range and charisma, I guess it can be argued that he is actually playing the same part in each film, with just a new name each time, kind of like a kung fu *Quantum Leap*.

When I started this project, it was the memory of a review of the films I read long ago that made me want to see them. What I remembered most was how the reviewer joked about how much surplus film stock Roger Corman must have had to make all these films. I remember thinking to myself, "How many films can they make about a guy ring fighting?" But after pParts 3 and 4, I realized this was not your typical franchise and that the films were not all just a series of ring fighting contests. After that discovery, I really wondered where each next film would go. In this case, in addition to changing up the story from the last film (which also involved arms dealers, mind you, but so do just about all of the *Mission Impossible* films), they seem to have given Wilson a makeover, including a fab new haircut and a stylish suit that just seems to make him look a little more glamorous that the first four outings. The whole film seems a bit glossier, more colorful, and less drab and threadbare than the early films.

This film really proves that Wilson could have been playing on the field with big boys like Van Damme and Seagal. It has tons of fights, a fantastic end boss battle against Steve James, and some great chemistry between Wilson and Duff (who looks gorgeous).

The film also has some really funny dialogue, the best being a bit with Wilson arguing with Duff, who is wearing nothing but a blanket: "So, you coming like that?" To which Duff replies, "I don't know, I may change into the shower curtain." With product like this, it's no wonder Corman kept greenlighting projects for Wilson, even if he did slap a *Bloodfist* tag in front of dang near every other film the guy made.

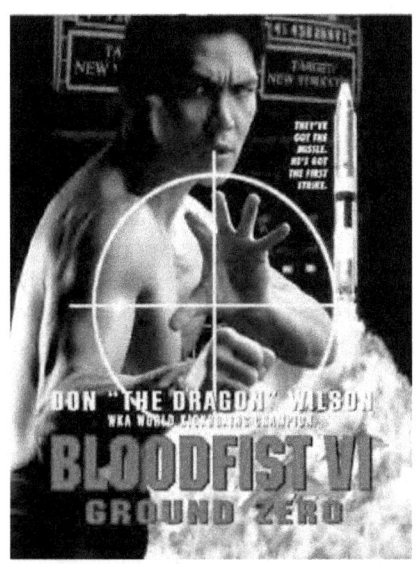

Bloodfist VI: Ground Zero (1995)

Army courier Nick Corrigan (Don "The Dragon" Wilson) stumbles upon an Islamic terrorist plot to hijack a remote Midwest nuclear missile silo and hold America's largest cities ransom for $100 million in gold.

This is a tepid *Die Hard* clone from Roger Corman's cash cow Don "The Dragon" Wilson that offers up modest thrills for action fans. If nothing else, the *Bloodfist* franchise really shows off Corman's genius. The man understood that no matter what story his latest Wilson film told, if he slapped *Bloodfist* and a number on it, folks would give it a rent. The franchise really racks up the film tropes: death sports, prison rampages, fugitives on the run, and, of course, *Die Hard* retreads. If you have a favorite action-movie archetype, there's more than likely a *Bloodfist* film aimed at you.

When I sat down to give *Bloodfist VI* a view, in the back of my mind was the nagging thought that this was bound to be the point at which the franchise would start to be a slog. Surprisingly, my concerns would mostly turn out to be wrong. It is actually a pretty exciting romp. It doesn't have the best fights of the series, and it may be about the cheapest-looking film thus far, but there is plenty of lively gunplay; entertaining, over-the-top villainy, and a long glimpse of Catya Sassoon's assets to make up for that. There's also some great fighter jet footage that I imagine is from some other more expensive film. Additionally, the film features a fun cast. Wilson is in top form and is backed by some great folks, including Wynn Irwin as sexist blowhard General Carmichael and Jonathan Fuller (*Castle Freak*) as the cocky terrorist leader Fawkes. There is also a fine stable of tough guys for Wilson to beat on, including Michael Blanks (*Dragon Fire*), Howard Jackson (*Disco Godfather*), Alex Desir, Dennis Keiffer (*Mortal Kombat: Annihilation*), and Art Camacho (who also choreographed the fights).

The film does have its shortcomings. Sassoon does not

bring her A-game (or even B- or C-game) performance, the martial arts bouts are very underwhelming, and how many times can you really use the same hallway set before it becomes a drinking game?

If the fights had been as much fun as the dialogue, this may have been the franchise's best effort, but sadly, it's more of a missed opportunity than anything else.

Bloodfist VII: Manhunt (1995)

After he rescues a beautiful stranger (Jillian McWhirter) from some lowlife bikers at a dive bar, Jim Trudell (Don "The Dragon" Wilson) finds himself a man on the run. Branded a cop-killer and a car thief and suspected of murdering the missing woman he saved the night before, he is now in a race to stay alive and clear his name while trying to avoid the police, the FBI, and a vicious gang of car thieves.

The year 1995 was very busy for Don Wilson. He appeared in five movies (*Batman Forever*, *CyberTracker 2*, *Virtual Combat*, two—count 'em, two—*Bloodfist* features), and the martial arts documentary *Top Fighter*. He also began his stint as a commentator for the UFC (Ultimate Fighting Championship). Perhaps having all these projects so close together was too much of a burden on the man, because he really doesn't seem to be giving this outing his full attention. While *Manhunt* has better production values and better fight choreography than the previous *Bloodfist* installment, the film (and Wilson) just seem to be going through the motions. It's the first film in the series that seems to be just a cut-and-paste version of the films that came before it. It's almost as if the script was written with lines cannibalized from the previous three films and then just jumbled together until it was enough to fill up 90 minutes of film stock. Wilson's co-stars, Steven Williams (tough-as-nails Captain Doyle), Jonathan Penner (cop-gone-wrong Johnny Marvosa), and Stephen Davies (sketchy Special Agent Craig), don't help matters much and come across like they are broad stereotypes in a parody of the genre rather than the straight-ahead action vehicle they are in. McWhirter's character is missing for so much of the film that she is more of a MacGuffin than anything else and doesn't get that much to do the few times she is on-screen.

When I began the very noble project of reviewing each and every one of the *Bloodfist* films (a project I undertook of my own volition), I

always expected it to become a drag at some point, and, to be completely honest, I thought I would hit that point by film three. The fact that I made it all the way to film seven before I started to really dread the notion that I had to try to write yet another *Bloodfist* review really says something about how decent the series turned out to be. So, here I am, with only one more film to go, and it is just now finally starting to become a chore to bring myself to watch and review any more of these—ah, well, I'm almost done.

***Bloodfist VIII: Hard Way Out* (1996)**

Aka: *Trained to Kill* (1996)

Rick Cowan (Don "The Dragon" Wilson), a former CIA agent-turned-high school teacher is trying to start a new life with his estranged son, Chris (John Patrick White, *Teaching Mrs. Tingle*), when his old life catches up to him and he is suddenly the target of an international hit squad. With both of their lives on the line, Rick and his son flee to Ireland to find who is trying to kill them and discover why.

Well, I have finally arrived at the last film in the *Bloodfist* franchise (so far, anyway; there are rumors of a possible new film, or they could just retitle yet another

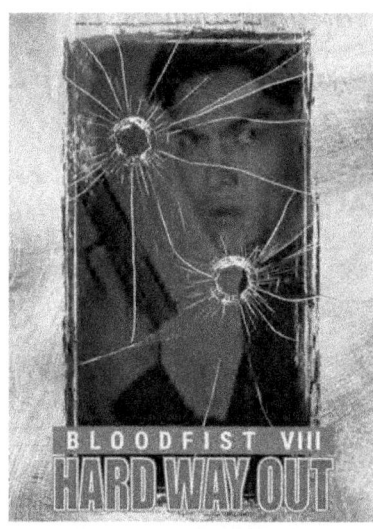

of Wilson's films) and—you know what? It wasn't that bad of a movie; not really a resounding endorsement, I know, but what can I say? It's been a long trip to get to this film, and I am more excited about being done with the series than the film itself. Like the films before it, *Bloodfist VIII* is chock-full of firefights, fisticuffs, and a few good explosions. And, like films before it, *Bloodfist VIII* has just enough of a storyline to keep the film moving from one action set piece to the next, but no real character development or great story revelations. It's pretty much just another Don "The Dragon" Wilson outing, one of many direct-to-video action efforts the '90s had to offer, and one of the more forgettable ones at that. It was a good run, but the well just went dry, and the bucket was busted to boot.

As a franchise, if nothing else, the *Bloodfist* films offer up a lot of variety and show that, with perhaps a little more money and talent behind him, Wilson could have been a big-screen contender. He had more charisma than Sho Kosugi and was a better fighter than Jean-Claude Van Damme, but he never had their polish, nor did he have the presence of Norris, Stallone, or Seagal. So, while he dominated the video shelves, he never became a big name on the big screen.

IT'S ALWAYS SOMETHING WITH A VIRGIN: BRINGING THE CONVENT (BACK) TO THE SCREEN

by Corey Danna

The title screen reads "1960" as a teenage girl, dressed in a Catholic school uniform, black leather jacket, and dark sunglasses, steps out of a car with a cigarette dangling from her mouth. She walks with purpose to the front doors of the St. Francis Boarding School, carrying a duffel bag and a can of gasoline. Once inside, she takes a monster swig of whiskey before laying waste to a roomful of nuns, using a baseball bat, the aforementioned gasoline, and a shotgun, all while Leslie Gore's "You Don't Own Me" plays. Thus, the tone is set for *The Convent*, written by Chaton Anderson (*Punk's Undead*) and directed by Mike Mendez (*Big Ass Spider!*), premiering on January 21, 2000, at the Sundance Film Festival. Word of mouth spread quickly, and the film seemed destined to become a cult classic. Due to circumstances beyond the filmmaker's control, there was a delay in getting the film a proper release. It never received a theatrical run, and almost two years later, it was dumped to VHS and DVD in the United States.

The Convent was first released in Europe, where it instantly connected with audiences long before it hit North American shores. In fact, the film was quite popular on the bootleg circuit at conventions, and director Mendez didn't seem to mind, saying, "At the time, I encouraged the fact it was heavily bootlegged. It was different then; there wasn't BitTorrenting. It took a long time from when it premiered at Sundance until its release." He continues, "Once it was out, I just wanted people to see it. People were trading tapes at conventions. I was never upset about it; I would autograph them. I discovered films the same way, like *Dead Alive* or *Meet the Feebles*,. So, to me, it was just really cool."

Almost 20 years later, *The Convent* is reconnecting with the same audience that embraced it all those years ago. Before discussing the present and future of the film, let's travel back to 1999, when a struggling independent film company called Alpine Pictures found itself with an opening in its schedule. ItA project had fallen through, and the company needed to fill the slot with a particular type of film: a horror movie. Chaton Anderson, who was working PR for

Alpine at the time, had an idea in her head, one spurred by personal experiences. As a teenager, she spent many nights trying to convince her friends to accompany her on an adventure. She had heard numerous stories about an abandoned property that was once known as the Good Shepherd's Home for Wayward Girls. It didn't take long before she and her friends broke into the property. "There was a groundskeeper who lived on-site in a little bungalow, but they were never awake or caught us going in," she remembers. "We'd heard that priests performed abortions in there and people had found fetuses in the walls. It was rumored that when the place was finally condemned, they found Satanists there. It had a really rich history and definitely felt haunted. This place was huge, a sprawling property over a couple of acres, and I saw things I would later use as images in *The Convent*." Anderson continues, "We have a beheaded Virgin Mary statue in the movie, and there were statues all over the property. Satanists had lopped the head off one, and it was just really eerie. The hard part was getting into the underground chapel, and we spent weeks looking for an entrance. We heard weird things, we saw weird things, but everything was boarded-up each night we came back. One night, the police came, and we had just made it down to the bottom. They didn't arrest us—we were given a warning—so I went back the next night. I found this spot where I had to crawl through, and the glass from the window above just shattered on my head. It didn't cut my head or anything, but it did get my arm, and we had to make a trip to the hospital."

Her script would follow a group of college kids who accidently unleash an unspeakable evil when they break into an abandoned convent. Before taking it to the company heads, she pitched her idea to Mendez, who was still a struggling young filmmaker, and the two were instantly on the same page. Anderson recalls, "Alpine had a project they were beginning to staff up for, and it was terrible. They even had a big-name writer come in to do a rewrite, and it was still terrible, and it eventually fell through. I had become close with Mike, so I pitched

All photos this section courtesy Chaton Anderson and © Alpine Pictures. All rights reserved.

my idea of zombie demonic nuns, and he loved it." Continuing, she says, "It took me a month to write the script, and I took it to Alpine, who loved it and were excited about having Mike on board. I had maybe a month to incorporate notes and do another rewrite before we moved on it. It all happened so fast and was very deadline-driven."

After the success of his first picture, *Killers*, Mendez could have moved up the Hollywood food chain, but instead, he had other plans. "Alpine Pictures picked up my first film, *Killers*, after it premiered at Sundance. That opened so many doors for me in Hollywood, but I turned them all down, the money and everything, because I'm a glutton for B-movies. I'll do a demonic nun movie instead! Chaton had the deal and it had to be done quickly," Mendez proudly states.

Alpine approved the rewrite and was ready to move on to the next phase: casting. Mendez reflects on the early stages: "My first film was basically a glorified student film, so, in many ways, *The Convent* was my first. I had never had to deal with making offers and stuff before, so someone from Alpine worked as a casting director. One role of real value, one we knew we needed a name for, was that of Christine. I knew it needed to be someone from the horror world and had to be a badass chick. The list was really short, but when I think badass chick, I think Adrienne Barbeau. She is a living legend, an actress every horror fan in the world loves and respects.

Mendez sent the script to Barbeau's agent and it eventually landed in her hands. Barbeau fondly remembers her first reaction on reading the script: "I started reading it right away, and I thought it was hysterically funny! The character of Christine doesn't show up until the movie is three-quarters over. I thought it all was very, very funny, but I couldn't figure out what they wanted me for. When I finally made it to her appearance, I realized I would basically be playing Snake Plissken. When I read her dialogue, all I could hear was Kurt Russell doing Snake."

In addition to Barbeau, there were two cop characters Mendez was looking to cast with recognizable names. He laughs when he recalls how he brought one of these actors in, saying, "Someone we knew was Coolio's pot dealer, so we offered him the role and a free eighth to come do it. He was game." Mendez would cast another genre legend as the second police officer: Bill Moseley. "This was before *House of 1,000 Corpses* and *The Devil's Rejects*, so Bill wasn't the name he is today. Most people only knew him as Chop-Top, but he was the cousin of someone at Alpine, and I was a fan. It really made no sense casting these guys, but who cares, they were so much fun!" During this process, they almost cast a really huge name to appear in the finale of the film, and it would have entirely altered how it concluded. "At one point, we were really close to casting Snoop Dogg in the movie. He would have shown up at the end of the movie to save the day. We had it where Christine would find herself in trouble and call her boyfriend at home, and it would have been Snoop. He would have shown up and saved everyone. It would have been pretty

spectacular, but everything happens for a reason, and I stand by the finale," Mendez reminisces.

The rest of the cast began to fill out, with fresh young faces making their feature-film debuts. Joanna Canton was cast as Clorissa, Richard Trapp as Frijole, Jim Golden as Biff, Dax Miller as Chad, and Renée Graham as Kaitlin. The character of Mo is a fan favorite and loosely based on a real person, Anderson explains: "Mo was based on a friend who went to the Catholic high school I went to. All of her banter was my banter, things I would actually say."

During the late '90s, Megahn Perry was the "guest star du jour" for WB, having appeared on episodes of its most popular shows, including *Dawson's Creek* and *Buffy the Vampire Slayer*. "When I was a kid, I played the goth girl a lot, though I'm not particularly goth in real life. I would say I'm more goth-adjacent, so I'm a total nerd, but Mo is the type of character I would want to be every day of my life if I could get away with it. She's way cooler than I am. We have the same sense of humor, but she can express it anywhere or anytime, any way she wants," Perry says. "I auditioned twice before they finally offered me the part. I think every actress my age at that time auditioned for the movie. I was so lucky to get the opportunity to do it. It was a seminal moment in my life," she remembers fondly.

The film features a pair of bumbling Satanists, Saul and Dickie-Boy. Mendez knew exactly who he wanted for the role of Saul: "He was always meant to be an idiot, but I knew if I brought in David Gunn, who was one of my best friends, he would do something really special with it." Gunn and Mendez knew each other from their Pasadena Community College days. Gunn was cast as one of the leads in his first film, *Killers*, but for *The Convent*, he would have to audition just like everyone else.

"Mike was my number-one cheerleader," Gunn offers, "but I still auditioned for the casting director and a couple of the producers before I landed the part." Gunn is a deep thinker, and he really took the time to analyze who Saul was and what would be the best way to bring the character to life. He relates, "Saul's a nut-job who's so dedicated to his fantasy life that, even when faced with the prospect of a real Anti-Christ being brought into the world, he still can't let go of his facade. At the same time, the real him is still there too; he's not a brave guy. I used to go to all the industrial clubs, and there were always these guys who would show up at the club dressed like Lestat. They'd be walking around the club, right, the place is hot, everybody's sweaty, and these guys were so committed, walking around like a 16th th century vampire. They'd be going up to girls who were dancing, doing the whole gaze with the eyes, and people were just looking at them absurdly. They were so committed to the illusion, and, in my mind, that was Saul."

The success of the Saul character was contingent on who they cast as his sidekick, Dickie-Boy. Anderson wrote the character a certain way, and not just anyone could pull it off. "I sat in on all the casting and even found some people myself. I was lucky enough to meet Kelly Mantle, who was the embodiment of Dickie-Boy, exactly how I had envisioned in my head," Anderson admits. Mantle was a young performer, and the first gig he booked after moving to Los Angeles was The Convent. He has since gone on to make history, becoming the first performer to be considered for nomination in the supporting actor and supporting actress categories of the Academy Awards for the picture

Confessions of a Womanizer.

When Mantle and Gunn met, it was apparent from the start that the two would have a chemistry that would light up the screen. "I adore David Gunn," Mantle reflects affectionately. "Chaton created this amazing (and hilarious) chemistry between them in the dialogue, so it was just a matter of bringing that to life."

At a certain point in the film, the comedic duo becomes a trio when the character of Brant comes between them. Liam Kyle Sullivan was a young actor and comedian when *The Convent* began casting. "I remember the audition being very well-directed by Mike Mendez," Sullivan says. "You could just feel his passion for the project when you entered the room. He gave me suggestions and I went with it." Incidentally, Sullivan went on to create one of the first true viral music videos with the song "Shoes," which has been viewed over 64 million times, making him and his character Kelly icons of pop culture.

When principal photography began, the stars aligned. The cast worked tremendously together, the effects looked terrific, and everything went according to schedule. Mendez takes us back: "We shot in August and it was very hot. We actually shot in the same place where they did the original *Saw*. There were quite a few horror movies shot there. *Leprechaun in the Hood* shot there after us. Eighteen days isn't bad, considering how independent films are shot these days; I haven't even had that lately. We were all really young, and there was just this really good vibe on set. I was pretty much left alone to make the movie the way I wanted to make it, so it was a really good time."

The film was shot in Los Angeles, and the location was everything Mendez had hoped for. Perry remembers it vividly, "We shot on some really shitty stages downtown. Three doors down from us, they were shooting porn. The shittiness of the stages did pay off because they were super creepy. They would shine the black lights into the sets, and it looked so great and unique."

Even though the film was coming together like everyone had hoped, it wasn't always easy. Anderson wasn't just the screenwriter, she was also the producer and played the character of Sapphira. Her experience was a bit different. She explains, "As the producer, I brought all the elements together, but the tough monetary decisions were made by the executive producers, and I had to execute their decisions. I was young and wasn't used to all the politics, so I had to be really gutsy. I wanted the film to be the best it could be, so I called in every possible favor I could. It was tough and there was a lot I had to deal with too." As Sapphira, Anderson was involved in some heavy FX scenes and still had to attend to her behind-the-scenes duties. "It was tough for me to appear in the movie and be one of the producers. It literally took eight hours for me to get in the makeup and maybe four to get out of it. I was running on no sleep, doing my duties on set as producer while in my demon makeup," Anderson states with some exasperation.

There comes a moment in the film when the first sacrifice takes place, setting the course for a showstopping moment: unleashing the demons on the unsuspecting teens. Once this scene plays through, everything changes in the movie, and, for the audience, it's when the ride truly begins. For the cast, they began to realize just how special this project was becoming. The shoot was grueling, they were working long days, and Perry was running on empty when this particular scene was shot. She states: "That's the scene where Mo asks Saul if he works at the Dairy Queen, which I think encapsulates the whole goth mentality of that time period. We shot mostly at night for days on end, and I was able to lie down in the middle of it. I was just thankful all I had to do was lie there. I was really, really tired. David Gunn and Kelly Mantle were there, and they were so hilarious. I just kept laughing at how funny everything they said was."

Perry isn't the only one to praise the talents of David Gunn, who really shines as the eccentric and misguided Saul. "I was so surprised with David during that scene because we didn't rehearse it and I had no idea what he was planning to do," Chaton Anderson says. "It was the funniest thing in the world to be able to work with all my friends in that scene. It felt really organic and in the moment.

Gunn, on the other hand, looks

at the scene a bit differently. "When getting into character, I just felt that Saul and Dickie-Boy would do this sort of thing weekend after weekend, and finally it works, even though they were probably just trying to bluff their way through it anyway. My question is, why would a girl as beautiful as Chaton be hanging out with these weekend Satanists? It's just hysterical," he laughs.

This scene is also the introduction to many of the brilliant and unique effects in the film, many of which had never really been seen before. Mendez explains, "Screaming Mad George had this punk band, and they did these onstage effects, and one of the things they did was have this black light-reactive makeup. And he also told me about these contact lenses that were also reactive to the black lights. I didn't have faith in CGI, so I figured the glowing-eye effect would probably look best if it was achieved on set. I decided to look into the lenses and makeup and thought it was really interesting and had never seen that before. It was a low-tech effect that just worked for us."

Effects artist Dean Jones has spent well over 30 years creating interesting and unique looks for film and television. Working under pressure and with limited funds was something he was quite familiar with, and he knew how to get more bang for their buck. "We created an interesting demon nun appearance using forehead appliances to create this evil brow on them," he explains. "We discussed using the black light effect on the demon nuns so that the white makeup, contact lenses, and blue veins that we airbrushed would pop."

The effect proved to be a huge hit with audiences, and Mendez was happy with how it all turned out. "I still don't think I've ever really seen it done in anything else," he says. "Even how they moved—I was attempting to make them look as if they were stop-animated. My second-unit director was the one doing it, and he sort of overcranked the camera. It wasn't quite what I was going for, but it was still unique and has held up."

"I was so jealous of Kelly," Gunn remembers with a hint of envy. "He got to dress up as a demon, you know, when he was the demon spawn. I loved that." Mantle responds quite boisterously: "UGH! I was in that makeup chair for six hours! I'm terrible at sitting still for long periods of time. But as tedious as it was, Dean Jones did an incredible job. I was in awe of his talents! Performing in the prosthetics was somewhat challenging, but I'm kinda used to the constraints because I do drag."

As challenging as it may have been, the final result looks pretty spectacular, and Jones still holds the creature in high regard. He states: "That was our 'hero' demon makeup! It rips from an embryonic sac, and then you get to see it in all of its glory. It really looked terrific, considering our budget."

When it came to scoring the film, Mendez wanted to take it in a different direction, far removed from the traditional ominous sounds. "I was looking for an electronic, industrial horror score," he begins. "This was Joseph Bishara's first horror film, and I had met him through Screaming Mad George. When we met, we just clicked, and till this day, he's one of my best friends—family at this point. The score he did for *The Convent* is so much different from what he's currently doing. Now he's known for stuff that sounds more supernatural or ghosty, so I'm curious if he could replicate that sound again."

Bishara is one of the most sought-after composers working in the genre today. *The Convent* might have been his first horror film score, but he's done some of the most successful horror films of the last decade, including the *Insidious* franchise and *The Conjuring* films. Bishara is still very supportive and proud of his work with Mendez. "Mike was clear from our initial meeting in wanting a mostly electronic, industrial-flavored score and to also play the more horrific aspects straight," he remembers. "Screaming Mad George suggested I meet Mike and put us in touch. I had also by chance just scored a drama from the same production company for director Philippe Mora. I remember Mike and I first met at this company's office, which was outfitted with castle sets from a medieval time-travel film they had made, and he asked me to do it that day."

As chance would have it, several years after scoring the film, the composer moved to a home where his neighbor ended up being one of the movie's lead performers, and she has nothing but praise for his work. Barbeau quips: "My neighbor, Joe Bishara, did such a wonderful score for the film. It really adds so much atmosphere to it. I'm not really into horror films, but I always hear my sons talking about how fantastic his music is."

Pictures like this can really bring fans together. Not only do they bond over their shared experience when viewing it, but the people who worked so hard to bring it to the screen still care deeply about their *Convent* family. Perry is the first to chime in: "Try putting me in a room with Mike, Chaton, Liam, or David. We all talk over each other, have the same sense of humor—everyone is hilarious, and they're a great group of people to improv with. Liam is still one of my best friends."

Gunn shares the sentiment: "Megahn was always making everyone laugh, and she was someone who really stood out to me. Adrienne Barbeau was such a class act, professional on every level. Her performance was of a certain caliber, and we all strived to be on the same level."

Mantle had a similar experience: "The friendships I made were awesome. Chaton and I are still super close girlfriends to this day." Veteran actress Barbeau has nothing but fond memories of her castmates: "I had such a great time working with Megahn Perry and the fellas. I also really loved doing my scene with Joanna Canton when she meets Christine for the first time—so talented. It was such an enjoyable shoot to be a part of."

After playing a couple of festivals, the film was eventually picked up by Lionsgate, releasing it on VHS and DVD. While the presentation it was given is rather respectable, it just never had a chance to garner a larger following. The fans who do love the film had always wanted to see another film, a sequel, prequel, anything. A couple years ago, it almost appeared as if their wish was going to come true. Mendez elaborates: "Chaton and I wanted to do a prequel, *The Devil's Convent*, but we were stuck in a rotten situation where she needed to get the rights and no one would give them to her. Since the original company is out of business and everything is owned by another entity, it's a rights issue to start, and then the next hurdle would be to get it financed. We have drafts of it, but it wasn't quite there yet."

Anderson sheds a little more light on the issue: "We didn't make money from the original film, and the producers did. They made it very difficult for us to get the rights. We haven't given up hope. Who knows what will happen in two years? We even wrote a sequel that was never made."

Mendez has this to add: "It would be similar in tone, but it was going to be Christine's story. We also had to make sure it would work as a stand-alone movie, because—let's face it—*The Convent* isn't a movie many people give a shit about. Thankfully, we have a core group of fans who appreciate it, which is wonderful. I don't think it was fully thought-out legally how we would get it done. It just turned out to be more difficult than Chaton thought to get the rights. If we are ever somehow able to overcome those hurdles, I would be down. I know there's a cool movie in there by taking the same concept and moving it to the '60s at a girls school with a demonic influence." Anderson remains optimistic: "It will happen at some point. We're just gonna have to wait."

For many years, the rights issue had proved to be rather confusing and aggravating for those involved. It had kept the film from getting a premium Blu-ray release or even being shown in theaters. "The original elements were being held hostage by a lab because the original company went bankrupt and stopped paying," Mendez explains. "So, the original negative was stuck in a place that wanted the debt to be paid before they would make an HD master of it. I'm not sure how much, something like $10,000 or $20,000, so they were holding onto it until someone was willing to pay it. Because of that whole chain of events, it wasn't really available anywhere. That's a frightening thing for a film, of being forgotten or lost. I really want to see this movie live on and not be forgotten."

Then, something truly amazing happened, and the fans were given an unexpected treat. In a handful of theaters across the country, *The Convent* was screened October 11, 2018, on a double bill with the film *Sweet Sixteen*. It was part of a series called *Retro Nightmares*, presented by the website Bloody Disgusting. Anderson and Mendez went to separate screenings, and the results were the same. "The crowd was so awesome! There's nothing like the energy of a crowd watching a horror film in a theater. We all had so much fun," Anderson recounts.

Mendez, who went to a different screening, says, "It was crazy to see it for the first time in nearly 20 years. In some ways, it's hard to watch something you made 20 years ago without cringing, but I'm thankful to say that, overall, it held up, and it was still funny, and we all had a great time. Much of the cast and crew were there, including Adrienne Barbeau. Hopefully, there will be more screenings like this in the near future."

So, what exactly did this mean for the future of the film? Mendez is happy to elaborate: "A company called Multicom picked up the rights after the original production company went out of business. The film has been restored to a 4K version, and it looks like we will finally be able to get it out on Blu-ray. 2020 will be the 20th anniversary of the film, and that seems like a mighty good time to do it."

With this recent breakthrough, it appears *The Convent* isn't going to be forgotten. It's going to be given a second life, which is long overdue. As for the cast and crew, their memories of being a part of this little gem will be treasured for the rest of their lives. Barbeau concludes: "I'm not a horror film fan, but the humor in *The Convent* really sets it apart from the others and makes it so special. It's a wonderful amalgam of comedy and horror."

Her insights really do peg what makes the film so special. For some involved, it was life-altering. Perry states appreciatively: "Hands down, the best experience I ever had making a movie. The friends I made making that movie all those years ago are still in my life now. I will forever be grateful for the film."

Gunn has only one last thing to add: "Being involved in *The Convent* really did amount to some of the best times in my life. It was an absolute blast to be on the set with everyone involved."

For Anderson, having given birth to the entire project with her script, it's far more personal. "Mike and I toured the world with that film! I'm so happy people are getting a chance to see it in theaters again," she finishes. "Mike and I have taken pieces of our lives and put it into the film and these other scripts. There's so much more story we want to tell, so who knows what will happen. I just hope people will continue to have a blast with it."

WHAT OUR FRIENDS ARE UP TO

We know a lot of interesting, talented people. Here are some of them.

DEEP RED Vol. 4, #2 – (Fantaco Press). The great Chas Balun may be gone, but his seminal work in legitimizing the horror genre via his writing will never be forgotten. Publisher Tom Skulan and editor-in-chief John Szpunar relaunched Chas's beloved *Deep Red* in 2018, and the newest issue hit the stands at the end of last year—and the first printing immediately sold out! Chock-full of fun articles, *Deep Red* #2 looks at the adult work of Ray Dennis Steckler, has some fun with *Cannibal Holocaust*, and offers in-depth interviews with *Frankenhooker*'s all-around nice guy James Lorinz and the legendary Tom Savini, as well as a roundtable discussion of *Combat Shock* and a rare piece from Balun himself! An absolute must for fans of the reddest kind of horror. Order yours from fantaco.net

SAVINI – THE BIOGRAPHY, by Tom Savini and Michael Aloisi (additional material). 2019 was a hell of a year for Tom Savini. It marked his return to directing (on Shudder's *Creepshow*), and he received a respectable homage (and cameo) in Netflix's *Locke & Key*. And now here's a real treat! This book has been in the works for some time (I saw an early draft at least 10 years ago)—obviously, because life is long and, when you're Tom Savini, filled with strange and fantastic twists and turns. The special-effects maestro, often called "The Godfather of Gore," invented techniques for onscreen murder that thrilled every horror fan growing up in the '80s. Savini talks about his desire to scare and thrill, his love of acting, his many influential friends, his friendship with George Romero, and many of the adventures and pitfalls he experienced while working in the movies. Told fairly linearly in Savini's conversational style, the book takes us through his formative years, the harrowing time he spent in Vietnam as a military photographer, and the Hollywood years. His notes and journals—through *Django Unchained* and *The Lost Boys: The Tribe*—bring the

reader almost up to date. The book is a handsome hardback, filled with color and black-and-white photos from Savini's vast archives. Reading the book feels like you're having a conversation with the man, and I can't recommend it enough. A must-have addition to your shelf, alongside his *Grande Illusions* books. Available through Amazon and DarkInkBooks.com.

decline. Once streaming popularized and streaming services were able to produce their own content, the need for independent movies seemingly vanished. Seymour interviews such indie mainstays as Lloyd Kaufman, Joe Bob Briggs, J.R. Bookwalter, Debbie Rochon, and others, all of whom share their stories of frustration. When Bookwalter talks about watching his titles vanish from Amazon Prime—once not only the chief model for exhibiting indie movies but also a chief source of valuable income—it would seem as if the industry is all but dead like Jacob Marley. Unfortunately, the viewer is left with little hope. We all have to rely on the marketplace to step up and fill the shrinking need for indie films with a new service, but the cost value doesn't seem to be too enticing as of this writing. This documentary is a fascinating and utterly depressing voyage into the state of independent art. Due for a release by Troma Entertainment later in 2020, *VHS Massacre* (both *1* and *2*) is important viewing for anyone in—or looking to get into—the indie film community.

VHS MASSACRE TOO (aka *VHS Massacre 2* [2020]) – Directed by Thomas Edward Seymour *(Land of College Prophets, Bikini Bloodbath Christmas).* Where the first *VHS Massacre* concerned itself with the death of the home video market and chronicling the decline and fall of Blockbuster Video, the second installment takes a close look at the veritable death of the indie filmmaking industry. Blockbuster's shuttering its doors across the country began the

SEX TERRORISTS ON WHEELS (2019) – Directed by Stefan Ruf, written by Ruf and John Herndon, starring Gary Kent, Justin Henry, Larissa Dali, Jecca Bitner. For this pure throwback to '70s exploitation, Ruf seems to have taken several chapters from Al Adamson's book to bring viewers a mean-as-nails, gory, violent adventure, with a vicious biker gang combatting Texas Rangers. The Sex Terrorists rape, cannibalize, and maraud their way across our nation's toughest state, but they meet their

match in mountain man Ezra (Kent), a half-blind Vietnam vet who can talk to animals and shoot the mites off a buzzard at 1,000 yards. There's little more to the plot than violence and anti-social behavior, but it would feel right at home between screenings of *Satan's Sadists* and *Psycho a Go-Go*. Kent, a veteran stuntman (his autobiography, *Shadows & Light*, chronicles his work with Adamson, Brian De Palma, and Richard Rush, and many of his stories inspired Tarantino's *Once Upon a Time in Hollywood*), plays Ezra with a whimsical touch and brings some gravitas to the film. Henry, as "Lobo the Wolf," is a particularly intimidating villain. If you're a pure-hearted lover of mean, nasty exploitation movies, here's a jim-dandy for you. Learn more at the Raw Cinema Facebook page: facebook.com/stefanrufmovies/

ESCAPE FROM THE DOMAIN by Michael Legge. Robert Morgan, the Last Man On Earth, discovers that the walking dead are the least of his problems when he finds himself bouncing from one implausible scenario to another. Voodoo, zombies, giant carnivorous talking plants. Maybe he shoulda stayed in bed.

Imagine if all those wonderful and awful public domain b-movies shared a universe. That's the marvelous premise of Michael Legge's new novel. With a whip-crack pace, the reader is dragged through plagues of the undead, giant leeches, hideous sun demons, and more adventures than you can count. It's a month's worth of late-night Chiller Theater episodes all in one book!

A filmmaker, actor on screens and stage—not to mention his alter ego, legendary horror host, "Dr. Dreck!"—Legge acquits himself quite well as an expert in classic low budget horror. If you're not sure which black and white marvel you and Morgan are tripping through at any given moment, the author provides you with a little guide (with pictures!) at the tail end of this slim volume. Available on Amazon.

I'D BUY THAT FOR A DOLLAR!

by Mike Haushalter

One of my favorite activities is to look through bargain bins and the racks of secondhand sellers to find movie deals. Whether it's a forgotten A-list title, blink-and-you-missed-it indie release, or last year's hot direct-to-home-video title, as long as it costs $2 to $5, it's bound to come home with me. But if it's less than that? Well, I'm willing to take a gamble on almost anything that's priced at a dollar and offers even a tiny bit of intrigue or interest. After all, I can't even rent most of these things for that price, and if they don't work out, I can sell them again. But when they do work out, it's magical. Here's a roundup of my latest finds, good and bad.

Cowboys and Aliens (2011)

The box says: "Daniel Craig and Harrison Ford star in this action-packed sci-fi western from the director of *Iron Man* (Jon Favreau) that critics call "wickedly original, unlike anything you've ever seen" (Jake Hamilton, Fox-TV Houston, TX). A stranger (Craig) stumbles into the desert town of Absolution with no memory of his past and a futuristic shackle around his wrist. With the help of mysterious beauty Ella (Olivia Wilde) and the iron-fisted Colonel Dolarhyde (Ford), the stranger finds himself leading an unlikely posse of cowboys, outlaws, and Apache warriors against a common enemy from beyond this world in an epic showdown for survival."

Why I risked a dollar: I love big-budget Hollywood disasters, and I had been actively looking for *Cowboys and Aliens* for some time when I stumbled upon three or four copies of it for a dollar,. all lined up in a row at my local Exchange. I scooped it up and put it on the stack, earmarking it for my annual New Year's Day viewing of the worst movie I could find.

Thoughts: Surprise, surprise! *Cowboys and Aliens* was not the disaster I was expecting it to be; in fact, it was a pretty fun thrill-ride. This is a great summer- blockbuster popcorn flick that just didn't find its audience. Sure, maybe my expectations were so low that a little bit went a long way, but in any case, I dug it.

Plus: Action-packed. Cool aliens and lots of good performances, including great work from Clancy Brown (*Highlander*), Sam Rockwell (*Moon*), Walton Goggins (*Justified*), and Adam Beach (*Windtalkers*).

Minus: Daniel Craig seemed to be coasting. The film has far more going on than it really needs. Meh script.

Shelf/Bin: It's a keeper, and in fact, I imagine I will upgrade to the extended cut or whatever they call the longer version (*Cowboys and More Aliens?*).

Frostbite (2005)

The box says: "If *American Pie* and *Animal House* cracked you up, *Frostbite* will knock you on your butt. Slacker Billy Wagstaff has a chance to become a world-class snowboarder when he's accepted into Pine Mountain Snowboarding Academy. But after a crazy night in a hot tub with babes and booze, he wakes up in a trashcan and out of the academy. That's when Billy realizes he needs to put his best foot forward and get back on the mountain. Featuring Traci Lords, gorgeous snow bunnies, and some of the best boarders in the world, *Frostbite* is a wild ride you won't want to miss."

Why I risked a dollar: I picked up *Frostbite* because I at first thought it was a horror film of the same title. I quickly realized I was wrong (really wrong, as the film I had mistaken it for is actually called *Frostbiter* or *Wendigo*) and that it was some sort of teen sex romp along the lines of *American Pie* or perhaps *Hot Dog…The Movie*, and I thought, "Oh, this might be fun."

Thoughts: Turns out I was wrong; it was not fun. It's pretty much just another rich kids vs. poor kids sports comedy, in the vein of much

better films such as *Caddyshack, Hot Dog...The Movie* (*Frostbite* stole a whole lot from this, no surprise), *Up the Creek*, etc.... I was not expecting much from this, and that is what I got, and a good deal less than that, in fact.

Plus: Some good snowboarding footage, some Playboy Playmate eye candy, and a few funny moments scattered throughout the picture. A decent cast highlighted by Peter Jason, Phil Morris (*Black Dynamite*), Adam Grimes, and Ron Zimmerman. Morris pretty much got me through the movie.

Minus: It looks flat, drab, and lifeless. Mostly unfunny, tired, overused story. Traci Lords. Lots of unlikeable characters.

Shelf/Bin: It's in the bag, baby....the trade-in bag. Yeah, this one was a once-and-done. It was work to watch it all the way through, and I can't imagine doing it again. If you have seen any of the films that inspired *Frostbite* (or even if you have), you are not missing anything by skipping it.

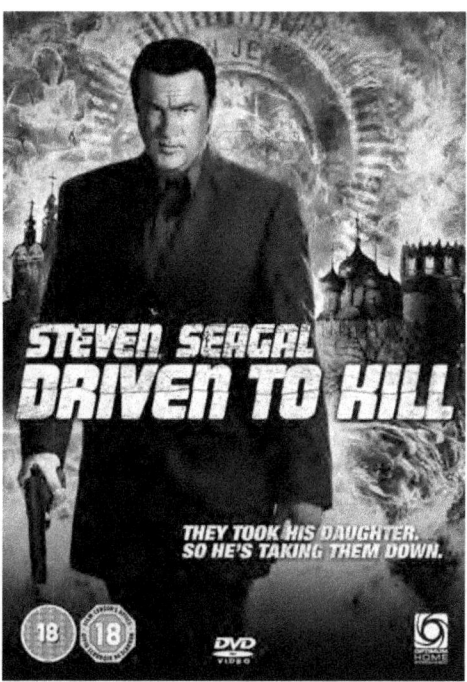

Driven to Kill (2009)

The box says: "Honor must be earned. Bullets, blood, bodies. International action superstar Steven Seagal is back...with a vengeance. *Driven to Kill* is a riveting action-packed crime saga that pits Seagal's lethal skills against a notorious criminal syndicate."

Ruslan Drachev (Seagal) is a highly respected former enforcer in the New York-based Russian mob who abandoned the gangland lifestyle years ago to pursue a peaceful career as a novelist. But after a brutal attack on his daughter—who was engaged to the son of a ruthless Russian nemesis—Ruslan must return to the sinister underbelly of his past and dole out his own merciless brand of justice.

Why I risked a dollar: It was the end of the Halloween horror-viewing season, and, after 50-plus horror films, I was looking to switch gears, and a Seagal flick seemed like the perfect start. Also, it looked a good deal like a *Taken* knockoff, and that means fun, right?

Thoughts: Above-average direct-to-video Seagal effort that probably could have garnered a modest big-screen release with a little more polish and ballyhoo. Gotta say I was pretty pleased with this one. It doesn't break any new ground and won't win any awards. B,ut, overall, the cast seems to give it their all, it's got a decent story, and it's action-packed. If you are a fan of Seagal, it's worth a look.

Plus: Plenty of firefights and martial arts mayhem. Fantastic cast of "hey, it's that guy"s, including Igor Jijikine (*Indiana Jones and the Kingdom of the Crystal Skull*) as head baddie Mikhail Abramov; Dmitry Chepovetsky (*Dead Silence*) as Mikhail's son, who wants no part of the family business; and Laura Mennell (*Project Blue Book*) as Seagal's endangered daughter.

Minus: A bit too much shaky-cam action. A lack of any standout hand-to-hand action. Seagal's Russian accent. Been-there, done-that revenge plot.

Shelf/Bin: Worth the money for a view and maybe even a keeper if you're a big fan of Seagal, but for me, this one is in the bin.

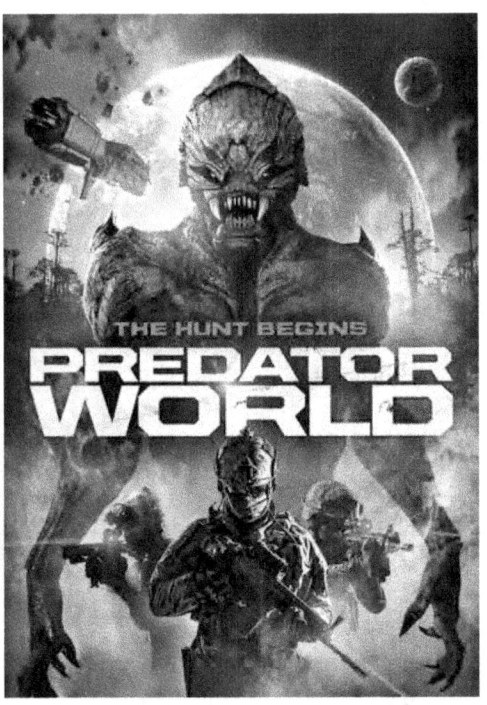

***Predator World* (2017)** (aka *Aliens vs. Titanic* [original title]; *Aliens vs. College Girls*)

The box says: "It bleeds, but you can't kill it! When the Titan 1C space cruiser, the most luxurious starliner ever built, is damaged during a meteor shower, with several survivors fleeing in an escape pod, their nightmare has just begun, as they land on a planet inhabited by a race of bloodthirsty aliens who methodically hunt them down one by one. If they ever hope to escape this predator world, they have no choice but to fight back with any technology they can find from the crash."

Why I risked a dollar: I love monster movies, and I love *Alien* knockoffs even more, so when I saw the box for *Predator World* on the shelf, I thought a *Predator* knockoff would be great fun.

Thoughts: Once again, I was wrong—very wrong. Instead of the low-rent sci-fi monster bloodfest I was expecting, the film turned out to be an overly ambitious low-rent softcore spoof of alien films. Now, I like vaguely funny T&A films as much as the next guy (if not more), but I am really not a fan of films lying to me about the content. *Predator World* was a title given to the film just to cash in on the 2018 release of *The Predator*.

If the film had been called *Aliens vs. College Girls*, I still may have picked it up (for a dollar anyway), but for different reasons. But, instead, I just felt tricked and not it a good way.

Plus: Fairly talented and attractive cast. Plenty of nudity. Good amount of blood and guts. Pretty keen monster costumes and puppets. Some good nods to better sci-fi efforts. A trailer vault with previews for nine Wild Eye Releasing flicks.

Minus: Bait-and-switch advertising. Low production values. Lame attempts at humor. Shitty music.

Shelf/Bin: My first thought was to kick this to the curb, as I was pretty angry about it not being more of an action-horror film. Instead, I am putting it back in the to-view pile and may give it another chance in the future.

Angel of Vengeance (1993)

The box says: "In the vein of *Hard Boiled* and *Naked Killer* comes this action-crime thriller in which two young women caught in a power struggle among a trio of mobsters must struggle to survive in a world run by vice and corruption."

Why I risked a dollar: Cheap '90s-era Asian action just seemed too good to pass up.

Thoughts: This is a schizophrenic Category III kung fu comedy that veers into darkness with the occasional vicious rape scene. Category III films often go in unexpected directions with odd tonal shifts, but this is so mix-and-match, it's practically a Godfrey Ho mashup.

Plus: A handful of decent martial arts punch-ups. A blind female kung fu master.

Minus: Long misogynist rape scenes. Forced drug addiction. Violence and brutality towards women. The funny parts are not very funny.

Shelf/Bin: This one is going in the bin, and then I am going to hose the bin out.

ALSO FROM
HAPPY CLOUD MEDIA, LLC

BOOKS

Written by writer/director, actor, stuntman, special effects guru, production manager Gary Kent, **Shadows And Light** tells of a Hollywood that was and still is, from the perspective of a man who has seen and done it all. Kent compiled credits on over one hundred motion pictures and won several major film awards. This book is Kent's homage to

the artistic, talented makers of magic, who began on the bottom of the dog-pile making biker flicks and nudie cuties and today find themselves on top of the Hollywood heap. The book is filled with memories, reminiscences, inside information, heretofore unknown facts, anecdotes and photos accumulated over forty-some years in independent, outrageous and courageous cinema. The books features stories of William Shatner, Ann-Margret, Brian De Palma, Bruce Campbell, Ed Wood, Charles Manson, Frank Zappa, Duane Eddy, the Hells Angels and others. This is the first printing from Happy Cloud Media, LLC, bringing *Shadows And Light* back into print with an updated Afterword.

A Whole Bag of Crazy: Sordid Tales of Hookers, Weed, and Grindhouse Movies, by Pete Chiarella. "I am known as 42nd Street Pete, a character that I created as a living reminder of that lost decade, the '70s. I was one of a million nameless, faceless kids with no direction and no future. We all had the ugly specter of the Vietnam War hanging like a sword over our heads. We weren't college material; we were clerks, gas station attendants, custodians, the like. Pretty much cannon fodder for the front lines. Most of us knew that we stood a good chance of being drafted

of the game. There are five forbidden films, when run together, can induce madness, or release the Dark Gods that created them, speaking through the psychopathic director. There is a man on the run, with a lost movie that others would kill to obtain. He barely escaped with his life. There is a tower, once housing for students, now a crumbling, rotting monument to film history, and the men and women who returned to the tower, to die watching their favorite films. Beneath the tower, there lies something made of light and shadow. It does not love its worshipers...

and coming back in a bag, so we lost ourselves in the explosion of drugs, alcohol, sex, violence, and music that were the '70s." Hustler, pot fiend, porn expert. Take a walk down a dark alley with 42nd Street Pete as he recounts his tales growing up on "The Deuce". Criminal activity, classic undesirable cinema, pot, booze, pros, cons. The '70s: uncut, uncensored. If you really remember the '70s, you were lucky to have survived them.

Hot Splices by Mike Watt. Featuring eight interwoven tales about the Film Addicts, the flicker freaks, the Cinephages—they devour film for the high, to connect to the art on the granular level...the bleeding perforations in their skin is just part

If you do not love film... If you do not wish to devour it as it devours you... If all you seek from film is entertainment... This is not the book for you.

ALSO FROM HAPPY CLOUD MEDIA, LLC

BACK ISSUES

#1: PREMIERE ISSUE!

Welcome to a brand new publication spotlighting the weird, wonderful world of "exploitation films". We sit back and discuss everyone's favorite sub-genre: the Lesbian Vampire Film. Interviews with "Ilsa" herself, Dyanne Thorne; plus "lost" interviews with Clive Barker and his *Saint Sinner* stars, Mary Mara and Rebecca Harrell.

#2: CRYPTID CINEMA.

All about cryptids of the cinema: Bigfoot, Nessie, The Mothman, The Yeti, The Pope Lick Monster—we got 'em all! Well, most. Plus, bidding a sad and fond farewell to George A. Romero.

#3: BIZARRO FILMS.

What makes a movie "Bizarro"? In this issue, we attempt to answer that question, with contributions from the authors of *"Bizarro Encyclopedia Of Film (VOL. I)"*, Heather Drain and John Skipp. PLUS: an exhaustive interviews with filmmaker Rolfe Kanefsky; Greg DeLiso and Peter Litvin (*Hectic Knife*), and an EXCLUSIVE INTERVIEW with Stephen Sayadian (aka "Rinse Dream", *Nightdreams*, *Cafe Flesh* and *Dr. Caligari*).

#4: ROCK 'N ROLL MOVIES.

A special 144-page salute to the rock 'n roll movie! Extensive interview with Paul Bunnell (*The Ghastly Love of Johnny X*); Jon-Mikl Thor and Frank Dietz (*Rock 'n Roll Nightmare*); *Slade in Flame* and an exhaustive account of AIP's *Beach Party* films; Plus: we say a tearful goodbye to our patron saint, Harlan Ellison. Finally, Richard Elfman drops by to say his piece about *Forbidden Zone*.

#5: ALTERNATE REALITY.

Warning: not a single title in this book is real. Half of the writers are fictional. Interviewee Larry Blamire (*The Lost Skeleton Cadavra*) is real, but the interview isn't. There is some evidence to believe that the Film Gods are real, but that's about it. We cover * The Beatles' legendary adaptation of *Lord Of The Rings*, directed by Stanley Kubrick * David Lynch ending the *Star Wars* franchise with his unusual *Revenge Of The Jedi* * The upcoming film adaptation of Archie Hall's *A Field Guide To Film Gods*. ALL HAIL CINEMAGOG!

#6: UNDERGROUND COMIX!

Did your old man throw YOURS out? Interviews with: Stephen Bissette, Howard Cruse, Trina Robbins, Mike Diana, Frank Henenlotter, Greg Ketter—plus Buddy Giovinazzo, Vaughn Bode's final essay, *Confessions Of A Cartoon Gooroo!*

Two Covers: COVER "A" with art by Mark Bode. COVER "B" with art by Will Eisner! (Sold Separately)

#7: HELL OR HIGH WATER - INDIE FILMMAKING!

Mark Savage (*Purgatory Road*), James L. Edwards (*Her Name Was Christa*), Gabe Bartalos (*Saint Bernard*), Carmine Capobianco (*Psychos in Love*), Henrique Couto (*Babysitter Massacre*), Revjen Miller (*The Adventures of Electra Elf*), the career of Scooter McCrae and his adventures with the British Parliament! Plus, we say goodbye to friend-of-everyone, DICK MILLER.

www.ingramcontent.com/pod-product-compliance
Lightning Source LLC
Chambersburg PA
CBHW071515040426
42444CB00008B/1654

HORSE RACING, BOOKMAKERS & GAMBLING

Today I drove past Wetherby Racecourse; bathed in the spring sunshine, it was a beautiful sight. Although I drive past it most days, I have never attended a race meeting there. A meeting had been held there the day before and the temporary yellow road signs had been left in situ instructing cars, buses and pedestrians where to go.

I love horse racing, I love the sounds, the smells and the atmosphere of a day at the races. I love to watch racing on TV and I love to go to meetings whenever we can, even though it is some time since we last set foot on a racecourse. When I retired from the Fire Service it was my intention to visit all the Yorkshire courses and watch the racing. Beverley, Ripon, Thirsk, Pontefract, Wetherby, Catterick, Redcar, Doncaster, and York. These were the plans before Bramley Dental Ceramics arrived.

As long as I can remember I have wanted a better understanding of the sport, so much so I once tweeted Mick Fitzgerald, the former jockey and now TV pundit, to ask if he knew of a book I could buy which would help teach me the basics. He did reply, explaining he thought Brough Scott had written one a few years ago. I have looked for it but so far haven't been able to locate a copy. I have even looked at the book 'Horse racing for Dummies' but it seems to be mainly about the betting and gambling side, which to be honest doesn't really float my boat.

I am not a gambler, call me tight or thrifty, call me what you will, but I am not a bookmaker's biggest fan as I loathe giving them my money. I would rather spend my money on a nice meal for Julie and me, rather than fund a nice meal for a bookmaker and his wife. People say having a bet adds to the excitement and enjoyment, that's fine and I don't have a problem with people who enjoy a flutter, but I don't share that pleasure. I much prefer to see the athleticism of the horses, the horsemanship of the jockeys, male and female, the excitement of the race, and watching the odds move up and down as other people place bets.

Bookmaking is not a profession I have too much sympathy for, the only people who benefit from gambling are the bookmakers or casino owners, admittedly a punter may get the occasional big win, but how much money have they already laid down to get to that point; as a punter knowing when to stop gambling and enjoy your winnings is a great skill. Bookmakers constantly advertise and suggest they give you everything, all sorts of deals which seem to be very attractive, when in fact they give you nothing. I do carry an internal wry smile when a favourite wins a race, meaning the bookmakers are losing or shall we say not making a lot. This critique is not directed at the individuals working within the industry, but rather at the concept as a whole. I have known some lovely people who are bookmakers. An acquaintance I played football with who was an excellent left back, in the days I foolishly believed I could play a sport which involved using a ball which had an equal bounce, when actually I was a lot better at sports which used a ball that's bounce was as unpredictable as me. He worked with his father as an on-course bookmaker's, and whenever we attended races, we would look for them and say hello. When I worked as a barman he would call in the pub after work for a well-earned pint. As I pulled his drink, I would ask him if he'd been working and which meeting he had attended that day, he would tell me York, Ripon, Redcar or one of the other many racecourses. Then I would ask him where he would be the following day and he would tell me, Doncaster, Pontefract or wherever. On more than one occasion, as he handed me his payment I would say,

"Go on, give me a top tip for tomorrow's racing," he wouldn't answer, silence, as if he hadn't heard my request or was simply ignoring me. I would move to the till to put in his payment, then as I returned to hand him his change, he would hold my outstretched arm, look directly into my eyes and with purpose say, "My tip for you, Andy, is keep your money in your pocket, why do you think I'm in the game?" Advice which has stuck with me to this very day.

He and his father were top blokes who I have a lot of respect for and never once begrudged what they did for a living. As I have said, I have no problem with the independent, small bookmaker; my beef is more about the profession itself, particularly the big national firms. Their advertisements are everywhere, TV radio, football shirts, newspapers, buses, billboards and sponsorship of major sporting events, luring punters in with their so-called special offers. Pay £30 in bets and get a £10 bet free, if you back

THE WORLD ACCORDING TO ANDY CARTER

a horse that doesn't finish get your stake back (obviously National Hunt) and if you sign up have the first so many races free bets. All these and many more offers as if they are doing the punter a great favour. This shows how the vulnerable can be drawn in to try to make a fast buck. It's all portrayed as what they can do for you, when it's all about the bookmakers and how they can get hold of your money.

Two examples of this, The Grand National, the world's greatest National Hunt Horse Race, 40 horses over 30 fences for four and a half miles. Probably the biggest challenge for any horse's strength and stamina. In this race the favourites always seem to be priced at very short odds four, five, six, seven or eight to one. In a race this long with so many horses over so many fences, in my opinion the favourites odds should be in double figures, ten to one at the shortest. Give the punters something, any horse no matter how good it is, in these parameters can quite easily be brought down, impeded or pulled up. Similarly, any long shot can also win just like Foinaven in the 1967 Grand National who came out best after the carnage at Becher's Brook which took out the majority of the field.

When a bookmaker advertises that they payout on five places, it should be noted that they pay out at fifth odds rather than the more usual quarter odds on each way bets, ensuring any payout is less than you may expect. You will never find a poor bookmaker – if the small independent gets a very large stake placed with his company, all he does is go to two or three other bookies and lays off the bet. They just can't lose! One bookmaker who came across as a nice guy, was whingeing in the press and on the radio that he had lost over £1 million when the jockey Frankie Dettori won all seven races at Ascot in 1996. Probably the one day in the whole history of horse racing the odds were firmly stacked in the favour of the punter, yet he comes out pleading the poor tale. Two decades later, he continues to engage in bookmaking with 80 locations at courses nationwide. He now considers it a hobby that supports his comfortable lifestyle. So, boo bloody hoo! That's what I say about his £1 million loss!

All the above is in my opinion part of the reason we have a problem with gambling addiction. Gambling is advertised as money for nothing, free bets, our odds are better than theirs and of course you can do all this via your mobile phone. When I was younger you had to physically walk into a bookmaker's shop to place a bet. It starts with a simple £1 on the nose or even £1 EW and then the dead cert (no such thing) comes along (see Top Banana) so £5 to win goes on to try and get back some of the money lost on the one- and two-pound bets previously. This trend just grows and grows, spiralling out of control, searching for the big win, which rarely comes and when it does it doesn't mean that much so the gambler strives for the next big win. Meanwhile the bookmakers' pockets or bags are full and overflowing with your money.

Gambling is very easy nowadays, especially online. Horse Racing, Football, Bingo, Casinos, Lottery, and other types can all be found online. A friend of mine would gamble on Serbian Basketball which gave him great joy. I have no criticism of the people in the industry, there are some lovely people working in it, but I have always advised my children if they want to make money through gambling be the bookmaker or casino owner rather than the punter. It's like my friend said all those years ago: 'Andy, keep your money, why do you think I'm in the business?'. From 1973 to 1982, I attended Bradford Northern games, both home and away, with my parents' friends. They often told me as a teenager, "Never gamble on what you can't control," which is the essence of gambling – chance! Now with this advice put together with my bookmaker friend would say to me in the pub, perhaps this is probably why I have the stance I do regarding gambling. My last thought is, have you noticed gamblers always tell you about their winnings and very rarely about their loses.

Remember 'Keep your money in your pocket'!

TOP BANANA

Top Banana was the name of a racehorse I will never forget. No! I didn't win a fortune on it so that's not the reason. It all started one Saturday morning many moons ago, Blue Watch at Bradford Fire station were just starting the day shift, parade and roll call had just been completed, and as we were gathering our fire kits together to enter the engine house to start carrying out our morning routines and inventories, one of the crew started to tell the story of what he'd been doing on his four days off prior to our return to work. He was explaining how he had been fitting a carpet for a stable lad who was employed by one of the many racing stables in Yorkshire. As he was completing the job and packing his tools away to leave, the lad was telling him about a horse running on Saturday called Top Banana and in his words it's a 'dead cert' and suggested he might want to have a flutter.

If you didn't already know, most firefighters are interested in any scheme which can make them a fast buck, easy money, so when the phrase 'Dead cert' was heard, interest was aroused and questions started to be asked.

"Where is it running?"

"Which stable is it from?"

"What has the stable lad got to do with this horse?"

"Where did he get the information?"
"Do we know who's riding it?"
"What time is it running?"
"Is it sure to win?"
"Should we back it and what's the odds?"

All these were relevant questions which were answered in a positive confident manner.

The conversation and further questions continued as the members of the shift drifted from the muster bay into the engine house to carry out their daily procedures. As they were being carried out and the minutes ticked on, it soon became apparent that the shift were more than interested in this new information and a fair amount of money was going to be put on Top Banana – £5, £10, £15 and even £20 was all set to be put on the nose of Top Banana, until eventually the whole shift of 15 firefighters were intending to have a gamble.

Now I like to think I know a little about horse racing and don't like giving bookmakers my hard-earned money (see Horse Racing Bookmakers and gambling). My bookmaker friend used to say when I'd ask him for a tip, "My tip for you, Andy, is keep your money in your pocket, why do you think I'm in the game?" Call it tight, frugal or even sensible, but I do not like to finance a bookmaker, why should I give him £20 so he can take his wife out that evening when I could take mine out with the same 20? When I saw the runners and riders of the race and realised there was a field of 27 horses, it was a seven-furlong sprint, and Top Banana's odds were by no means odds-on, or even short, alarm bells started to ring in my head. I wasn't convinced but couldn't be seen not to be taking part, so my bet was a miserly £2 each way. Later that morning as one of the fire engines was returning to station after attending a small rubbish fire, the crew called into the bookies armed with betting slips and copious amounts of cash to back Top Banana which was of course a dead cert.

Saturday on a fire station is by tradition floor washing day when the engine house and muster bay floors get a right good soaping, squeegeed and rinsed with a hose reel so they are clean throughout the following week. As this hive of activity was carried out between fire calls, there was a buzz of excitement and anticipation in the air at the obvious pending financial success that the watch's new sweetheart Top Banana was going to bring to us all. We sat down to dinner and the murmur of expectancy was getting stronger as the time approached. Two o'clock arrived and the TV room was bursting with inquisitive firefighters, as the countdown to the race began.

"That's it there, number seven!" were quotes heard as the horses were walked around the parade ring.

"Well at least it's got four legs."

"It looks better than a Blackpool donkey!" and "It looks in good nick."

Were all comments made as the firefighters watched intensely at the television eagerly waiting to see if this dead cert would deliver its promise.

They're off!! As the firefighters roared their encouragement, the 27 horses galloped down the straight track in two distinct groups. One half of the field down the stand side and the other half down the far side, with one or two straight down the middle, jockeys searching for the perfect ground for their charge.

"Come on, Top Banana!"

"Come on, boy! Keep going!"
"Where is it?" and
"What colours is the jockey wearing?"

were shouts of motivation being directed at the television. Then that was it, two and a half minutes and seven furlongs later it was all over, the result was announced needlessly as we all saw it for ourselves, Top Banana was not in the frame, it's probably still running now, with the first four horses confirmed and Top Banana never mentioned. With the race finishing there was a stunned lull of silence as the realisation that this 'dead cert' called Top Banana was nowhere to be seen! The watch personnel couldn't believe it, all the build-up and expectation throughout the day, all the hopes of money making and the apprehension of success vanishing before their very eyes, as gradually and with mounting momentum the venom turned toward the tipster.

"You little twat! You said it would win!"
"I lost 20 quid on that useless nag you said would win!"
"Oy you, ya little prick, you owe me a tenner!"

Were some of the comments and insults the amateur tipster had to endure. For the rest of the tour of duty he kept himself out of the way, giving it a wide berth you may say. His defence of "I didn't tell you to back it", "it was only what I'd been told" and "I lost money too" did not abate the masses. Consequently, the fire engine never called back to the bookmakers for any winnings.

Four weeks or so later I was at the fire station, we had just finished the fire engine daily checks and were getting ready for drill when I came across the tipster in the muster bay filling his fire boots with hot water and a five-litre bottle of bleach by his side.

"What are you doing?" I questioned with surprise.

"Trying to get the smell out of my fire boots," he replied.

"What smell?" I asked.

"Them twats!" he said raising his eyes to the ceiling to identify the rest of the watch upstairs. "One of them has put bananas in my fire boots and I have been on leave for the last 20 days, so the bananas have rotted and my boots stink!"

"Oh dear," I said with some heartfelt sympathy as I walked into the engine house trying to keep my guffaws of internal laughter under my breath.

As far as I am aware he never tipped a racehorse again in the whole of his fire service career!

THE CHOCOLATE BOX

In my early days on Blue watch at Bradford Fire Station there certainly was a rivalry between all four watches. I would describe the relationship with White watch and Green watch as a healthy rivalry with mutual respect, but with Red watch it was dislike probably best described as a loathing. The reason behind this watch unrest was down to the two Sub Officers on each shift. These two junior officers certainly didn't see eye to eye, there was many a morning as Blue watch arrived at work to take over from Red watch, loud and raised voices could be heard from down the short corridor emitting from the other side of the closed door of the station officer's office as the two individuals were giving it hammer and tong about some disagreement over something the respective watches had or had not done.

Consequently, each watch would stand with loyalty behind their own Sub Officer which matured into each watch not liking each other. I personally had no problem with the members of Red watch; in fact, I ended up joining them as they needed a driver, 11 years into my career which was frowned upon by some of my Blue watch colleagues. In those days our fire helmets were made from cork and due to usage in fire situations they were susceptible for the yellow paint to crack and fall off. One morning I got into work to be told by Red watch's Sub Officer he had repainted my helmet and all I needed was the West Yorkshire Fire Service badge transfer to put on the front. My helmet looked fantastic, he'd done a real professional job, it looked like new, I was thrilled, and I considered this act to be well over and above the call of duty. With the watches' tit for tat wind ups being order of the day, Red would play a joke on us, so we'd retaliate and vice versa. On weekends part of the watches' routines was to carry out cleaning duties as the station cleaners didn't work Saturday or Sunday. One Sunday morning as Red watch come on to take over from Blue watch, they pointed out they were unhappy that the toilets had a very strong smell of bleach, so the next few occasions Blue watch did the cleaning of the toilets and shower areas they used neat bleach, so the fumes were overpowering and eye watering. The attitude being 'if they want to complain we'll give them something to complain about'.

The story I am about to tell began two or three tours prior to the incident being unveiled. We arrived at the fire station to hear venomous noises emanating from the Station Officer's office, nothing unusual there. I can't remember the problem but something Blue watch had done had offended Red watch and so the two sub officers were fighting each watch's corner with vigour. After parade and checks we retired to the canteen for tea break before drill. All the talk was about the morning's disagreement, and it soon turned round to suggested ideas for revenge. This was carried out with great hilarity as unrealistic ideas were dismissed and laughed about. Red watch had a chocolate box which was always locked between shifts; this was an old metal army ammunition container which was opened on shift and bars of chocolate sold at cost to watch members. As Blue watch was discussing revenge I simply said,

"Why don't we put their chocolate box in the oven?" The reaction to this suggestion was one of great mirth and laughter which soon subsided, and the idea dismissed as ridiculous never to be mentioned again.

Two or three tours later as Blue watch were arriving on station to start days and Red watch were finishing their last night shift, I walked into the watch office before parade as usual to be confronted quite aggressively by a very bombastic, belligerent member of Red watch.

"You, ya little shit, do you know owt about it?" he said in a very loud, forceful manner. "'Cos if you do, I'll beat your little brains out!"

Totally bemused and taken back by this unusual welcome I managed to ask, "Know what about what?"

I can't describe how I felt when I heard the explanation. It was like being hit by a wrecking ball and knocked over by a feather all at the same time, plus I had to keep my composure so my 'little brains' would not be pulverised.

"Some bastard has put our chocolate box in the oven."

WOW!! Shock!! Realisation that someone unbeknown to me had put my idea into operation and I truly didn't know anything about it. My answer was very weak and quiet as I couldn't let it slip I had knowledge of where the idea had come from.

"No, I don't" to which was answered with,

"Good! And if I find out you do, I'll crush ya!"

Well, there was a threat, as I walked out to escape the distasteful, noxious and unpleasant environment, more a case of self-preservation rather than a want to leave. The cat was out of the bag, and I knew where the idea came from but never believed after the response it got when I'd suggested it that it would be carried out, I was absolutely gobsmacked and I had done nothing wrong.

Parade was called and the officers had decided to dismiss Red watch as quickly as possible to stop any potential confrontation. Then after the roll call, we were asked directly,

"Does anyone know anything about Red watch's chocolate box being put in the oven?"

Silence! Not a movement, nothing in response, if anybody did know there was no admission coming forward. Then eventually after what seemed like several minutes of calm, questions started to be asked.

"Why do they think it's us? White and green have both worked since we were last on station."

"Perhaps they did it themselves to make us look bad, I wouldn't put it past that lot."

And many more questions were submitted.

Then I thought of a question which of course I already knew the answer, I asked, "Are you sure it was actually put in the oven and not accidently left on the food warmer, the top can get very hot?"

The Station Officer answered with authority, "Andy, I can assure you it was put in the oven and not just left on the food warmer, I've seen the contents and everything inside it is destroyed."

That was that, we continued with our duties, the incident was discussed many times with great joviality that someone had got one up on Red watch, but no one came forward and with the watch defending itself to the hilt there was not a lot else which could be done.

Many years later the perpetrator did come forward and admitted to the deed. He explained when he heard my idea, he thought to himself it would be a good ruse. He had intended to put the box in the oven at a very low heat for a short period of time, five or ten minutes, just long enough for the numerous bars of chocolate to be melted, misshaped but still edible. Unfortunately, after the box had entered the oven, he got called out to a fire call, was distracted and forgot about what he had done. As it was a Sunday the cook for the day had ramped the oven up to full heat, gas mark nine ready to cook the Sunday dinner Yorkshire puddings. When the culprit returned to station he remembered the box in the oven, estimating it must have been in there for well over half an hour. Accompanied by another firefighter both wearing oven gloves, they retrieved it and put the container in the freezer to try cool it down rapidly. I don't know why they did this, perhaps they thought the exposure to extreme cold would somehow reverse the damage caused by the exposure to extreme heat. Of course, the box was padlocked and couldn't be opened for the contents to be examined, so it was just left back in the place it was kept as if nothing had happened. Nobody other than Red watch saw the reaction when the box was opened; sometimes for a practical joke to be successful the punchline is not witnessed.

The incident at the time cost Red watch money, £25 was estimated, this was reimbursed by the station's sports and social club. The joke didn't stop there – at the time the brigade produced a weekly newsletter which announced activities, achievements and awards from stations and departments within the organisation. A couple of weeks after the chocolate box incident it was advertised in the newsletter that Red watch at Bradford Fire Station was collecting empty chocolate bar wrappers for charity and would be grateful for any contributions. This anonymous announcement led to Red watch receiving envelopes filled with hundreds of chocolate bar wrappers through the internal mailing system for weeks, they received that many they had to publish their own announcement that 'due to the fantastic response they had received enough chocolate bar wrappers and didn't need to be sent any more'. Today, many years after the event even the members of Red watch can see the amusing side of the events. Perhaps they wish they'd thought of them first.

At that time of the watch warfare between Red watch and Blue watch, from a Blue watch point of view it was a great practical joke even though no one was aware who had actually carried it out. It was designed to be done in jest, to cause the minimal irritation, grief and annoyance for Red watch resulting in great laughter, never was it intended to cost Red watch or the chocolate vendor money. Unfortunately, due to the nature of the job, a fire call, forgetfulness and Yorkshire pudding day, the result was slightly more severe than originally planned.

BLEND OR SINGLE MALT

Firefighters always seem to get a laugh out of very trivial incidents on station. Once the drill session, work and duties have been completed on a daily or nightly basis, there is free time for firefighters to kill in between fire calls. Consequently, this is when practical jokes, wind ups and even justices after perceived wrongdoings would be carried out. These instances certainly brought the team closer and tighter as a unit when it came to the important issues of firefighting and other incidents. There is no better feeling than when running into a burning building, as everybody else is running out, knowing and trusting your colleagues behind you are there and will support you with everything they've got.

During a tea break, the watch was discussing whisky, comparing blends, single malts, Irish whiskey, and bourbon, debating which had the better taste. Each member of the watch had their preferred brand, and opinions on how it should be served. Some individuals preferred their drink neat, while others liked it with water or a mixer. Some enjoyed it with ice, and some were indifferent and would consume it in any manner it was served. A few could not tolerate the beverage at all and would refrain from drinking it under any circumstances. The discussion was proceeding at quite a pace as different labels and makes of whisky were being vocally compared as to which was the best or at worse a good one. After a while the Sub Officer piped up with quite a sweeping statement.

"I can tell the difference between a single malt compared to any blend!"

This declaration stopped the conversation in its tracks as disbelieving firefighters reacted with claims of,

"Bollocks!" or

"Don't talk shit!" and

"Dream on! That's impossible!" but the Sub Officer was adamant, he had drunk enough whisky in his lifetime and was able to decipher the difference between a single malt and a blend.

Eventually tea break finished, and as the firefighters sauntered downstairs and into the engine house to start the day's daily duties there was an air of disbelief as they digested and questioned the Sub Officer's claim, comments of,

"There is no way he can tell the difference between a blend and single malt" and

"I don't care how much he has drunk in his life, that can't be done!"

The fire engine required its weekly clean and testing but while this was being carried out the focus of chatter was the Sub Officer's claim. It was while the valeting of the appliance was in full flow that a plan was beginning to formulate and put this proclamation to the test. It began as one member of the watch said:

"We should call his bluff somehow so he could prove the claim," as he removed rolls of hose from the central locker.

"Yes, let's see if he can do as he says," said another, while he was armed with a rag cleaning another locker. The conversation persisted as the plan gained momentum and soon the details were confirmed, and this very important piece of market research would develop into reality the following night.

Alcohol is strictly banned on a fire station but surely once this significant experiment was explained it would be overlooked this once; also, which if any senior officer would find out. This rule was the only pending flaw in the plan but after detailed discussion it was considered a minimal risk worth taking. After all, not two years prior, bars were commonplace on fire stations.

The following night shift duly arrived with eager anticipation. All the relevant equipment for the experiment was gathered and stored behind the redundant bar on the third floor. The evening's parade and checks were fulfilled with conversations focused on one event and one event only. The time and place was confirmed, 2300hrs in the old bar, dependent on fire calls. This gave plenty of time for all the evening's drill and work to be completed and for supper to be consumed in a leisurely rather than rushed pace.

Eventually the time ticked round to 2245hrs when all the personnel with an interest gathered at the venue. The experiment had been set up on an old green baize card table where three whisky tumblers sat. One stood behind a piece of card marked 'A' and a second behind a card marked 'B'. Both contained a measure of whisky. In between them both was a third glass half filled with water. At one side of the table were two bottles of whisky, a bottle of Bell's Whisky, the blend, and a bottle of Glenfiddich, the single malt. A stainless-steel bucket was situated at the side of the table. All was set up as the Sub Officer strode into the room, akin to a prize fighter entering the ring. Cheers and hollowing welcomed him as one firefighter massaged his shoulders. He was shown to his seat in front of the three glasses. The room hushed in anticipation as the rules were explained by a senior firefighter picked to be the adjudicator.

"As you can see, Sub" he said, "there are two glasses containing a measure of whisky; one is a blend, the other is a single malt. The glass of water is for you to clear your palate between tastes, and the bucket is the spittoon. The whiskies used are Bell's and Glenfiddich," as the adjudicator pointed to the two bottles on the side to emphasise the point.

"Ooh! I like those two!" said the sub. There was a sigh from the audience as they realised, he must be familiar with the two whiskies on offer.

The official continued, "So, you have a sip of glass 'A', swill your mouth, have a sip of glass 'B' then give your verdict as to which is which."

To be fair the only flaw in this experiment was the fact that even if he didn't have a clue of the difference, it was a 50:50, heads or tails moment. A correct guess at the end of the day could prove to be right.

"Do you understand the task?" the adjudicator questioned.

"Yes!" replied the Sub.

"Then, in your own time, begin!"

The audience leant forward in anticipation as the Sub Officer raised glass 'A' to his lips.

"Mmm that's a nice whisky" was his comment as he picked up the glass of water, had a gulp, swilled his mouth and swallowed. The spittoon was not required, much to the disappointment of some of the onlookers. Then for glass 'B'. After a large sip he swilled it round his mouth and stated he liked that whisky too.

"Well! Which is which?" asked the adjudicator. The audience held their breath with great anticipation.

"Glass 'A' is the single malt and glass 'B' is the blend!" he triumphantly announced with an air of confidence.

Instantly the silence was shattered with a union of laughter and guffawing. Firefighters had tears rolling from their eyes, some to exaggerate a point were on their backs with legs in the air, holding stomachs, creating a scene of complete joviality. Confused and dismayed by this reaction, the Sub Officer shouted,

"What, what's funny?"

Following additional inquiries to understand this response, the adjudicator raised his hands to quiet the audience. As the laughter diminished, he made an announcement.

"They were both the same whisky!"

Crescendo! The laughter was reignited with new vigour at this revelation.

"Well, you bastards!" retorted the sub officer with a tone of self-conscious embarrassment and confusion.

"You bastards! Dress for drill! dress for drill!" he threatened. With impeccable timing the bells went down for a fire call and the room dispersed as the watch descended the poles with sounds of delight, joy and laughter.

The lesson learnt from this whole exercise is. When you work on a watch at a fire station it is prudent not to make sweeping statements you cannot realistically prove!

PUBLIC SPEAKING

Accustomed as I am to public speaking over my years, I have found myself more than half a dozen times stood in front of a large congregation making a speech. My recollection of the first time was at the Phoenix Park Rugby Club annual dinner in 1980 at the Norfolk Gardens Hotel. The club's under 19s Colts squad decided to attend the dinner and awards night. We thought it would be a good idea to present our two coaches with a gift, a token of our thanks and gratitude for the time, effort and commitment they gave to coach our enthusiastic group. We had a collection and with the proceeds one member purchased two smart Pringle jumpers, having had a quiet word with the committee to inform them of our intentions, who thought it was a damn fine idea and gave us a slot on the evening's itinerary to present the gifts to our two loved coaches. Who was going to do the speech and presentation was the next question? The captain, the obvious choice, was a great rugby player and leader, but was quite shy and introvert off the field. He made it quite clear it wasn't something he felt comfortable doing. I don't know why or the reason, but I heard myself saying, "I'll do it!" and once you volunteer you are stuck with it, so I became the elected candidate.

The night arrived and was attended by officials, guests, players, families and friends of the club, all dressed in dinner jackets with bow ties or suits and the ladies in posh frocks. A very pleasant evening was being enjoyed by all. Soon came my time to stand up. I made my short, prepared speech, the substance and contents of which I can't quite remember. I know I mentioned a couple of funny stories involving us and the coaches, most people seemed to be laughing. I acknowledged their importance and the appreciation of all the squad and called them both up to present the two items of cellophane wrapped knitwear. There was a standing ovation with cheers and whistles which was tremendous. I had nerves, I think this was quite visible, but as I sat down the relief mixed with the adrenaline rush was overpowering. The rest of the evening concluded with other awards presented followed by guests on the dance floor or at the bar. I was approached by the guest of honour, the first team captain and the club chairman who each over the evening showered me with praise, admiration and compliments about my performance, which made me feel very proud, humble and content.

Now to the first of my best man speeches. I have only been a best man twice… Both times for the same groom. For his first wedding the bride and groom were meant to marry 12 months prior to the date of the actual wedding, but to the dismay, despair and downright anger of everyone involved the groom got cold feet and cancelled. Of course, this didn't go down particularly well with the bride and her immediate family. So, when the occasion was rearranged for the following year, I discovered writing the speech quite daunting. The two major rules I have learnt about public speaking are: one, don't go on too long, and two, never insult or belittle any member of you audience. As a best man insulting or embarrassing the groom is an exception and expectation. Every guest at a wedding is there to have a good time and will almost always laugh and empathise with your speech if you follow these two rules. The wedding was held at a venue which the previous week had hosted Princess Diana at a charity function, held in a posh and very plush marquee attached to the main building. The wedding party was asked if they would like to use this facility which they agreed to. These facts became the basis for my speech; a delayed wedding held in a tent.

I wrote the speech and read it over the phone to Julie who gave it a lukewarm reception to say the least, one step short of rubbish. Well, that didn't do much to strengthen my confidence. The day arrived and I carried out my best man duties to the best of my ability. We all descended on the luxurious tent after the matrimonial service and sat down to a delicious top-notch meal. The groom's father stood up and said a few words, followed by the groom. My turn was coming, the nerves were jangling, my stomach was churning, and my brow started to perspire and glow. Then I heard the words:

"Ladies and Gentlemen. Andy the best man has a few words to say!"

Wow! It's me, here's my time. Will the guests like what I've got to say? It's not compulsory to be funny, but it helps. I started off a few best wishes sent by card from absentees. One card was huge, approximately three feet by two feet filled with good wishes from the pupils at the bride's school where she taught. I was so nervous the card, because of its size, was shaking when I picked it up and I struggled to read the main message. The groom's brother who was sat in front of me spotted this and in a loud heckle shouted,

"A bit nervous I see, Andy!" which didn't help my nervousness. The previous day I had written my speech and as the wedding had been postponed the year before I had grilled the paper it was written on and soaked it in coffee to make the appearance of old parchment paper. After the card readings I heard myself say,

"I now have a few words to say; I wrote this speech last year but had to put it away. I have since found it in the back of my underwear drawer so I can deliver it today." This was the moment, when the audience saw the parched, brown and singed paper the speech was written on they roared with laughter. I glanced down the top table to see the bride's mother laughing with tears in her eyes. Ok, I thought that joke would go well or plummet into silence, to see the mother of the bride laughing at a joke which referred to a very stressful time eased my nerves and settled my stomach. From that point the rest was relatively easy. The bride was well known for her dislike of the great outdoors and her love of home comforts, so I referenced that because the honeymoon wasn't booked until the summer, they would be spending their wedding night here in the tent. I produced props, sleeping bag, stove with tin of beans, trowel with toilet paper for latrine purposes in the nearby woods, wellingtons for the walk to the woods and other tools and equipment for their romantic overnighter in the tent. I was aware of the laughter but because I was concentrating on the task in hand, I didn't appreciate how well the speech was being received. I followed this with a few digs and embarrassing stories about the groom, toasted the bridesmaids, and sat down after about 25 minutes to a standing ovation again. Throughout the evening the compliments and praise I received from the guests made my chest swell with pride like the rugby club speech some eight or so years earlier. The only disappointment for me and the wedding party was the fact the whole performance had not been filmed. From purely a self-indulgent reason it would have been nice to have seen it from the audience's position.

The second wedding for the same groom took place some years later and was a more informal affair. After the church ceremony the guests assembled at the bride and groom's house and garden for the celebrations. I found this speech one of the easiest I have recited because by this time I was attempting to follow in my father's footsteps and write rhyming poetry. I have read my own poems at speeches for the dinner celebrating the success of our first Firefighters Charity calendar, my retirement party, Dad's sixtieth birthday, bizarrely my sixtieth birthday and of course at the groom's second wedding. As is custom, I began with cards of best wishes from absentees, then I told a longish joke about an American poetry competition which got a good laugh and served as an appropriate introduction to my speech which I had written in rhyming poetry. Once again when I'd finished, I received a very warm reaction with applause and whoops aimed my way. Wow! Perhaps I may be good at this.

My favourite and indeed the best speech I recited was for Mum and Dad's Golden Wedding celebrations at a local golf club. Unfortunately, due to nerves I messed up the opening joke. I was meant to say,

"Ladies and Gentlemen, before I start Olivia would like to say a few words." Then after days of practice Olivia who was five and a half would stand up and say the phrase,

"A few words!" which should have got a good laugh to start proceedings.

Instead, I messed up and said, "Before I start Olivia has something to say." Bollocks! No punchline for Olivia but she dealt with it well. She performed her part perfectly and said,

"A few words!" then like Alfie at our silver wedding party she went on surprisingly to tell Grandma and Grandpa how much she loved them, and they meant a lot to her. I never saw this coming as I presumed she would just carry out the one line then sit down. My speech itself was received tremendously, I had them rolling in the aisle, making jokes and telling funny stories at my parents' expense. At one point I filled up with emotion which was totally unexpected, but I managed to forge through. Again, the reaction from the audience afterwards was mind blowing. Dad had written his own speech, decided he couldn't follow my performance, so stood up and ripped his notes into tiny shreds. This was met with another crescendo of laughter.

It seemed I was getting a reputation for delivering speeches. One day a friend came to me and told me he had been asked to be best man at his mate's wedding, and would I consider writing his speech for him? I was amazed and honoured that somebody thought I could achieve this challenge. He armed me with information about his groom, and I wrote the speech. I did not attend the wedding but was told it was received with a fantastic, overwhelming reaction. Whether it was disclosed that I'd wrote it and not the best man I don't know, perhaps he just enjoyed the credit and adulation on my behalf.

In my time of performing speeches, I have had one noticeable failure. Friends and guests were very polite about it, and some said charming and favourable words, but you know within yourself when it has not gone well; the resigned embarrassment and shame still haunts me today. I was asked to do a wedding speech as a guest. The reason being the groom, groom's father and best man were all adamant they would not get up and speak. Call it nerves, shyness, even embarrassment, but they would not stand up, so would I please? This didn't fit well with me; I didn't want guests who hadn't a clue who I was think I was gate crashing the event. I was assured this would not be the case and was cajoled into doing the speech. Remember the two rules, keep it short and don't upset anyone. Well, I broke both! I think my problem was I was so honoured to be asked to cover three speeches I put too much effort into my composition. This led to a speech which went on nearly 45 minutes, far too long, but to add fuel to this mistake when I arrived at the wedding reception after the service, I was informed that the three individuals would be making speeches after all. Let's think about this, I had written a speech to cover three others, for them to change their minds. Looking back, I should have withdrawn my composition because by the time I had sat down after delivering my words the speeches had lasted well over an hour, and the audience were becoming bored. My other mistake was when I got a single heckle and insulted the audience member. I'd been to a firefighter's retirement function a few weeks earlier and the speech maker was heckled by a colleague. In response he retorted, "I was going to do an impression of an idiot, but you beat me to it!" This was hilarious at a firefighter's retirement but was never the best or wisest thing to be repeated at a wedding when most of the guests are total strangers and are just willing for you to shut up and finish. Oohs and gasps from the audience as tumble weed meandered across the floor of the room… awkward!! As mentioned, I was assured, I'd done well with my words and box of props, but deep down I knew this was not my finest hour.

I have performed my own groom's speech which involved a till roll with the statement, "I have a few thank yous to make" as the roll was launched across the room giving the illusion the list was endless and would take hours to read through. Also, as previously written about, I did one at our silver wedding celebrations. (The speech which was never delivered.) When I get up to speak the nerves get to me every time and I do show symptoms. I can shake, slightly perspire and there can be a wobble in my voice, it does ease as I progress into my text. As much as I enjoy the adulation and praise after delivering a good oration, the disappointment, embarrassment and guilt when it doesn't turn out as perceived is humiliating, overwhelming and not very nice. Remember, if you are asked to do a speech or say a few words at a wedding or any other function: keep it short, keep it sweet and never, never insult members of your audience.

DESERT ISLAND DISCS

I enjoy listening to the radio programme 'Desert Island Discs'. When I first started listening to it, I would make a beeline to the episodes featuring guests I had heard of. I soon discovered that some of best episodes featured guests I didn't know. Two specific shows that spring to mind featured two surgeons, David Nott and Henry Marsh. Both being high flyers in their field and were very interesting to listen to, with very powerful stories. David had been and worked in war zones across the world, carrying out operations where needed. He told the tale of operating on a badly injured child in a makeshift operating theatre in a hotel in Sarajevo, when right at the critical stage of the procedure all power was lost due to the bombing, as the hotel was under attack, all the operating staff left due to this imminent danger except him and his anaesthetist. Eventually the power was restored, and the operation was successful. He also told of the time he had to operate on a casualty in Syria who was a member of the rebel group Isis surrounded by the patient's armed colleagues unable to speak in fear of them finding out he was a Christian Doctor. He explained how he felt the first time he had to drill into somebody's skull for the first time, and on his own, solo you might say, without a senior consultant there overseeing what he was doing. He had to do this to save a life and just trust in his knowledge and training to carry out the procedure, I do remember it concluded in success. The details of these stories were very powerful which made for gripping listening. The other guest Henry was also a brain surgeon with an equally fascinating story. He described the challenges involved in deciding whether a patient should undergo life-saving surgery that may result in severe disability, noting that these are complex decisions faced by professionals in this occupation. At times, the music selections are outside my usual preferences; however, the purpose of the programme is for guests to choose tracks that hold personal significance for them.

Due to my enjoyment of this radio show I have often dreamed of being asked to appear on it myself and if invited – not a chance – which eight songs would I choose? Which book would I take? Which luxury item would I select? And which disc would I save from the waves? So, I have tried to pick my selections, which like most of the programme's guests explain is not the easiest of tasks. When you have listened to 60 years of music and all you can choose is eight tracks it is not that simple. I thought it might be a good formula to pick one disc from each of my seven decades of life, but when I got to the noughties, teens and twenties of this century I couldn't find anything which had any significance to me. Whereas there are numerous to choose from, from the seventies, eighties and nineties. Anyway, after much thought and deliberation here is what I chose followed by the reasoning behind the choice.

Discs
- Morningtown Ride – The Seekers
- Won't Somebody Dance With me – Lynsey de Paul
- Caroline – Status Quo
- You Shook Me All Night Long – AC/DC
- You Make Me Feel (Mighty Real) – Sylvester
- Hold On Tight – ELO
- Everybody Hurts – R.E.M.
- Take The Long Way Home – Supertramp

Book
- The complete works of Anthony Buckeridge 'Jennings Books', but if this is not allowed and I can only have one book it would be:
- Jennings Goes to School by Anthony Buckeridge

Luxury
- Endless supply of paper, fountain pens and ink

Save from the waves
- Hold on tight by ELO as it reminds me of Julie

THE DISCS

Why these? I hear you ask. Each tune has played a massive part in my life. In some cases, the bands have played a major part, but I only wanted to choose one track per band, so I had to choose my favourite of Status Quo, AC/DC, Supertramp and ELO. On the other side of the argument I had to omit some great artists who have all played a major part in my music listening life, because eight choices is not that many. So, I must apologise to artists like Rick Wakeman, OMD, Nile Rodgers, Bruce Springsteen, Fleetwood Mac, Dire Straits, Black Sabbath, and many others.

Morningtown Ride, The Seekers (1964)
This is probably one of the first songs I became aware of as a small boy. On a Saturday and Sunday morning in the late sixties we would as a family listen to Ed 'Stewpot' Stewart's Junior Choice, a two-hour request show aimed at families with children. Every time this song came on, I loved it, if on any weekend it wasn't played, I felt hard done by. It is a beautiful tune which as a child I couldn't listen to enough. According to my father, my earliest preferred song was 'San Francisco' by Scott McKenzie. He recalls that I would sing along whenever it played; however, I have no memory of this myself.

Won't Somebody Dance with Me, Lynsey de Paul (1973)
This disc was my first bought 45rpm single record. Purchased at Fairbank and Harding's music store in Pudsey for the princely sum of 49p. At the time 49p seemed extortionate for a small vinyl disc carrying two songs (A & B sides) but with a lot of nattering and persuading Mum relented and purchased it for me. A heartfelt sad song about a girl left on her own with no one asking her to dance. Perhaps a common occurrence at the weekly disco or party.

Caroline, Status Quo (1973)

My favourite Status Quo track which helped to initiate my interest in the heavy rock genre. I have spent many a happy time sat on the toilet playing imaginary drums while listening to this record. A friend, also a massive Quo fan, and I would also headbang to it as we charged around the Abbey pub in Bramley after last orders, having spent the evening drinking there. This was our regular weekend haunt when we ran the service crew at Hunters Grieve Scout Camp. Looking back, this seemed to be more about entertaining the locals with a bit of immature exuberance rather than anything else, and this was always the chosen Juke Box track.

You Shook Me All Night Long, AC/DC (1980)

This track is on the list because AC/DC is one of the bands I have a passion for, and this is my favourite track of theirs. I have been a big fan of them since Bon Scott was the lead singer, who tragically died in 1980. I have been to his grave in Fremantle Cemetery, Western Australia, to pay my respects and stood by his statue in the town a few times. I don't really know what it is about this track from the Back in Black album, but every time I hear it, it just makes me feel good. AC/DC underlined my love for the heavy rock genre.

You Make Me Feel (Mighty Real), Sylvester (1978)

This record represents my disco years of the late 1970s and early 80s when we would go night clubbing to Belinda's, Intime, La Phonographique, Cinderella's and Rockefeller's and the Mecca, all in Leeds. I have a copy of the 12" single version of this thanks to a close friend who introduced this record to me when we attended Airedale and Wharfedale College. When played it just makes you move.

Hold on Tight, ELO (1981)
This record reminds me of Julie. During our early years of dating, we would play this song on the car stereo and sing it at the top of our voices while driving home at night. We sang along as we engaged in a form of seated dancing in the car. The song takes me back to very happy times, with the love of my life.

Everybody Hurts, R.E.M. (1993)
I discovered this track when attending the biannual 'Jamboreast' district scout camp in 1993 at Buttermere Lake in the beautiful Lake District. The Venture Scout Service team would play the newly released album Automatic for the People by R.E.M. while they were washing up the camp pots, generally tidying the cooking area, and carrying out the other Venture Scout duties. To me most of the music on the CD was just background noise but if I was within earshot when this track came on it would stop me in my tracks, and I would just melt. It is one of the most beautiful pieces of music I had ever heard. I am very fond of ballads, and this is a fantastic ballad, probably in my eyes or ears my favourite of all time. I have requested this is played at my funeral, and if my wish is granted the congregation will be in floods of tears, not necessarily due to my demise, but more hearing this tremendously solemn and melancholic tune.

Long Way Home, Supertramp (1979)

Supertramp is possibly my all-time favourite band. I have loved and enjoyed their music all my life. Particularly the period before Roger Hodgson left the band after the Famous Last Words Tour in 1983. I went to see them at Earls Court during this tour, and they were brilliant. I have all the early albums on both vinyl and CD, with Paris being my favourite live album, followed closely by Crime of the Century. Once again there are numerous songs of Supertramp I could have picked but this one from the albums Breakfast in America and Paris is probably my favoured piece. The harmonica intro sends shivers down my spine.

THE BOOK

The full works of Jennings by Anthony Buckeridge or Jennings Goes to School (1950)

Jennings goes to School has always been my favourite book even though it is a children's story. I was introduced to Jennings and his best pal Derbyshire when my fourth-year junior schoolteacher at Waterloo would read it to the class. He had a fantastic talent of reading a story and bringing the characters alive with his voices and descriptions, it could at times be mesmeric to a then ten-year-old boy. This in later life saw me collect the whole series of 'Jennings' books, including many first editions by attending book fairs to seek out any copies of the Anthony Buckeridge stories of Jennings and Derbyshire.

THE LUXURY

A Fountain pen with an endless supply of ink and paper.

I had to think long and hard about which luxury I would take with me to the island. Pillow and bed with fresh linen was up there along with an endless supply of Timothy Taylor's Dark Mild from a hand pump. I decided a fountain pen with paper and ink would be my choice so I could write and sketch about events and experiences on the island.

The disc I would save from the waves if all were lost at sea would be Hold on Tight by ELO. This by no means is my favourite record but as pointed out previously when hearing it the connection this song brings to Julie and the happy times belting it out at full volume in the car would be priceless, instantly bringing back happy memories and putting a smile on my face.

All the above would be the contents of the show Desert Island Discs featuring Andy Carter.

Well, You Can Dream, can't you!

DEAD CATS UP TREES

There is a common misconception that all firefighters are good for is rescuing cats from trees. The standard answer when this is queried is 'How many dead cats have you seen in trees lately?'. The reason there are no dead cats in trees is that eventually when they get hungry or desperate they somehow manage to get themselves down. We are a country of animal lovers who hate to see animals in distress, so sometimes firefighters are called upon to show compassion.

Like most people in life, the majority of firefighters are animal lovers, and some aren't bothered by them. Bradford Fire Station had a station cat called 'Blackie'. She lived on the station but was certainly an outside cat. She would come inside to be fed and sleep in some discovered warm location, but most of the time she was outside reducing the local rodent population. In her later years some less sympathetic firefighters would take great delight in occasionally locking her overnight in the ADO's office which didn't stress the feline as she would sleep, but she had a habit of defecating in the gaffer's out mail tray. This thoroughly pissed off the boss but created great mirth among the firefighters.

Cat, dog and other animal rescues were not too common for a city centre fire station, but we did get a few. The majority of which had amusing endings. One of the first incidents I attended which involved an animal was at a house fire. As we approached the incident, we could see the glow of the flames reflecting in the night sky. The property involved was an upstairs maisonette, the resident was a man who was a hoarder and known to suffer with mental health issues. It was quite a large but straightforward incident which we soon had under control. While I was inside the property wearing breathing apparatus and holding a hose reel jet, I couldn't work out why the floor had a cushioned feel under foot. The reason became apparent as the job concluded – the flat was filled with black bin liners crammed with rubbish, newspapers and other hoarded items. There wasn't a visible piece of floor to walk on in the whole first floor flat. When the fire had been extinguished and the smoke had somewhat dissipated, we became aware of a very large, distressed dog sheltering, hiding and very frightened underneath all the bin liners. Luckily for him he was in an area of the property not affected by the fire, which had ensured his survival. A unique problem became apparent, trying to settle down and coax a fearful canine is in normal circumstances relatively easy – "come on, fella, it's ok, come on, let's see you", all said in a calm sympathetic manner is usually the method used in managing the situation, but the large mongrel was terrified, scared, confused and very nervous. He had just experienced being trapped in a major house fire and trying to persuade him you are friendly and only there to help while wearing a breathing apparatus mask is not too convincing. The poor thing must have viewed us as some sort of alien, an invader from another planet, certainly not a more familiar friendly faced human being. Smoke was still within the property and although it was lightish, an air supply was still required.

So, what to do? The dog was in such an agitated state we couldn't get near it, so we had to leave it alone being aware of its presence.

The Station Officer decided we needed professional help so radioed control and requested the attendance of a vet. As we waited for the vet we continued with damping down duties and clearing away some of the masses of overflowing black bin bags giving the angry frightened dog a wide berth. By the time the vet arrived on scene the maisonette resembled a burnt-out shell, with badly charred roof joists exposing the twinkling stars in the clear dark night sky. The job was finished apart from the need to extract the dog. The vet was briefed about the conundrum, there's a dog inside shaking with fear, he won't let us anywhere near, he snarls and bares his teeth when we approach. Surprisingly the dog didn't bark too much, he was very quiet throughout his whole ordeal.

"Not a problem," said the vet as he turned into his opened hatchback. "I'll just sedate the animal and bring him out but first I need a volunteer."

One of the more experienced firefighters was, shall we say, 'volunteered', thinking he would be there to assist with carrying the dog out… oh no! The vet turned round and spoke.

"My intention is to sedate the dog using this syringe, if by any chance I miss, slip or fall and this drug enters my body, you immediately plunge this" as he held up a second syringe "anywhere into me. I don't care where it goes or how you do it so long as the contents are delivered into me." So, he stood there with two needles in his hands and gave the second to the volunteered firefighter. That is what happened: the dog was sedated, there was no need for the second syringe and the animal was transported away in a dog cage situated in the rear of the vet's car. The firefighters cleared up the burnt-out mess, musing about what would have happened if the first syringe had gone into the vet. The conclusion being it's as well as it didn't.

One Saturday evening after pub closing time the bells went down, and all the firefighters headed down the poles into the engine house.

"Pump two only" was announced over the Tannoy.

"Cat stuck in tin can, Old Miller Dam Public House" was the further information. We climbed into the cab and set off while donning fire kit not sure what was in store for us. We arrived at the pub which was shrouded in darkness, questioning whether this was a false alarm or not. The front door opened and an elderly, rotund gentleman sheepishly waved us in. Four of us raced in and were confronted in a dimly lit bar area by the landlady holding what appeared to be a dead cat with the whole of his head inserted into a Whiskas cat food tin. Among the crew were sniggers, smiles and titters as the scene was quite amusing and appealed to the firefighter's sense of humour.

"Stop laughing!" snapped the landlady. "It's not funny!" Well, it was actually but we complied with her wishes.

The Sub officer took hold of the lifeless feline which could only have been a few months old, then he sent one of us out to the fire engine for the tool kit. As the other two tried to calm the distressed landlady down, who by this time was convinced her beloved new kitten was deceased. She had tears rolling down her cheeks as we calmly pointed out that cats sometimes play dead when trapped in darkness, and as the pub was dimly lit, there was no light at the end of the tin and the kitten was still breathing this was probably the case. As this was being explained and the toolbox was arriving, the Sub Officer had spent the time discreetly teasing the kitten out of the tin. Eventually with no other intervention the kitten was released, shook its head, meowed and immediately started to purr as it nestled into the safe fire tunic covered arms of the Sub officer. Of course, by now the tears, sadness and concern of the landlady had changed into smiles, happiness and relief as she suddenly realised the funny side of things. After a few cuddles the kitten was placed back into the landlady's loving bosom. There was a sense of embarrassment as the couple realised they had called a fire engine with five firefighters to release an over eager kitten from the tin of cat food it could not wait to eat. We assured them both this was not a problem; it is our job to help people in distressing situations; we were just glad we could be of some assistance. Obviously on our return to the station the atmosphere in the cab was full of hilarity, jokes and humour about the death-defying rescue of a kitten stuck in a tin.

The most bizarre call for an animal rescue came many years later. I was the driver of the Hydraulic Platform when late one evening about 2130 hours the bells went down.

"HP only!" was the announcement over the Tannoy so I headed to the appliance via the poles, while the leading firefighter went to the printer for the job sheet. I opened the doors, started the engine and switched on the blues as the LF jumped on the wagon.

"Where are we going?" I asked.

"Bingley's area," he said unconvincingly.

I pulled out of the station then questioned, "What's the job?"

To which he replied, "I can't work out whether I'm reading this properly."

"What do you mean?"

He had quite a perplexed look on his face. "Well, it says here 'animal rescue' bird stuck in tree!"

"Bird stuck in tree?" I queried with surprise. "Don't birds live in trees anyway?"

"Exactly!" he said. "That's what I thought, how can a bird be stuck in a tree?"

We couldn't work it out what we would be confronted with. All through the journey we tried to come up with possible scenarios, some funny, some fantasy and some just ridiculous, but none seemed plausible.

"Bird stuck in tree? Mmm bird stuck in tree?" What could this possibly mean? Perhaps, and we thought the most likely reason was false alarm. What right minded member of the public call the fire service on the 999 number to report a bird stuck in a tree? As we pulled up outside the property, we had convinced ourselves this was a wind up.

The LF dismounted the appliance and went to the front door of the address given to investigate. After two or three minutes he returned, hauled himself into the cab and said, "It's all suddenly become very clear."

"Is it a false alarm?" I asked.

"No, far from it, you see that tree over there?" he said, pointing at a large oak tree some 50 yards down the road.

"Yes," I replied.

"Well, if you look closely at the very top of the tree you may make out a large bird."

After a bit of staring and squinting I managed to make out the silhouette of something about 40 feet high on a branch. "Ah yes, I think I see something."

"Well, that is some sort of buzzard and the guy who lives here is a bit of a bird of prey enthusiast. He was flying one of his birds for some evening exercise, you know like Casper did in the film Kes, well the bird landed in that tree and its jessies have caught on the branch and it can't fly off."

"Ah," I said, "bird stuck in tree, it's all bleeding obvious now!"

Initiating the rescue I sited the HP, the gaffer and the enthusiast who was wearing a large gauntlet with a dead mouse in his fingers, went up in the cage to the top of the tree, untied the jessies, fed the mouse to the buzzard and down they came with a large bird of prey stood on the client's gauntlet looking as uninterested as if it was an everyday occurrence. The owner expressed sincere appreciation for our assistance in recovering his bird. He was still thanking us as we set off back to station. That was the day we successfully rescued a bird from a tree... bizarre!!

It was a bright sunny afternoon, and we had just arrived back at station after completing some fire prevention work. As we were making our way to the mess for a well-earned cup of tea, the control line rang. It rang through the station with its own unique tone, so it was instantly recognisable. The usual comments of 'what do they want?' and 'It'll be a missed AMS!' (additional management statistic) logged after every turn out, so although the firefighters, well aware Control had phoned the station, they were not really concerned by this regular daily occurrence and continued with the important task of tea and coffee making. About five minutes later, as refreshment was being consumed the Tannoy crackled into life.

"Water tender crew to the appliance."

The crew rose from their chairs and strolled downstairs to the appliance bay, as it was clear that the call was not an emergency, voicing the occasional comments regarding the inconvenience at the loss of a drinks break. I was driving with two firefighters in the rear and a leading firefighter in charge. As I boarded the appliance the leading hand was already sat in his seat.

"What we got?" I enquired.

"Cat stuck in a tree" came the reply.

"Cat stuck in tree?" I questioned. "We don't attend them; how many dead cats have you seen in trees lately?"

"Exactly," said the LF, "but a senior officer is in attendance with the RSPCA, a vet and the owner. Apparently, it's a young kitten and it's been up there a couple of days."

"It still won't die up there," I said very unsympathetically, "and if it does gravity will take over and the poor mite will fall out."

"I agree," he said, "but a senior officer has mobilised us on a silent approach, with no lights, horns and at legal road speed to see what can be done."

We arrived at the scene, and was met by the officer, vet and RSPCA official. Having alighted the pump, we had a group conflab to discuss ideas of how to remove the cat from the tree. Twenty-five yards down a tight side road was a 60-foot sycamore tree, with a small black and white kitten perched quite happily on one of the top branches. How do we get it down? It was out of range for the hydraulic platform and the line rescue team would not be able to get up into the tiny branches and twigs towards the summit of the tree. The senior officer suggested we could blast the poor animal out with a jet.

"A jet?" I queried astoundingly, unable to hide the surprise in my voice.

"Do you realise what sort of pressure the pump would have to deliver to get a meaningful jet up to that height, never mind the jet reaction a branch man will have to control."

"Yes, we do, but with the permission of the owner and the approval of the RSPCA it seems to be the only solution possible," said the gaffer.

"Wont we kill it?" asked one of the crew.

The RSPCA officer joined the conversation saying, "It is a possibility, but cats are quite resilient, and the owner has given consent. If we do nothing, we could end up with a dead cat in a tree!"

"That'll be a first," I quipped, "but it could also be dead on the ground."

The vet, who had been listening, added, "It may sustain an injury from a fall which I can sort out, but I don't think it will die because of the fall."

At that the decision was made: we would attempt to blast the poor thing out of the tree. Luckily for the kitten, if there was much luck, it was so far up the tree a jet would only soak it and knock it off balance rather than firing it out of the tree like a bullet from a gun, launch the poor mite through the air and land one hundred yards away on a nearby football field.

We set into a hydrant to feed the pump and ran hose down the narrow road. I attached the water supply and put the pump in gear. Three to five bar pressure would be a normal delivery to a branch, but this could be so much higher. As I was doing this the two firefighters came to the appliance and started unloading a large yellow salvage sheet.

"What do you need that for?" I asked.

"The gaffer wants us to stand under the tree and catch the cat."

"You've got to be joking, you'll never catch it and you are in for a right soaking, who will be on the branch?" I asked.

"The LF and the gaffer" came the answer.

"A gaffer on a branch? This I've got to see," as we laughed in unison. I did ask why we needed a salvage sheet and the reply I got was the fact that a small crowd of onlookers had gathered, and it would display compassion toward the unfortunate animal. The fact it would be a futile act which would only succeed in drenching two innocent firefighters seemed to be irrelevant and discarded. It was always stated at Training School 'If you don't like getting wet you shouldn't have joined' and this would confirm that statement.

"Water on!" came the command from the branch men so I increased the revs of the pump and watched the water spew from the branch. They raised the jet towards the tree, and it was obvious to me there was not enough pressure, so I upped the delivery to six bar. This would be a challenge for one branch man, but the LF and gaffer seemed to be managing. The jet was still short of the kitten, so the message came through to increase pressure. Up and up, I raised it, six-point five bar, seven bar, eight bar, and nine. At this point the branch crew were really struggling to hold on. Meanwhile the two firefighters holding the salvage sheet were receiving a soaking of tempest-like proportions which made me chuckle inside. At 11 bar the jet managed to reach the kitten and dislodged it from its perch, it fell bouncing off every bough on the way down. It landed on its feet and immediately absconded at great speed, terrified. Its reunion with tera firma was nowhere near the waiting salvage sheet being held by two drenched and very wet firefighters!

Everyone seemed pleased with the outcome except perhaps the kitten. As we had finished stowing the hose and other equipment onto the pump, the senior officer approached us and thanked us all for our efforts; he also informed us the kitten had returned home, was as wet as a drowned rat but was happily tucking into a bowl of cat food as if nothing had happened.

THE DAY BEFORE MY WEDDING

Having watched Gavin and Stacey's wedding a few nights ago I started to think about my own wedding. The seventh of July 1990, without doubt the best day of my life. Olivia asks, "What about my birth?" to which I reply:

"That was a good day, but it was the result of me and your mother getting married."

She seems to have accepted this fact, and I don't now detect a glum face and a humph! Anyway, back to the story. My wedding day started the night before as I am about to disclose.

Mick, my best man, Kevin and Jim, my two ushers, were staying with me that night in our first house on Grange Avenue in Thornbury. I had already had two stag nights, the first in Bradford with all my colleagues on Blue watch at Bradford fire station, the second was in the Railway pub in Rodley with my friends and acquaintances. I didn't want a third and specifically not on the eve of the wedding as I wanted to feel fine and dandy to enable me to enjoy every minute of the big day. I had made this quite clear to the wedding party as the four of us wandered across the road to the Junction pub for a quiet drink. (No such thing!)

We were joined by Donald, my soon to be father-in-law – The Junction was his local even though it was about three miles from his home in Rodley, he would be in there most nights drinking while playing darts and dominoes. Also, Alex a Scotsman who is always up for a good night had walked from his house in Pudsey to join us. Of course, and is it any wonder with both Don and Alex involved, the quiet drink turned into quite a long session. By the end of the night the whole pub was aware I was getting married in the morning, well 1500hrs to be precise and all these strangers were either wishing me good luck, best wishes and some commiserated with me. As we left, in quite a merry state, I asked the landlord if he had a spare till roll for an idea I had for my speech; he obliged saying it was his wedding present to me and the only condition was I returned to tell him how the day went; consequently, I did return on numerous occasions. My idea was to announce I had just a few thank yous to make which won't take long, then launch the till roll across the floor giving the illusion I was going to be there for hours with a massively long list to read out. Having parted company with Don and Alex, I found out the following day that Alex had fallen into a bramble bush on his way home and was covered in little scratches all over his body. It was a warm July evening, and he had been wearing shorts and a tee shirt. Poor fella, when I saw him, he did look a mess but luckily his suit covered most of the evidence.

The sleeping arrangements for the four of us that night were Mick and Kevin slept in the two single beds in the back bedroom, while Jim and I shared our double bed in the front bedroom, I think the three of them drew straws and Jim lost. Everybody seemed happy with this arrangement, so we all retired to slumber looking forward to my big day tomorrow. Jim was six foot tall and weighed about 17 to 18 stones, he could be described as a big unit. I woke up not too far into the night because Jim was snoring away with great volume, as he had trouble with his breathing and his left elbow was embedded into my right temple as I lay on three inches of bed mattress. His size, along with his state of unconsciousness, made it impossible for me to move him and as I wanted to be as fresh as possible to enjoy my wedding day, what could I do? Realising I had a sleeping bag stored in the little box bedroom I quietly got up, found it and went stealthily downstairs into the dining room. I shut the door, put down some cushions off the settee and rapidly fell into a deep peaceful sleep for the rest of my last night as a single man. Never once did it cross my mind this may cause alarm and panic the following morning.

As the sun rose – well it had been up for hours – on the morning of my wedding day there was dread, fear and worry rattling around the house on Grange Avenue. Jim had woken up to discover I was missing; he raised the alarm with Mick and Kevin to questions of

"Where the hell is he?" and

"Do you think he's done a runner?" answered with statements like

"You were sleeping with him; how can you lose him?"

I was nowhere to be seen or found. I don't know to this day why the dining room wasn't checked, but it wasn't. I was oblivious to all this panic and was still in the land of nod, dreaming of my intended beautiful bride, totally unaware of what was happening on the other side of the shut door. For the others, who by now had visions of me running round Thornbury in my boxer shorts with pre-wedding nerves and cold feet, it was a very worrying start to the glorious day. Ringing Julie was not an option as they didn't want to distress her, but they did ring my parents to ask if they were aware of my location. Followed by strict instructions not to inform Julie.

Eventually I woke up, bleary eyed and hair a mess, I opened the dining room door to be confronted by three headless chickens who looked as if they'd seen a ghost.

"Where the hell have you been?" I was asked.

"Asleep, why?" I answered.

"What, in there, why?"

"Yes, because I couldn't get the snoring rhinoceros' elbow out of my temple, and I needed sleep."

Of course I was totally unaware of the stress, confusion and heartache I had caused by just searching for somewhere to have a sound night's sleep.

The distress was soon forgotten as we laughed and tucked into a full English breakfast, as the tale of the missing groom became the talk and joke of the morning. Parents were phoned to be informed I had been located, and embarrassment subsided as they asked themselves why they hadn't checked the dining room. It is all now a happy, funny memory of the start of our special day which would develop into the best day of my life!

MY WEDDING DAY

After the drama of the missing groom, the atmosphere in the house that morning changed very quickly, from one of stress and worry to one of excitement and anticipation. Once the wedding party had been reunited, we all had a good hearty full English breakfast – considering the previous night celebrations we were all surprisingly sprightly and feeling quite well with no hangovers, headaches or upset stomachs. With breakfast consumed and washing up completed, we headed to the family home at Hillfoot Drive from Grange Avenue to get dressed into our wedding suits. This was done early at the request of the 'video cameraman' who wanted to film us leaving the house and setting off to church in my best man's father's Jaguar. He explained he couldn't be in two places at once and if he filmed us at the correct time of departure, he couldn't be down in Rodley filming Julie and the bridesmaids leaving for the church. So, we carried out a dress rehearsal which was filmed as if it was real, after which he set off to Julie's house and we came back from round the block to get ready properly for the trip to St Wilfrid's Church in Calverley.

The two ushers Kevin and Jim were brilliant, I couldn't have asked for two better groomsmen. They spent most of the morning running round like blue arsed flies, sorting flowers, presents and other small but important tasks requested by me, my parents and Julie, who had phoned once or twice. All this left Mick, my best man, and me to concentrate on getting shaved, showered and dressed into our top hat and tails, well morning suits, at a slow, relaxed and leisurely pace. I had that much time I managed to write my speech on a till roll enabling me to perform the visual joke later. I must say we did scrub up well and looked very smart, I adored being the centre of attention, I lapped it up and it made me feel very important that day! The wedding service was due to start at 1500hrs, we look back on this in later years and wish we had started earlier, perhaps 12 or 1300hrs as the reception and the evening celebrations were slightly pushed together and overlapped. This did not by any means spoil the day, but the extra couple of hours may have allowed the day to be run at a slower more relaxed pace.

Eventually, the groom, best man, and two ushers were ready and gathered in the kitchen. My father gave me a piece of advice that I will never forget. Although he says he does not remember saying it, there are witnesses, namely the wedding party. He said, "Now then, son, let me give you a little advice: you will spend the rest of your life trying to work out the logic of a woman and the day before you die you will be no nearer, so don't bother!"

In these days of Political Correctness this advice could be interpreted as being sexist, and mildly misogynistic, but 1990 was a different time and they were uttered with the best intentions, slightly jocular, tongue in cheek and to be honest quite wise, just as females have similar opinions of males. I can assure anybody reading this no malice was ever intended and the advice was received in the spirit it was given. I presume similar advice could be given to any bride on her wedding day about the failures of her future husband. With that the four of us left the house, got into the Jaguar for the second time and proceeded to the church this time for real. Calverley Parish Church here we come.

Would you believe it, we arrived at the church slightly late; shouldn't it be the bride who is traditionally late? In real terms we weren't late as Julie hadn't arrived, she was sat with her dad in the back of a white Rolls-Royce, passing the Thornhill Arms as we walking down the path to enter the church, so it was close. Even so, the photographer still wanted to take photographs of us four as arriving guests were all eager to give me their best wishes and good lucks and comments on how smart I looked. I walked into church and killed a little bit of time going round some of the congregation to say hello, as Julie and the bridesmaids were having their pictures taken outside. My stomach was going round like a tumble dryer, I considered myself to be the luckiest man on the planet, about to marry the girl of my dreams. What did she see in me? I must be doing something right. Then someone whispered:

"She's here! Julie is here."

Wow!! The anticipation went through the roof, the feeling beat a lottery win (allegedly), or any winning goal for City at Wembley, a feeling I'd never experienced before, or since! I joined my best man at the front of the church and waited.

Then it started, 'Here comes the bride' butterflies, the nerves, the anticipation, the excitement, the pride and the honour were off the scale, all battling to be the predominant emotion. I knew I shouldn't, but I couldn't resist, I looked round and saw her, this beautiful young woman, all in white, moving gracefully towards me, with Donald, her father, by her side. She was stunning, surrounded by a shimmering, hazy fog like an actress in an old black and white movie. As she glided towards me the awe of beauty consumed me, it was mind blowing, she was walking down the aisle to be with me for the rest of my life. I was brimming with pride; my chest was expanded like a strutting cockerel. I was stood tall, taller than a short person should be. I was king for a day and no one and nothing could stop me. It was brilliant, this feeling was better than becoming a father – that feeling was close but not quite there. Olivia and Alfie both complain that their birth should mean more, until I point out it was me marrying their mother that was responsible for their births, so there!!

The vows were said and the rings exchanged, surprisingly I kept my composure throughout, then we were escorted up the nave to the altar for prayers. We knelt and the whole church fell silent, suddenly the quiet was shattered by a crescendo of two-tone horns, sirens and bull horns from outside. I whispered to Julie, "The boys are here!"

They couldn't have timed it better, because if the congregation had been in full voice singing no one would have heard them. In fact, two pumps, the turntable ladder and the hydraulic platform had all turned up to see us exiting the church, but as luck would have it, they got a fire call to some high-rise flats at the exact time we had knelt for prayers, and the noise was them turning out. I was disappointed we'd missed them as I would have loved a picture of me and Julie stood with the watch on the decking of the turntable ladder. C'est la vie! Pump 2 (The Water Tender) did return from the false alarm, so the watch was represented as we exited the church.

Register signed, then the slow stroll, arm in arm down the aisle and out of the church ready for the group photographs. There were a few complaints about our photographer and his rude attitude. We never noticed any impoliteness, and, in his defence, he just needed to get the different photographs done as it was starting to rain. When the photographs were produced later, we were over the moon and thrilled with them, so to those who complained or were enraged by any rudeness my answer is tough, it was our day, and the results were very much worth it. Photographs completed and confetti thrown, we found ourselves sat in the white Rolls-Royce on our way to the reception at the Guidepost Hotel on Common Road in Low Moor, Bradford. This was the first time all day it was just the two of us, when we had plenty of time to discuss our day's experiences so far, because the journey lasted quite some time due to being driven very slowly to the venue. The driver explained it was slow so we could enjoy the car and the ride, which was fantastic, but painfully and embarrassingly unhurried. It would have been better going the long way round faster, that would have done the job!

The welcome at the Guidepost by the management was excellent, they knew us both as we would regularly attend for our Sunday dinner with my cousin and wife. As guests arrived from the church, with the ushers and best man having sorted out the travel arrangements ensuring all guests were able to get from church to the reception, we had a few more photographs taken including ones with Granny May, followed by a sherry reception while everyone was assembling. Then the traditional line up was set up, where the bride and groom, parents, bridesmaids, best man and ushers met the guests, who were then shown into the dining room to be seated at their designated places. Once everybody had taken their seats, Julie and I were introduced to the room by the Master of Ceremonies, a Frenchman called Jean-Pierre. He announced in a very thick French accent,

"Ladies and Gentlemen, please stand and welcome your bride and groom, Andrew and Julie!"

We still mimic him and his Frenchness today over 35 years later. Everyone enjoyed the three-course meal before the speeches and funny bits began.

Donald stood up to make his father of the bride's speech; it was short, quiet and to the point, so much so many guests missed it. He had been worried sick and lost sleep over making his speech for weeks prior to the day and couldn't get through it quick enough. When he sat down you could literally observe this heavy burden lift from his shoulders as he sank another pint of Guinness with relief. I was then introduced and rose to deliver my speech, which was mainly a list of thank yous. I had asked the landlord of The Junction the night before if he had a spare till roll and when I got up to speak, I started by saying,

"I have just got a few thank yous to make," then promptly threw the till roll across the room. This gave the impression I had thousands of thanks to make, meaning I would be stood there for hours. It thankfully achieved the intended laugh from my audience.

My first task was to present Donald with a birthday cake as it was his 51st birthday. We thought we had this all arranged but when I mentioned this in my speech the management seemed to go into meltdown. I didn't want to say the words 'Birthday Cake' as I didn't want Don to have an inclination of what the surprise was going to be. There was staff running round like headless chickens, from where I was stood there was obviously blind panic behind the scenes. Eventually after what seemed like an age the cake made an appearance and as the laughter subsided, I presented it to Donald as the guests sang happy birthday. I then continued to read from the long list of thanks, including Mum and Dad for having me, my beautiful wife Julie for taking on the challenge of me, the stripper on my stag night and the vicar for sorting out a potential disaster, which I had to explain. We went to see him not long before the wedding day and one of the questions he asked was if we'd had our banns read at the church in Thornbury, my parish. When we told him we were not aware of this, he sat back in his chair, with a frustrated and slightly angry look, sighed and stated,

"Oh no! In that case you can't get married!"

Julie's shocked, drip white expression was unforgettable; a snapshot of it would have been priceless. All she could think about was the fact that all our guests had purchased new hats and frocks. The vicar took what seemed to be an unhealthily long time to get to the point where he told us we could apply for a special licence to attain permission. Wow! The relief was immense, and we knew he'd given us a major bollocking, but problem solved, and the blood returned to Julie's face.

Back to the list, I had another three presentations to carry out. Jim, one of the ushers, had asked me to present an eternity ring to his wife, it was a year to the day that they had got married (it didn't last an eternity, I think they were divorced within three years). I also presented a bouquet of flowers to Mr and Mrs Smith who had sold us our first house on Grange Avenue; it was their 50th wedding anniversary. Finally, I presented the best man and ushers with their gifts of thanks. I had my audience laughing and guffawing, and before I sat down, I told them to enjoy the rest of the day and the night party as they would see me as they had never seen me before, to which some wise Alec heckled,

"What, sober?"

The surprise was going to be that me and the best man would be dressed in dinner suits with bow ties, a first.

Once again, as Mick was delivering the best man's speech the Guidepost staff were in a panic, because like most weddings we were running late. This was the main reason when looking back we should have married at 1200hrs. They were panicking because they needed to change the room back into the restaurant for the booked evening diners. In fact, staff had started preparations before Mick had finished speaking.

My wife and I retired to the bridal suite to catch our breath and for me to get changed into my dinner suit. Julie said she would stay in her wedding dress until 2100hrs so the evening guests could see her wearing it, then she would get changed and party, and we did! We didn't stay in the bridal suite too long, I remember lying in the corner bath with a bottle of champagne while freshening up for the night do. The evening celebrations turned out to be a 'Reet gud do', it was held in a downstairs bar, and the dance floor was a covered swimming pool, it wasn't a small room, but I would describe it as cosy. At 2100hrs on the dot Julie disappeared to get out of her dress and true to her word we danced the night away. For the early part of the evening several male guests went missing – they were discovered crammed into a room watching the 1990 World Cup 3rd and 4th place playoff game between Italy and England. The following day was the World Cup Final when West Germany beat Argentina 1-0.

Eventually the evening came to a reluctant close as all the guests left or retired to their pre-booked rooms. Julie and I made our way back to the Bridal Suite, discussing the possibility of divorce which would enable us to go through it all again, along the corridor, up the stairs and we arrived at the suite door. The Bridal Suite awaits! The rest I leave to your imagination, cos I ain't telling you owt! Only,

THIS WAS THE BEST DAY OF MY LIFE!!!

EXAMS

My relationship with exams over the years has not and has never been good. I must stress all I am about to say is not anybody's fault but my own, I am a firm believer you should take responsibility for your own actions, perhaps in this case responsibility for my inaction would fit slightly better. The word exam has always sent me cold, even as I write this the hairs on the back of my neck bristle with unease, the words, test, quiz, or assessment sit in my mind much more comfortably. I don't understand what it is about exams I find so terrifying, perhaps it's the pressure you're put under when you're young. Statements from adults about how important they are, how you should work hard for your exams and if you don't pass you will come to nothing, are all pressures thrown at unsuspecting minds.

All this even before you are exposed to the exam experience. Candidates stood outside the exam room with nervousness in their hushed voices, claiming they had not revised when in fact they had, and you admitting you also had not revised when in fact you hadn't. The slow shuffle into the large hall or gym to find your place at the allocated position. The atmosphere of the exam room, the tension in the air, the quiet whisper as candidates need some question answered by the invigilators and then you all sit down in isolation at a small table with only your pen and thoughts for company. Sat in a room of hundreds not allowed to talk, waiting for the delivery of an exam paper anticipating the pending instruction to start. All this added together makes a sterile, pressure induced environment all with the knowledge that if you don't perform for the next two or three hours you are on the road to ruin, no job, no career and no prospects.

At school the general rule of thumb is you work for two or three years on not one but several subjects, with mountains of information thrown in your direction, to be tested and examined in two maybe three hours on any random topic within that specific subject. So, you sit in the exam room, waiting for the paper, pleading with the mythical gods it contains questions about the subject you just luckily happened to read about in the previous weeks, this to me is a massive lottery. Teachers and lecturers spend weeks trying to predict and inform you what questions may be asked on the paper, observations like

"They have not asked this question for a few years, so it may be on the paper this time," or

"This question is a favourite so you might have a look at that," are all intended to give you a heads up, so your revision focus is on these few questions that are rarely on the paper. Then you are told to study previous years' papers just in case the exam board repeat a question asked five or so years before. Do these pieces of advice and information make the exam easier or is it a mild form of cheating? It doesn't seem right to me that you're supposed to study large subjects, only to be examined across a few hours which has such an influence on the rest of your life.

My problem is not only the examination surroundings and tense atmosphere within the room, but my lack of preparedness. The cliché is 'Fail to prepare, prepare to fail'. How do you revise? What do you revise? How much did you revise which never appears on the examination paper? I never had a lot of instruction on how to carry out these skills, I think exam technique is taught a great deal more to the youth of today than when I was in the same situation. Revising wasn't enjoyable for me; I lacked the patience and focus to study uninteresting subjects for hours on end. When I read a newspaper or magazine article, I often get three-quarters of the way through it, lose concentration, put it down, and do not finish reading it, boredom sets in. When I did revise, I didn't seem to have the ability to retain the information, so consequently I would look at, and work on the easier parts of the subject which was neither use nor ornament. Like I said, this is nobody's fault but my own.

My first experience of the word 'exam' was when I was nine or ten years old. I had participated in piano lessons from the age of six, I attended half-hour lessons once a week, and I did enjoy playing the piano, but was never the greatest practiser in the world, in fact I was probably the worst. After a while, each time I left home to go to piano lessons my mother would say "Ask the teacher about your exams!" What?! I was doing this for fun and enjoyment, why would I want to do exams in it? This put me right off, in fact it panicked me, so I decided the easiest way out was to quit and run away. Which is what I stupidly did. I used the excuse with my teacher I would be going to secondary school and ironically would need spare time to do my school studies. The biggest surprise was when I told my parents I wanted to stop, expecting huge resistance which never came, all they said was "OK" and accepted my wish. In hindsight, I believe they wanted to get rid of the piano to create space, save the weekly cost, and because getting me to practise was a daily struggle. They would tell me to do half an hour practice which would be set on the oven timer in the kitchen, this timer had a loud alarm which could be heard all over the house. I would set it, start the practice, playing easy, known pieces then when my parents were upstairs or in the garden, I would sneak from the lounge into the kitchen and move the timer forward a few minutes, then return to my so-called practice. I got away with this for some time until the day I pushed it too far. Not for one minute did it cross my mind they may have checked their watches when I set the timer, so when I moved the timer on, then on and on again, the alarm would sound, and I would shout 'Finished' and eagerly head for something better to do. This was the quickest half hour in the history of time, as it only lasted 19 minutes and when I was questioned about how come I'd finished so early my defence that the clock didn't lie, or perhaps your watch is wrong, wasn't quite the convincing argument I was after. The final straw was the day I was practising the piano as Dad was descending the stairs and he thought to himself, 'that noise doesn't sound like any sort of practice', so he burst in to the lounge and caught me facing the bay window, with my back toward the piano, watching the kids playing out on the street, and my arms reaching round randomly plinking the keys. I think this convinced him the piano was not for me. Ironically, a few years later I became a huge fan of Rick Wakeman, one of the greatest pianists of modern times. It would have been nice to have the skill to emulate some of his work in a small way.

My first experience of an exam situation was when I sat my 'O' levels; these were never going to go well as I had certainly failed to prepare. We were not taught how to revise effectively. What to revise seemed to be a bit of a lottery all put together with my personal disinterest in revising, it may come as no surprise I didn't do very well. I recall queuing outside the school gym, waiting to enter the intimidating venue. The nervous chatter among candidates justifying their lack of revision. I struggled with this process for over a month, and it came as no surprise when I received my results, I had achieved diddly squat, nothing, just one 'O' level and that was English. This may be quite amazing to you who have read any of my stories, with my poor spelling and grammar. I am convinced the examiners felt sorry for me, so awarded me the one 'O' level as a consolation. English? Me, now there is a surprise!

Consequently, I re-sat four 'O' levels 12 months later at Airedale and Wharfedale College. Here the exams were held in a cold, dank, smelly miserable community hall off campus which didn't help with the already oppressive ambience. This was all irrelevant and no excuses as once again my preparation for the exams was next to nil. College was where I discovered drinking, smoking and girls. Exams, as a free spirited 17-year-old with little responsibility and no revision skills was not a major priority. Mistake! Big mistake! Despite my initial confidence, I unfortunately failed all the four 'O' levels when I received the results a few months later.

Working life began in 1979 at Leeds University where I believed, naively, this would signal the end of examinations. Oh no! How wrong was I? They sent me to Bradford College on day release to study for a BTec in Textile Colouration.

Embarrassingly it took me eight years to complete a four-year course, never failing the same year twice. The Textile Department didn't really seem too interested or bothered about my day release course, therefore I wasn't either. Yet another mistake! The assessment side of the course was quite straightforward, it was the examinations and the environment I struggled with, as my preparations became less and less, the exams became harder and harder. While attending Bradford College one of the chemistry papers I sat was the lowest point in my examination history. I entered the challenging setting and took a seat. We were instructed to fill in the front of the answer book, Name, good start, candidate number, course and subject. I opened it up at the front page, ran my thumb down the inside spine to keep it open, then wrote number one in a bracket '1)'. When instructed I turned over the question paper and read the whole of it from front to back. It felt like it was written in a foreign language. I didn't understand any of the questions, so I put the question paper into the answer book and left the old hall, feeling embarrassed and ashamed.

On to the Fire Service, end of exams? Oh no! At training school we had an exam every four weeks of the 12-week course. These were small affairs done in a classroom environment. Less stress, less oppressive atmosphere and a more relaxed approach. Also, the revision was structured and because we were disciplined, we revised together as a team helping each other out. The fact this was a career I had craved since being ten and had an insatiable strive for knowledge, made preparation more appealing and interesting. On the day of our final probation exam, there was a sense of relief. During the week leading to the exam, the emphasis was all about the paper and what questions would be on it, the instructors were desperate for us to pass. One day prior to examination day an instructor accidently, on purpose, left a copy of the exam paper on the desk at the front of the classroom, so we could have a look at the questions. I made full use of this event and revised each of the questions to near perfection. In the exam itself, which was the easiest I'd ever sat, one recruit had an enquiry about question four. The instructor addressed the room clarifying the confusion in the question, as the rest of the recruits looked perplexed and confused about what he was explaining. It soon became apparent the recruit with the question had been handed a different paper to the rest of us. He was asked if he wanted his paper changing but he refused, having confidence to carry on with another paper. If that had been me with the alternative paper, I would have panicked, every question I had focused on in revision would have been different. Eek! Close call! At training school, we were told we may as well sit our Leading Fireman's exam, because of the knowledge we had gained we would breeze it. I did enter it, and I didn't breeze it; I was never told how I had done in the exam, I just know I failed it. Promotion within the fire service never interested me, all I wanted to do was be a good firefighter and drive fire engines. This being the main reason I have never sat an exam since. I have done many courses which usually resulted in a small test or assessment, but never since the late eighties have I sat in that intimidating oppressive environment that is an exam hall.

    I believe that examinations are nothing more than a memory test, this is no disrespect to those who enjoy them and are successful in the process. My reason for stating this is

I know of two specific candidates who in the classroom were brilliant, very intelligent, very studious and knowledgeable, but put them in an exam environment and they both would completely fall to pieces. One would have beads of sweat on his forehead as the nerves, anxiety and trepidation would get the better of him. It was known if this individual was in your exam group the good thing was you wouldn't come last. In conclusion I have no excuse for my failures in examinations, it was all down to me, I repeat 'Fail to prepare, prepare to fail'. I was never taught revision techniques or how and what to revise. The volume of revision needed failed to hold my concentration and enthusiasm. What to revise for an exam was somewhat of a lottery, knowing which area of a large subject you need to learn which may or may not be on the paper. For me, assessments are a better judgement of someone's knowledge rather than two or three hours of mental torment sat in an intimidating exam auditorium, in total silence with a paper in front of you and only your pen and thoughts for company.

Exams? Not for me!

FIRE HEROES... OR NOT?

The summer of 1995 was the hottest on record, July and August saw wall-to-wall sunshine. There was no rainfall, leading to low reservoirs, a hose pipe ban, water rationing and parched desert-like ground conditions. All these criteria did not make being a firefighter's life comfortable. Bonfire night is traditionally the busiest day and night of each year with crews turning out over 50 times a shift, but because of the 1995 weather conditions for over a 30-day period it was kind of bonfire night every day. As I arrived at the fire station to start my shift, I knew what was in store. After the parade and checks of equipment we would stow the fire engines with sandwiches, snacks and water, fully aware we would not be returning to station once the fire calls had started. In those days fire engines didn't carry drinking water so to compensate for this inadequacy we used the 20-litre bottle from the station's drinking water dispenser. It was not ideal as we were unable to keep it cool due to the high temperatures, so as the day and evening proceeded the liquid would turn lukewarm, which wasn't pleasant to drink, but at the end of the day it was hydrating if not refreshing. Since 1995 bottled drinking water is now standard on fire engines for crews' rehydration. After the pumps were loaded, we would carry out a quick drill and then prepare for 1100hrs. The kids were on school summer holidays so the fire calls would start at around this time when the little blighters had left their homes to play out after breakfast. I am not suggesting for one minute that all the fires we attended that summer were due to delinquent children, but it was suspected they did cause a large majority. So, the first shout would be around the 11 o'clock mark and that was it, we wouldn't stop till the end of shift. The whole brigade was so busy the staff in the Control Centre were having to prioritize calls, meaning bin fires, small rubbish fires and other minor incidents would be delayed as fire crews would be needed to attend more serious events.

On the day in question, 21st August 1995, nothing was unusual, all the routines had been carried out with no indication of what was to happen that afternoon. Over the years this was one of the best characteristics of the job, it proved to me that no one ever knows what is in store for them on any particular day or in fact the next ten minutes. How many times do people get up in the morning ready for the day ahead, only not to return to bed that evening, because of some untimely event. Eleven o'clock came round and the bells went down as predicted, to shouts of 'here we go' and 'see you tomorrow' aimed at the crews manning the special appliances. We attended bush fires, skip fires and grass fires one after another. In and among these calls were the usual fire alarm actuations, a malicious call or two, and refreshment taken between each mobilization.

We had just finished packing equipment away after putting out a large grass bank and bushes when we were mobilized to the former St Blaise Middle School on Rooley Lane to reports of a building fire. St Blaise was an unoccupied school, but half the property was being used by Gregory Middle School as their premises had been destroyed by fire months earlier and were waiting for their new school to be built. So off we went, blue lights flashing, horns shattering the relative afternoon tranquillity towards the reported building fire. As we approached, we could see smoke on the horizon, suggesting this could be a going job. The driver shouted to us in the back: "It's a goer!" making us aware to be ready as we arrived. It was the school holidays, and the majority of the buildings were uninhabited, so security made entering the grounds tricky. We had to get through two lots of bolted gates which were dealt with using large bolt croppers releasing the chains. By this time, we had been joined by two other fire engines. Crews were dropping hose off the wagons ready to get a flowing water supply to the incident from hydrants beyond the school perimeter.

Eventually the fire engine pulled up on the disused playground ready to pump water. The building in front of us was of a typical 1960s school design, a two-storey construction with ten classrooms, five either side of a lengthy corridor, mirrored on each floor. Flames were spewing out of the classrooms on the first floor. Quickly enough water had arrived onto the fire ground and rapidly fed into the three fire engines standing on the redundant play area. Firefighters were running hose toward the burning building demanding "Water on!" as the revs of the pumps increased with noise. Suddenly four jets of water were aimed through the shattered windows on the first floor. After about 30 minutes or so when the jets had knocked the flames back from the outside, the Station Officer approached me and my more experienced colleague Dave, pointing to the protected stairwell on the left-hand side of the structure, and said, "Will you two gain entry into that staircase with a jet, climb to the first floor and start fighting the fire down the central corridor?"

"Yes, Boss!" we replied in unison. This to me seemed a natural course of action; the jets had reduced the intensity of the fire on the first floor, the smoke emitting from the outlets was thinning but the fire was still burning within, so action was needed to complete the job. So as we acquired a charged hose, two other firefighters were breaking the door down so we could advance up the stairs.

Arriving on the landing I looked down the corridor leading off the stairwell and saw fire the full length but by no means was it intense. It was as if paper had been strewn all over and was the source of any flame. The smoke was thin, so vision was quite easy. With hose in hand, I crouched down behind the door jamb and opened the branch. Water shot out straight down the passageway with enough pressure to quickly hit all parts. Soon the fire was extinguished but was still alight in each of the ten classrooms. I turned to Dave and said,

"Come on, let's advance down this corridor and hit every classroom as we pass, we will soon have this fire out."

His reply probably saved our lives. He said, "Before we do, I'll just nip back downstairs and get a fire ground radio."

Good point, I thought, but did we really need it? As things turned out yes, we did; a lot of times you cannot beat the voice of experience. Off he went leaving me crouched, turning the branch on and off sporadically.

Dave arrived back up the stairwell after about five minutes armed with the required fire ground radio. At this point my eagerness to get into the corridor and singlehandedly put this

fire out was reaching the thrill threshold. Dave stood behind me as support and shouted,
"Right then, here we go."
"Ready," I replied as I put my foot forward into the corridor from the landing.
BANG!! Wow!
"What was that?" I shouted.
"I dunno" came the response.
The explosion shook the building and virtually in the same shocking moment very thick black smoke was slowly billowing up the staircase towards us, filling the air with an acrid bitter smelling environment. I'm sure I saw the jaws of death within the surging rolling black mass of darkness.
"Oh bollocks!" Dave exclaimed. "What do we do now?"
"Not a problem," I replied. "We can get out using that door behind us."
About 15 yards down a link building corridor the other side of the stairwell was a door; it looked flimsy, so I was quite sure if it was locked, we would be able to smash through it. I put down the branch and led the way to the door. It was unlocked but as I opened it, we were confronted with a wall of breeze block. This was the point between the in-use Gregory Middle School and the abandoned St Blaise Middle School. Now we seemed to be scuppered. Our escape route was blocked by thick black smoke, which was getting thicker as it percolated into the link building where we were now situated, and the other means of escape was breeze blocked up.
By now the misty, smoky atmosphere was developing into a thickish foggy smog and of course we were not wearing Breathing Apparatus. Retreating down the corridor towards

the thick smoke and developing dancing flames, we tried to open a couple of windows. The first one was nailed down but the second one opened, so I put my head out to gasp at some less stale air. I was leaning out of the window and gave an odd cry for help, but this was unnecessary due to the fact Dave had alerted the fireground that we were in a sticky situation. I was asked later if I had at any time felt concerned or even frightened. My answer was a definite no, as I knew as soon as the firefighters outside were aware of our plight the fire would become a secondary priority with our rescue suddenly becoming the sole focus of every attending firefighter.

As I was leaning out of the window there was a tap on my shoulder. I turned round to be confronted by a firefighter dressed in Breathing Apparatus.

"It's your lucky day," he said cockily. "I've come to rescue you."

"How do you propose to do that?" I asked with sarcasm.

"I'll lead you out," he replied hesitantly.

"So, do you want me to hold my breath down two flights of stairs, through thick black smoke or have you got a BA set hidden behind your back?"

The realization in his eyes told a story. I really did appreciate the fact he had entered the building to rescue me, but I did think it needed a bit more thought. As this conversation was happening, a 135 ladder was quite amateurly being pitched to the window – 135 means 13.5 metres which was far too big for the five metres needed to get us both out. Consequently, the ladder was pitched at a very near horizontal angle. The ladder crew consisted of three firefighters from another station and one of the Bradford crew. He was that frustrated with the pitching attempt once it was in place he stormed off in disgust. Although the ladder was at an awkward angle, it did give us a means of escape which we both eagerly used to abscond from the corridor which was becoming increasingly thick with the black smoke.

The message was sent that 'all persons were now accounted for' as we both walked round to the front of the building to report to the Officer in Charge. He told us to have five minutes as we gulped water from the lukewarm 20-litre water container. This was to remove the acrid taste of smoke from our mouths and rehydrate after the experience. I never felt any detrimental effect from being in this incident and consequently was willing to get involved with firefighting duties. I returned to the end of a hose to pour water into the ground floor of the building. At this point it became quite clear to me how serious the explosion had been. When I had entered the protected stairwell there was no sign of fire on the ground floor, but now as I fought the conflagration black smoke, and 20-foot flames were spewing out at a volatile rate, I realized what a near-miss this incident was. Eventually, with the fire now well under control, the night crews arrived on the fireground to relieve us and allow us to return home.

The following day I arrived at the fire station ready for the new day ahead. All the talk was about the job at the school the previous day. As checks were completed, Dave and I were summoned to the Station Officer's Office. When we entered there was the Station Officer with two others.

"Good morning, gentlemen," said the gaffer. "Here are two reporters from the Telegraph and Argus who would like to interview you both about yesterday's fire at St Blaise School. Have you any objections?"

"No, none at all," I said, and Dave nodded in agreement. I didn't really comprehend why the press was so interested in a fire which really in my opinion was of little importance at a disused school. There were no casualties, no fatalities and no real damage as the school was due to be demolished. I gave the reporters my account of the incident and a photographer was sent to the station shortly after. I was naively unaware of what was to come, believing there would be a small paragraph in the paper later that day.

"Fire Heroes!" have you seen it?" shouted a colleague from across the yard. "Fire heroes, it's here in black and white" as he waved a newspaper in the air above his head.

"What are you talking about?" I enquired as he arrived next to me.

"Look here, you've only gone and made the front-page headline news." He thrust that day's copy of The Telegraph and Argus into my hand. Sure enough on the front page of the paper under the headline 'Fire Heroes' was a picture of the school on fire, another showing firefighters pointing jets towards the burning building and one with me and Dave posing in fire kit with yellow helmets in hand with a long report explaining how we were minutes from death. How we escaped our ordeal, had a glass of water, leapt back into action and continued fighting the blaze. Wow! Talk about press sensationalism. When I'd read the report, I said,

"Perhaps there was no important news today." I was slightly embarrassed but then again had a feeling of pride being recognized for the job we had done. This I think was my 15 minutes of fame.

That was the day I became a fire hero, though perhaps looking back the headline should read 'Fire Fools', 'Fire Idiots' or just no headline at all. To enter a burning building with no Breathing Apparatus and no fire ground radio was wrong and quite a silly thing to do. Dave and I had done nothing erroneous; we were just following orders, and it never crossed my mind that the task in hand along with visual conditions neither would be needed. We were just going to put out a smallish conflagration to reduce any further fire spread or development. In defence of the officers in attendance who would know there was a gas supply into the deserted school? Who would know the gas main was live? And who would expect or consider it to explode? As I've said many times, no one knows what will happen in the next ten minutes. A sobering thought struck me, if we had been wearing BA or carried a fireground radio we would have advanced down the corridor and would likely have been situated right above the explosion. The fact we were delayed while Dave returned to the fireground probably saved us from serious injury or even death. Then the headline may have been totally different

Fire Hero!...not me!!

VINEGAR, HAGGIS AND FISH

Every day on a fire station there are two parades, one at the morning shift change and one at the evening shift change. After the off going watch has been dismissed a roll call is conducted when the fire fighters of the new shift are given their duties for the day or night ahead. This includes the officer in charge of each appliance, the driver of each appliance, the BA wearers on the pumps and other operational duties. Two other roles are designated on parade, Dutyman whose responsibilities include answering phones, answering the door, welcoming visiting officers complete with salutation, ensuring the offices are clean and tidy and ensuring breathing apparatus cylinders are filled with air. The second role is that of Kitchenman sometimes referred to as Orderly, these duties include ensuring the kitchen is tidy, pots are washed up, kitchen floor mopped, assisting the cook and emptying kitchen bins.

Although on a fire station there was an unwritten rule that you don't mess with colleagues' food, the kitchen and mess areas were many times the fulcrum of practical jokes and wind ups. This may be because the geography of most fire stations has the kitchen right alongside the mess room where the firefighters would congregate for meals, tea breaks and downtime. A lot of jokes and teases were down to individuals' habits, foibles characteristics and mistakes. When I joined Blue watch from training school and had my initial interview of welcome from my new station officer, it was pointed out that the watch could only take the piss out of what they know about you, so be careful what you divulge.

On one nightshift a firefighter came into work complaining he had bumped his head, and it was quite sore. So, after parade and checks we sat him down on a chair in the mess room and members of the watch wrapped his head with brown paper and proceeded to douse him in vinegar as per the nursery rhyme of 'Jack and Jill'. At the time this seemed to be a great idea with the prospect of a good laugh, but the consequence was the station had a stench of vinegar for most of the evening, and the victim and his hair still smelled of vinegar after several showers trying to eradicate it.

Another of the many tales concerning food was when it became apparent one of the watch members was dating a Scottish doctor who worked in one of the local hospitals. She would ring up the station and ask to speak with him with a very strong and rich Glaswegian accent; this was long before mobile phones. When the phone call was announced over the Tannoy, it would be done imitating the broad Scottish brogue, which would gain a laugh and titter. It was decided for one dinner time the following tour we would eat haggis with tatties and neaps. The ingredients were purchased, and the preparation finalised for the watch to feast on this traditional Scottish banquet. There was one problem, as a member of the watch pointed out – he suggested the haggis should by rights be piped in. Next follows an example of firefighters' imagination when developing a wind up. The tallest member of the watch dressed up wearing the iconic Tam O' Shanter hat with long orange hair emerging down the back and sides. A dog's tartan blanket brought from home wrapped round his waist with his trousers rolled up above his knees as to represent a kilt and a tartan tea towel hanging over his shoulder. What about the bagpipes? I hear you ask. Not a problem, and with a touch of genius they were constructed using an empty one-gallon green plastic fuel container, two mop handles stuck in the can neck, the drones resting on the firefighter's shoulder and a short piece of rubber piping exiting the can into his mouth as the blow stick. Stuck on the front of the can with copious amounts of sticky tape was a short piece of dowel with felt tip dots drawn down it to represent the chanter, the pipe with finger holes. Then on cue a recording of 'Donald Where's your Trousers' was put on the CD player as the procession entered the room. This included one firefighter holding a silver tray with the haggis on it, followed by the pretend piper with two escorts. On appearance the mess room descended into a crescendo of cheering, clapping and singing to the tune enquiring the whereabouts of Donald's troosers. All this time, work and energy given to receive one small minute of laughter because one of the team had a Scottish girlfriend.

Another example of this was when an example of greed had to be dealt with. Every Friday dinner time it was ritually written in tablets of stone it had to be fish and chips. The kitchen man or mess manager would collect numbers in the morning as to how many firefighters required fish and chips for lunch, with or without mushy peas. During the morning this oceanic feast would be meticulously prepared. Batter mixed, fish counted, potatoes peeled, chipped and peas steeped. As the time for serving approached, it would be announced over the Tannoy 'dinner is served' so the watch members would appear from their duties and congregate in an orderly queue at the serving hatch eagerly waiting for the pending culinary delight. Numerous times one member of the shift, who had a self-centred, arrogant and selfish attitude to most things in life, would join the front of the queue, scan the battered fish on the plates and picking the largest fish would lean across the food and grab the plate saying,

"I'll have this one!" Chips and peas would then be added and off he would go to sit down and enjoy his meal.

This behaviour was quite rightly frowned upon and the individual concerned having a thick skin just deflected any jibe, comment or anger sent in his direction. So, it was agreed among the watch personnel it was time to teach him a lesson. The plan was hatched, it was done with MI5 precision. Every detail was meticulously worked out and rehearsed until the day of the event. As normal the watch was asked who wanted fish and chips, as normal the kitchen man and cook prepared the meal and as normal the watch was summoned to the kitchen hatch to line up in wait for the food. Now all that was needed was the victim to play his part and sure enough right on cue he did. He joined the front of the queue, picked the largest battered fish, got his chips and peas and went to sit down. Now if he had been more observant, he might have noticed the big smiles, nudges and joyful murmuring from the rest of the shift as they waited in anticipation for the reaction. Then it came in a loud and surprised tone.

"Oh, you Bastards!!" was the statement as he tried to cut into his large fish which was in fact a piece of battered cotton wool. The watch was in hysterics, lads guffawing, some bent over double with tears of mirth rolling down their cheeks. Comments of:

"Serves you right!"

"Greedy Bastard."

"Enjoy your fish?" and

"Serves you right for pushing in!" were sent in his direction.

Red-faced and embarrassed, he sheepishly joined the end of the queue to replace his cotton wool fish with one that had been swimming in the sea days earlier. Needless to say, the fish he got as a replacement was noticeably smaller than any of the others served that day. He had learnt his lesson and jumping in front of the queue was never exercised again.

THE FAMOUS GREENOCK MORTON

Many English football supporters have a favourite Scottish team. Be it Celtic, Rangers, Stenhousemuir, Cowdenbeath or Hamilton Academicals. The two formers due to reputation, the three latters due to unusual names. Since 1988 my favourite Scottish team is the famous Greenock Morton for no other reason than we have family friends who live in Greenock.

In my youth as my interest in sport, particularly Rugby, Football and Cricket developed, I couldn't get enough. I would watch it, read about it and listen to radio programmes dedicated to it. On Saturday afternoons long before I attended live football matches, I would eagerly watch the football scores come into the BBC TV programme Grandstand via the teleprinter, followed by the reading of the classified results. These would be read out from League Division One, down to League Division Four, then on to the Scottish Football league results. Most results would appear with some marked with the letter 'L' indicating a late kick off, with the result not yet confirmed, some marked with a 'P' meaning postponed or an 'E' for evening kick off. On these team listings, although it never stood out, I was aware of the team referred to as Morton. As far as Scottish team names go, as a youngster

I thought this was quite a plain and boring name. I didn't know anything about them, where they came from, colours or ground, nothing, just the uninspiring name Morton.

This illusion stayed with me until 1988 when we went on a family holiday to Dunoon. We drove to Scotland to catch the ferry across the river Clyde from Gourock to Dunoon. Mum and Dad have some lifelong friends who live in Gourock, the next town along the coast from Greenock, and using the ferry was too good an opportunity not to visit. While driving along the coast road I spotted a set of football ground floodlights which intrigued me – I wasn't aware of any football team west of Glasgow. If I'd have been in Ayr, Hamilton or Kilmarnock, it would be obvious whose ground the floodlights belonged to, but I was in Greenock and had never heard of a Scottish football team bearing that name. This fact had me racking my brain, who could it be? So, I asked my dad's friend the question.

"As we drove through Greenock," I said, "I noticed some football ground floodlights on the left, which team plays there?"

"That is Cappielow Park, the home of the famous Greenock Morton," he answered.

It hit me like lightning and suddenly it became clear, the Morton referred to on the classified football results on a Saturday evening was in fact Greenock Morton and that characterless name for a football team 'Morton' instantly had an air of wonder, intrigue and fascination. From that moment on Greenock Morton became my second love in football behind my cherished Bradford City FC.

Every Saturday after watching Bradford City at Valley Parade, I would get home and look for the Greenock Morton score of that day. Our friends in Gourock would send me cuttings from the Greenock Telegraph and other Morton-related memorabilia. In 1997 we acquired a new family PC and among other IT tasks I enjoyed using it for letter writing, one of which I sent to Greenock Morton FC explaining that I am a fan who lives 230 miles away in Bradford West Yorkshire and had watched and kept an eye on Morton from afar and would love to visit at some time in the future. I sent it off with little hope of receiving a reply. A week or so later a lovely letter arrived through the post from a man called Gary W Miller, the commercial manager of Greenock Morton FC, inviting me to Cappielow Park to see the 'Mighty 'ton' play a fixture of my choice.

I picked a date and fixture, which fit with my fire service shift pattern, Greenock Morton v Hamilton Academical, and arranged board and lodgings with our friends in Gourock. I invited Dad to join me, not for the game, which was not his cup of tea, but to ride shotgun and spend the weekend with his lifelong mate. We arrived on the Friday dinner time; I left Dad in Gourock and went to Cappielow to meet Gary. He welcomed me with open arms and proceeded to give me an impromptu tour of the stadium. This was fantastic; I was made to feel very important. We talked about football, his passion for Greenock Morton FC was insatiable, he was also interested in my knowledge of Bradford City. I was shown the Board Room, Changing Rooms, the Kit and past programme store. It was brilliant, I was introduced to more official areas at Cappielow Park in two hours than I'd ever managed in two decades at Valley Parade. When the tour had finished, Gary invited me to spend the evening with him at The Spinnaker Hotel from where he ran the Greenock

Morton Fan club. I accepted the invite, and we had a great evening talking football with Greenock Morton fans who were as interested in Bradford City as I was in Morton. Eventually the evening drew to an end and I arranged to meet Gary at the main gate on Sinclair Street the following day ready for the game.

Morning broke on the day of the game, it was a bright and sunny day as I was transported to Cappielow Park by one of our friends. I met Gary as planned and he instantly treat me like a guest of honour; it was marvellous, he escorted me straight to the hospitality suite and bought me a beer. I was introduced to the sponsors and officials before sitting down to a pre-match meal served by a lovely lady called Sharon, who I found out was Gary's wife, Greenock Morton was a real family affair in the Miller household. After the delicious meal Gary took me to the changing rooms and introduced me to some of the payers, Dave Whylie the goalkeeper, Warren Hawke and Harry Cullen who at the time was my favourite player, a few photographs were taken for recollection purposes. Then having wished them good luck and a good game I was escorted back to the board room for another drink before being shown to my seat in the director's box ready for kick off. It was a very entertaining game, end to end, full of incident and Morton won 3-0. After the game I had a couple of post-match drinks enjoyed with members of the board who enthused enormously about the fantastic performance and win. The day ended all too quickly, but before I left Gary took me on one final treat to meet the manager Billy Stark in his office. Billy had obviously been well briefed about who I was, where I was from and why I was there as we chatted football and other subjects for a good 20 minutes. In his career he had made 503 senior appearances and played for St Mirren, Aberdeen, and Celtic; ironically, he had also represented Hamilton, that day's opponents, 14 times. This was the cherry on the cake, what a lovely end to a great day. Gary and I said our goodbyes and his last words were 'Andy, don't leave it too long, please come and visit us again'.

I accepted Gary's invite and visited Cappielow a couple more times, the second of which was like the first, with visits to The Spinnaker Hotel, tour of the ground and hospitality. On this occasion I went armed with Bradford City merchandise including a pennant which was hung on the wall in the trophy room alongside other football club badges. It rained all day and all night, so I rang Gary to confirm the game would be on, which he assured me it would, stating Cappielow has remarkable drainage. When I met him at the main entrance and saw the pitch it looked in remarkable condition considering the amount of water which had fallen on it over the previous 24 hours. Morton was playing Ayr United that weekend and once again won, 2-1, so everybody was telling me I must be the lucky mascot as I had never seen Morton lose.

The last time I saw Gary was when Greenock Morton had an away fixture against Clydebank. Although it was a home game for Clydebank, they had no ground of their own so were tenants at Dumbarton's Boghead Park, which I discovered to be a very appropriate name. The ground was a good 40-minute drive from Cappielow, and I had been on the phone to Gary more than once in the previous week as he had arranged a place for me to travel on the Spinnaker Hotel Greenock Morton Fan Club's minibus to the game.

He told me where to meet a guy called Jock who was the organiser of the travel, as he was expecting me. Gary then explained where I should go once I had got off the minibus on our arrival at Boghead. The minibus was full, and ladened with blue and white scarves and banners, a real party bus. The trip to Boghead was full of singing, football conversation and optimism. My situation and the reason for being there fascinated the other fanatical Morton fans on the coach and my story filled the time of the journey. On arrival at the ground, as instructed by Gary I told Jock,

"If I'm here when the bus leaves after the game, so be it, but if I'm not here when you are ready to leave go without me."

I wasn't too sure why I had to tell him this, but he accepted it with slight confusion in his voice. As instructed, I left the bus and made my way round to the main stand; my name and details had been left at reception and I found myself being escorted to the boardroom. As I was shown through the door, Gary spotted me and strode over with purpose, shook my hand and said, "Andy, I am so glad you made it". He seemed delighted to see me. He introduced me to board members of both clubs and told me to help myself to the hot buffet and free bar. I sat in the director's box and witnessed the 0-2 win for Morton. I had retired to the boardroom at half time to enjoy a cup of coffee and a pie, chatted to one of the young Morton players' parents and had a thoroughly great time. After the game it soon was time to go, and as I was thinking of racing back round the ground to the minibus, Gary approached me and said,

"Andy, I've had a word with Billy Stark, and you're invited back to Cappielow with me on the players' coach."

Wow! You could have knocked me down with a feather! So that's why I had to give the message to Jock. It was brilliant, once again the players were interested in my story and other than playing, they made me feel like part of the squad, it was fantastic. All thanks to Gary W Miller, Mr Greenock Morton! As I got off the coach at Cappielow I thanked Billy Stark and said my goodbyes to Gary having absolutely no inclination this would be the last time I would see him. When I got home to Bradford, I wrote a letter of thanks to Gary in appreciation for all he had shown and done for me. He replied acknowledging my thanks and suggested in his letter things were changing at the club with its sale and staff restructuring.

I don't quite know whether this was the reason, but it certainly played a small part in me not contacting Gary again. Then, tragically the day came in 2004 when I received a phone call from our friends in Gourock informing me it was reported in the Greenock Telegraph that Gary had passed away at the age of 35 due to a heart attack. I was devastated, although we hadn't been in touch for a couple of years, I still considered him to be a close football fan friend who went over and above the call of duty to make my experiences with the famous Greenock Morton greater than I could have ever perceived as a result of me just writing a letter all those years previously. Gary was described in the Greenock Telegraph as Mr Greenock Morton which was an accurate and fitting tribute to a great man.

Thank You, Gary W Miller, R.I.P.

AGE

Age is a counting system and a process which has never concerned me. When I was young and growing up, I was taught it is tradition to celebrate each period of 12 months as a birthday. Imagine if we had been told to celebrate every period of 24 months, all of us would be half our current age, the only downside to this theory is that by the time we reach 45, we will be dead or nearly dead. You see, counting systems are all relative, yet some people can become really stressed about their age, which I cannot understand; they go to extreme lengths to move mountains in trying to stop or alter the process which in my mind is pointless, accept who you are, how you look and be happy with your appearance. Some people may suggest this is easy for me to say because I am told regularly, I don't look my true age, but once again this is only appearance camouflaging a fact. I think a person's appearance can be affected by habit, smoking, drinking and drugs can have a detrimental effect on an individual's complexion. As I grow older my mind thinks I am a lot younger than my body allows me to be. In my head I don't feel any different to how I felt when I was a 30-year-old rugby player and would love nothing more than to play one more top-level rugby game, but then I have a word with myself as my brain realises my body will disagree.

One big tackle or one scrum could seriously injure or even hospitalise me, and if I was lucky enough to avoid injury, because of the exertion and physicality required, I would be black and blue due to the old age ease of bruising and not be able to walk for a week. The reality far outweighs the fantasy.

Signs of age can develop as we grow older, involuntary noises made as my body struggles to bend down, rise out of a chair, or getting up from low level, which can feel like ascending Everest, is something I find happening more frequently as I rapidly race toward those twilight years. Aches, pains and fatigue are symptoms we complain about more and more often as our bodies progress through the decades. Then you develop this problematic habit of falling asleep for no apparent reason, it's not too much of an enigma when done at 1600hrs in the afternoon with only close family around to witness it, or between the hours of 2100 and 2200 missing that TV programme you have waited all week to watch. The embarrassment arises when this happens in front of invited guests at home or inconceivably out at friends' houses or attending special parties. No matter how you try and fight this habit of inconvenient rude slumber, it seems you are powerless to stop it from happening, giving the illusion the event or celebration is monotonous or boring, which is never the truth. We tend to suffer more medical issues and take a larger cocktail of drugs and tablets, is this all a sign of the body breaking down due to the fact the aging process is taking us towards the natural end? Younger people standing up to offer you their seat in a waiting room or on a bus, with your initial thought being 'Wow do I really look that old?'! Looking in the bathroom mirror each morning gives other clues you are aging, what happened to that young face, taut skin and nicely coloured hair? Discovering one day it has metamorphosised into an old face, loose wrinkled skin and a grey or even balding head.

Although this process has never bothered me, it can creep up behind you and smack you right across the back of your head; this experience has happened to me on more than one occasion. The first time I experienced this sensation, was the evening we were sat on the fire engine ready to start the nightshift, contemplating life and generally discussing topics of the day, when one of the young firefighters in the back put his head through and asked the Officer in Charge (OIC):

"If we get turned out this evening, would it be ok to call in at the local car dealership as my wife is attending the launch of a new car model?"

"If we are passing it may be a possibility," the OIC answered.

As luck would have it, we attended a skip fire not far from the Dealership and as we were making up the hose and equipment the OIC turned to me and said,

"Go back to station via the Dealership as the young lad wants to see his wife."

As we approached the showroom, two ladies were stood on the pavement, waving at us, one was recognisable as the young firefighter's wife and the other was a very attractive, smartly dressed female companion. As I parked the fire engine at the kerbside, the two ladies approached the wagon, one proceeded to the rear of the cab to talk to her husband which left the other stood right outside my window. We started chatting which was very pleasant with such a sophisticated and distinguished lady, we both found the short conversation easy, sincere and full of humour, while the two newlyweds were discussing newlywed issues. Me and my newfound friend were getting on just fine when the OIC said,

"Come on, Andy, we best return to station."

Reluctantly we said our goodbyes as I started the engine ready to pull out and return to base. As I steadily entered the traffic for our homeward journey I shouted into the back,

"Hey, mate, who was that lass with your missus, she was a bit of alright, wasn't she?"

And here's the punchline:

"Andy, that was my mother."

BANG!! That smack right across the back of my head, as I instantly realised, I am older than one of my colleague's parents which was quite unsettling, and not the best feeling in the world. The sense of bewilderment and realisation was overwhelming, as the phenomenon of aging had never seriously occurred to me until now. This epiphany was indeed a sobering wake-up call. To try and ease my obvious mood of despondency the young firefighter stated, "She did have me when she was 15," but somehow this fact did not have the uplifting or calming effect he intended.

Similar situations have occurred multiple times since. I encountered a former scout in the supermarket, and we discussed past experiences and memories of camping, climbing, and hiking with the other scouts. This individual was 13 or 14 when I was his leader, so when he mentioned he had just turned 50 the week before, BANG! that smack across the back of my head hit me again. Trying to understand age and age difference can be frustrating and perplexing, understanding it as a process which cannot be stopped, can take time to comprehend. One Sunday morning we were detailed to carry out a Hazardous Materials (Hazmat) scenario for that day's drill session. This involved two firefighters being dressed in breathing apparatus and large green chemical protection suits; while they were being dressed ready to deal with the supposed chemical spillage, the rest of the crews were setting up the washing off area, which consisted of taping and coning off dirty and clean areas, building a temporary dam with a salvage sheet, a run out hose reel with detergent and brushes ready to clean and decontaminate them both of any possible chemical they picked up during the drill scenario having completed their investigatory tasks. This session is designed to evaluate the crew's ability to execute the Brigade procedures for real Hazmat incidents. After the two firefighters in chemical protection suits finished their investigations and information gathering, they approached the dam to begin the decontamination process. To ensure this decontamination procedure is carried out systematically and thoroughly, there is a designated Decontamination Director which on this occasion was me, who displays large cue cards instructing the suited firefighters to wash off in a predetermined order. The director shows each card one by one, and after the instruction is completed, he drops the card to the ground before showing the next directive. As I was carrying out this procedure, I happened to mention, I must look like Bob Dylan in his music video for the track 'Subterranean Homesick Blues'; it was just a general observational statement referring to what I believed was a famous piece of music video which everybody must be aware of. This prompted a question which floored me rather than slapped me across the back of my neck, when the young firefighter standing next to me enquired,

"Who's Bob Dylan?"

"Who's Bob Dylan?" I repeated incredulously. "Who's Bob Dylan, are you serious?"

"Yes, I have never heard of him," came his response.

"You've never heard of Bob Dylan, the most genius, poetic, song writing superstar of the folk-rock genre in music history."

"No, I don't know who you're on about."

I thought he was taking the piss, but this was a classic example of the generation gap, I couldn't quite believe there were people on this planet who had never heard of Bob Dylan, but then again why would he? Throughout the young firefighter's 24 years of life, Bob Dylan would hardly if ever have featured, and similarly this firefighter would know of world famous Youtubers and Influencers who I would not be aware of. Consequently, there will be people reading this piece who are also wondering who is Bob Dylan?

Other evidence of the generation gap is when you suddenly realise you are the age you remember your parents being, or worse your grandparents. I am now well over 60 years old, and I remember writing a rhyming speech for my father's 60th birthday celebrations, I can also remember going swimming with Granny May (Mum's mother) when she was of an age like me now, perhaps younger. This thought is quite sobering as these people for many years seemed so much my senior, yet one day you wake up realising you've caught them up. Did their outlook on life mirror how I see it now, did they do daft things as I have done as a senior in society or were they always on that perfect pedestal I viewed them being on when I was so much younger? On my first day working for the Textile Department at Leeds University, my immediate boss Jack Jones' first words to me were,

"Eight years to do, then I'm off!" Doing the maths this made him 57, which is an age I have passed with interest. I was 17 when he said this, which made me feel very young as he appeared so old. When I was in my youth and parents or friends of parents celebrated their Silver Wedding Anniversaries, they always appeared to be very old, but I celebrated my silver wedding over ten years ago, so it makes you think how old do I appear to the youth of today? I mentioned these few examples to my father who responded by suggesting I should try living with the fact of having a son who's retired. I know I retired from the fire service at a young age, 53, but even so this is another example of how the ageing process is relentless, and how the feeling is not unique to me, others experience the same and maybe this is why the counting system of age can really affect some people's comprehension. It is often said 'Age is just a number' so perhaps we should look at it like this and just accept it. Possibly, this is the problem, a mentality issue. We are taught from being young it can be rude or offensive to ask people, particularly ladies, their age, why? Surely it is a fact to be proud of, not be ashamed or embarrassed by. When you do have the courage to enquire a lady's age the usual answer is the question, 'how old do you think I am?'. The dilemma with this question is, do you risk offending someone by guessing their age incorrectly or do you flatter them by suggesting they may be an obviously unrealistic younger age, making them feel good but missing the truth? You can't win, so perhaps the best policy is to never ask.

I have found from experience there can be some advantages with the ageing process, I do seem to gain some respect from most of the younger generation although I don't think my generation receives the same amount of respect we gave the generations above us. Could this be down to lack of discipline, upbringing, and suspicions, or just youngsters enjoying more freedoms, who knows? I first noticed this as I approached retirement from the fire service; in a discussion with the Chief Fire Officer, he asked me what changes I had noticed throughout my long service and experience. I explained I felt as a firefighter with all the firefighting knowledge, experience, knowhow and understanding I had obtained in my career, I never got the same amount of respect from the younger members in the service as I gave senior firefighters when I was a young novice, whether this is a society trend or it was a problem unique to me I'm not too sure, but it did become a noticeable tendency the nearer I got to retirement. Other advantages of age can involve financial gains, qualifying for free prescriptions just at a time when you need tablets most, bus passes, senior rail cards and subsidised tickets for concerts, football matches, the theatre and cinema all are welcomed consequences of ageing. All these features are positives, but it doesn't make you feel any better. Looking back 30 years, which was not that long ago, past holidays, history making events, friends and incidents are all vivid memories – the worrying opposite is when looking forward 30 years, realising your demise is not too far away.

So, in conclusion, age has never bothered me, but sometimes it can creep up and smack you across the back of your head. It is a counting process we can't stop, resisting it is futile, so don't waste time trying; alternatively, embrace age, accept it and use it to your advantage. Enjoy every minute of your experiences, don't worry about something you have no control over and celebrate each birthday as if it is your last as it could well be, no matter what stage of life you are at. The saying goes, 'Grow old gracefully' and why not? There isn't a soul on this planet who will not experience ageing if they do grow old, and there has never been anyone to my knowledge who has stayed young or lived forever, so why do people feel they can be the exception?

FOR THE LOVE OF BEER!

I had my first taste of beer at the age of 14 when I entered a pub and naively asked for a pint of beer, and to be fair I was very underwhelmed. I didn't like it and couldn't understand what all the adult craving was all about. Consequently, with a group of school friends we discovered cider which was sweet and easy to drink. In our mid-teens we held house parties, attended by no more than a dozen of us. We would arrive armed with two litre bottles of Woodpecker cider, cheap and easy to purchase from the local off-licence. Of course, according to the law of the land this was strictly illegal due to our age, but in the mid-seventies it seemed a blind eye was turned. Other ciders consumed were Old English, Bulmer's, and Strongbow. I can't remember an occasion at these get togethers where any of us got extremely drunk, but it must have happened with hangovers to be nursed the following morning.

On reaching 16-years-old I ended my time as a scout at Fourth Pudsey which didn't have its own Venture Scout Unit, so like others before me, I progressed into the Pudsey District Venture Scout Unit. Becoming a member of this Unit opened my eyes to the adult world. My first camping trip away with the ventures was to Beasley Camp Site, situated at the top end of the Ingleton Waterfall Walk. The itinerary involved arriving at the campsite on Friday afternoon, pitching our tents, then heading to the pub. Saturday hike to and climb Ingleborough then to the pub. Sunday we had to rise early, strike camp as we had an appointment to go shooting with the Army Youth Team at their firing range. The details, explanation and arrangements for this adventure really did appeal to me, and I eagerly looked forward to it for many weeks. All kitted out with tent, walking equipment and provisions in my rucksack, I was put in a car and transported to the campsite. It was obvious to me the priority was to get to the Craven Heifer Public House in Ingleton as soon as we possibly could. On arrival at the pub the venture scout leader approached me and said,

"I'm very sorry, Andy, but because you are only sixteen, I cannot allow you to drink alcohol as it's against the law."

"That's OK, I will just have soft drinks," I said, fully understanding his reasoning.

One of the other members of the unit heard this conversation and interjected, "If he's going to drink pop, they serve cider here, surely it's OK for him to drink that?"

"Yes, I drink Woodpecker cider at schoolfriends' parties," I said following the lead.

The leader relented and agreed to let me partake in drinking at the same rate as my peers, after all it's only pop! In the 1970s cider was generally considered to be an apple juice with a slight kick, by no means was it thought of as an alcoholic drink. Factually, Woodpecker Cider has an ABV of 3.5%, which is very similar to the beer I was not allowed to drink. It was forbidden for me to drink when in reality I was drinking. The night progressed, playing pool and drinking apple juice with a kick, I loved it, the banter, the laughter and camaraderie as a 16-year-old among adults was very gratifying. Of course, the major negative with this environment was the fact that for the first time in my life I got extremely drunk, paralytic in fact. Never had I consumed so much alcohol in one night, but it was only apple juice. My body and its systems had never experienced anything remotely like this sensation which could make you fall over involuntarily. Unbeknown to me the very worst was yet to come. I haven't a clue how I got back to my tent, but somehow, I managed it and instantly hit the world of slumber fully clothed.

After a night of broken sleep, I was woken up by the sound of hens clucking. My head was thumping and my stomach churning like a washing machine on slow cycle. The incessant noise of clucking and cooing was going straight through my brain with zig zagged vibrations. At a very slow, sluggish pace I managed to move and unzipped my tent to be confronted by a flock of hundreds of hens pecking the ground and being responsible for this continuous din, jangling every sinew in my body. As I stuck my head out into the cold morning air to investigate, I was pecked on the nose by an inquisitive fowl wondering what this most unusual sight invading its space was. Then I realised how I was feeling, the peck woke me up to this foggy headache, fuzziness, a sensitivity to the morning light, nausea and lethargy, oh I did feel rough. Eventually as I exited my tent to meet the others this awful feeling didn't seem to bother anyone else. We went into the village to find a breakfast, I was told not to worry, a good feeding would make me feel better. Oh no it didn't! Watching my new mates tucking into a full English greasy breakfast made the nausea unbearable. I managed a coffee and then got back to the tent where all I wanted to do was lie down and die. Yes, like everybody else who was young and has suffered this physical endurance, I did utter the words "Oh I'll never drink again!" that day was a write off. I never did climb the second highest peak in Yorkshire and refrained from attending the pub that evening. Will this awful feeling ever go away? I rose on Sunday morning for the trip to the shooting range which I was immensely looking forward to, but still I had a fuzzy, foggy head. A hangover for nearly two days was not nice, but it was an experience. The next time cider touched my lips again was some 30 years later, the day Alfie was born.

After a few days the hangover from hell was soon forgotten. As I progressed with age the White Cross public house in Pudsey became my second home along with my group of closest friends. Tetley Bitter was the brew to drink, I did like this amber coloured liquid, but it was not the bee's knees. I was still searching for an ale that I would enjoy more than anything. That moment was not long in coming. When I dislocated my shoulder playing rugby, I was off work for a few weeks. I had an older friend who was a travelling salesman, and he suggested that while I was convalescing why not join him on a couple of his rounds in Lancashire and call somewhere for a pie and a pint at dinner time. This would get me out of the house and keep him company between appointments. We spent the morning calling into two or three of his customers, he dealt with business while I sat in the car listening to the radio, as dinner time approached. We stopped at a pub he knew of for lunch, he ordered his drink, a pint of Tetley's Dark Mild. Without thinking when he asked what I would like I just said, "I'll have the same please." This was a strange comment because I hadn't a clue what I'd ordered. Wow!! How glad was I I'd followed his lead. I took one large gulp of this new to me alcoholic beverage and it was like nectar from the gods, a lightning bolt moment. I couldn't believe it, there was a beer I could enjoy, it was delicious. It was like an epiphany; a realisation that led to all I ever drank in the White Cross and other Tetley establishments. Tetley hand pulled Dark Mild was my all-time favourite alcoholic drink; unfortunately it is very rare now, if you can get it at all.

Throughout this period in my life, I expanded my geographical horizons, camping, hiking or just holidaying in different locations around the country. I discovered the local brews of each alien area tasted 'shite' and with Tetley's Dark Mild becoming rarer and harder to access, I changed my drinking habit. I discovered Guinness to be an enjoyable, palatable drink and quite consistent throughout the land, don't get me wrong there is good and bad Guinness depending on how well it's kept, looked after and served, but generally it was quite uniform. So, unless dark mild was available, my drink of choice became Guinness.

I drank Guinness for over 25 years until the day I was sat in the Masons Arms in Cowbridge, Wales, chatting and sharing a pint with my cousin Peter. I was explaining the fact that other than the odd brew I found most beers around the country are shite.

Then came the realisation, an opening up of my perspective when Peter said, "I hear what you say but I look at it in a slightly different way. Rather than thinking alternative beers are shite, I consider them to be different. As much as I enjoy a pint of Tetley's, because Yorkshire is where I hale from, if I'd been born and brought up in South Wales, Cornwall, Kent, or Cumbria, the local brew would most likely be my beer of choice. Which consequently triggers the question, is there such a thing as a 'shite beer'? They are all different which are not necessarily compatible to our taste."

These were some of the wisest words I think I'd heard in years, 'not shite, different' which changed my whole philosophy and outlook. The whole point of beer festivals suddenly had an understanding, they were not arranged so punters could drink as much as possible, but for punters to taste different beers from around the country, sometimes continents, and form an opinion of their likes and dislikes, hence often you receive a half glass pint glass on entry.

A firefighter colleague approached me one day and said, "Andy, next Friday it's the Bradford Beer Festival at the Queens Hall and a lot of the watch are thinking of going straight from work, are you in?"

"Yes!" I responded. I thought this would be a great opportunity to test out the new philosophy discovered in Cowbridge a few months earlier. Friday came and about a dozen of us left work and meandered across town to the Queens Hall. We paid a fiver admission, received the commemorative half pint glass, a programme listing all the beers on offer with descriptions, and the card which covered the five pound to pay for different drinks. This was my first experience of a beer festival, and I loved it. Barrel after barrel behind a counter with far too much choice. So how do I choose? Programme notes, type of beer, alcohol by volume (ABV) and name all guidance and evidence of which to choose. With 'different not shite' ringing through my head,

I chose a dark beer, which was certainly different but also enjoyable. This was where I discovered I prefer darker beers to lighter hoppy ones.

As I was partaking in my fourth half pint, one of my work colleagues approached me and said, "Come on, Andy, we're off to The Bod for karaoke and proper beer, it's all shite here!"

"No, it isn't, it's different and the whole idea is to find one or several you like," I answered, my argument falling on stony ground.

"Rubbish! Karaoke and lager it is for us!" he responded.

"Lager?" I questioned. "Pop for grown up boys?" Of course this was only my opinion, but it still had no effect and off they went with minds made up. Only two stayed, stating they thought my logic was quite good and we had a marvellous evening trying different types of ale.

All this contributed to my newfound love of real ales, and micro-breweries and micro pubs started to spring up all over the place. These establishments allow the customer to taste any of the brews the publican has on offer before purchasing a pint. My personal choice is for dark beers, dark milds, stouts and porters, but I do enjoy pale ales, IPAs and ruby beers as long as they aren't too hoppy in taste. I prefer a malty beer rather than one which has a potent hop taste. Since Tetley's hand pulled dark mild has disappeared from general sales, my favourite beer now is Timothy Taylor's dark mild. If they sell beer in heaven this would be the beer I'd drink. Timothy Taylor's brews are all very good in my opinion, the brewery does not produce a bad beer.

So, in conclusion, is there such a thing as a bad beer? In my judgement the answer is a simple no! There may be beers out there that individuals don't like, but that does not mean it's substandard or poor. If beer in the barrel is not kept and looked after properly, this can constitute into an unpleasant pint, not necessarily making it a bad beer. As mentioned, I am not a fan of lager, it's too gassy and blows me up; having said that I do drink it abroad. On 18th August 2013, on the suggestion of a work colleague of Julie, I joined the app, Untappd. This tool allows you to log and score all new beers tasted and drunk and share your opinion with friends. As I write this the app tells me I have tasted 1,391 different beers from all over the world and out of a top score of five my average score reads at 4.06, with very few scoring lees than 3.5, suggesting that in my own personal research there is no such thing as a shite beer, they are all simply different!

HORNBLOWERS

We had a new recruit join us on Red Watch at Bradford Fire Station. He was a young university graduate who had decided a career in the Fire Service was his chosen path in life, following in his father's footsteps who was an officer in a neighbouring brigade. He was a very intelligent young man and through his probation period on the watch it quickly became obvious he would go far. Unfortunately for him, some of the tricks and pranks played on young recruits were so designed they could play on the most intellectual of minds. He joined the shift on the tour between Christmas and New Year but we had bumped into him in town when our shift were on their pre-Christmas drinks and he was out with his fellow recruits on their training school leaving drink before they all joined their new fire stations. He came over as a very pleasant young man.

Back at work on the tour before Christmas, we were discussing what wind ups we could design to throw the new recruit into the realms of confusion. It quite quickly became obvious it was going to be harder than originally thought. All ideas thrown into the mix were pulled apart because of floors identified in each plan. The only pretence agreed on was that one of the older members of the shift would play the alcoholic as he had done in the past with previous recruits.

This wheeze involved the member of the shift walking round with a whisky glass containing a measure of cold tea which resembled whisky, whenever he was in the company of the recruit. This would be accompanied with comments in the order of 'don't tell anyone, son' or 'just having a quick snifter' and 'keep it to yourself' as he tapped his nose with his finger. Another piece of evidence to keep this charade going was when the older fireman opened his locker as the recruit was passing several empty beer bottles would fall out and rattle across the floor. He would then exclaim "Ah! I was meant to get rid of them, bugger!" then he'd turn to the recruit saying, "don't tell anyone, kid, our secret", with a nod, a wink and another tapping of the nose. Unlike the old days, pre-1987, alcohol was strictly forbidden on a fire station, so these efforts put the recruit in a very awkward position. Should he report it and experience the wrath of a senior fireman or should he do as asked and 'not tell anyone, kid' – oh the dilemma! Apparently, this deception was maintained for a good few months until the recruit was well established as a watch member.

Every piece of fire brigade equipment has what is called a standard test. This is where each piece of kit is tested either daily, weekly, monthly, quarterly, six monthly or annually dependent on what it is, how often it's used and how important it is. This includes everything from fire engines and ladders to BA sets and first aid kit. All equipment is also standard tested after it has been used. On fire engines we carry a pair of railway warning horns, these are for use at incidents on railway lines. Two lookouts would be sent up and down the line, and when a train is approaching they would blow on the horns with all their might to warn crews, who then clear the lines until the danger has passed. In these

THE WORLD ACCORDING TO ANDY CARTER

modern times for health and safety reasons trains would be stopped, eliminating any potential risk to firefighting teams. In 27 and a half years' service I only had to use these horns once. I was on Blue watch in my early days, and we were using the 'divisional spare' fire engine as our usual pump was away in the workshops being repaired and maintained. Unfortunately, the two-tone horn on this reserve fire engine had one of its tones missing, so instead of sounding nee nah, nee nah it would only produce nee... nee... nee. This was very embarrassing attending fire calls with only a nee and no nah. So, in his wisdom my sub officer asked me to stick my head out of the rear window and fill in the missing nahs with the railway warning horn, which I did. It sounded ridiculous nee pherr, nee pherr, nee pherr. It just didn't fit, and it was physically tiring. This exercise didn't last long, and the horn was soon put away, never in my career to be used again.

The tour after the New Year celebrations just happened to start on a Saturday. We had done the daily checks and were all sat in the mess room discussing the few annual and six-monthly standard tests to be carried out that day. The new recruit was downstairs in the engine house being instructed by one of the leading firemen on different pieces of equipment. It then came up in conversation that we hadn't performed a wind up for the new recruit. Well, it suddenly seemed obvious to me.

"Why don't we tell him that on the first Saturday of the year we have to do an annual standard test on the railway warning horns?" I said.

"But there isn't a standard test for the railway warning horns, we just blow them now and again on the daily checks to make sure they work," was the reply.

"I know that, you know that, but does he know that?" was my riposte. My mind was working overtime, how could we make this work? Between the fire station main front door and the major road junction of Nelson Street and Croft Street were three minor road junctions where Caledonia Street, then 75 yards further on comes Duncan Street, then 75 yards or so Adelaide Street before landing at Croft Street. Why don't we stand at the main door with a fire ground radio, send the recruit to the junction of each of the four streets, instruct him to blow the four horns, two from each fire engine, then we report to him by radio whether we've heard them or not and if so move on to the next junction and repeat the task. If we hear the horns at all four junctions, they will have passed the standard test. Brilliant!! What a great idea, let's go carry it out. So we drank up our tea and left the mess room giggling like excited schoolgirls with the prospect of getting a laugh at the expense of this unaware recruit.

We found the recruit and explained what he needed to do which he accepted with a very unsure and unconvinced manner. He'd never heard of a standard test for railway warning horns and was not sure we were being serious. Outside the weather was awful, it was raining with monsoon-like venom. No wind just heavy vertical rain, it was as is proverbially described as stair rodding. The recruit asked if we were just doing this to make him get wet? Oh no, no, no, was the answer, but this did bring up a problem of how to convince him to carry out the task. Sometimes to ensure a practical joke works there comes a point where you must sacrifice yourself so the intended punchline can be achieved. Never being one to shy away from getting wet and being told throughout my career 'if you don't like getting wet you shouldn't have joined', so for the sake of a joke I said I'd go with him. This, the recruit admitted later, was the clincher. If another fireman was going to get wet too, it must be procedure.

We both dressed in full fire kit, yellow helmet, tunic, boots and wet legs (over trousers). Acquiring the four horns and a fireground radio off we went out into the biblical rain on our way to Caledonia Street. On arrival I informed the watch by radio the horns were about to be blown, and the recruit proceeded to sound the horns one at a time. When all four had been deployed our colleagues at the station confirmed they had heard them all so the recruit and I walked at a brisk pace to Duncan Street to repeat the procedure. By now we were soaked, rainwater dripping off our helmets, tunics absorbing copious amounts of water and our boots successfully keeping our feet dry from the gallons of standing and running water. We felt like and possibly looked like a pair of drowned rats. After completing the test at Adelaide Street, I instructed the recruit to march onto the major junction where Nelson Street met Croft Street and complete the procedure as I was getting too wet and was returning to station. He proceeded to Croft Street where he blew the horns for a fourth time. As I was returning, I heard the horns without looking back and a broad grin crossed my face. I looked up at the station to see firemen leaning out of the second-floor windows applauding and guffawing that such a simple wind up had succeeded, even if it did mean I got soaked.

This though was not the conclusion, we rang brigade control on the direct line, this was a red phone straight to control, affectionately referred to as the bat phone. We explained the charade being carried out on the station and asked them if they could ring back in about 15 minutes to inform the station, they had received a call from a member of the public reporting a sighting of some lunatic dressed as a fireman blowing some sort of bugle, making a right racket in the pouring rain. The control staff, always eager participants in any station wind up, duly complied, so as the recruit returned to station drenched, the bat phone and the final touches of the plot was enacted. At this point an Irish member of the shift exclaimed in his strong Irish brogue,

"I tink he's had enough now!" but the wind up was already complete. The recruit took it all in good humour and still refers to it as a fond memory. He deservedly went far as he now is a high-ranking senior officer, proving we all start at the bottom.

THE SPEECH WHICH NEVER WAS DELIVERED

The year 2015 was a year of celebration, I retired from the West Yorkshire Fire and Rescue Service on May 31st after 27 and a half years' service, so we had a party to celebrate the end of my firefighting career. It was a good party, but the better party was held at Woodhall Hills Golf Club in Calverley, Leeds to celebrate our Silver Wedding Anniversary. We had sent out invitations, booked the venue, organised the catering and the DJ and were really looking forward to an evening of celebration. It was a great party, the food was a hog roast and the DJ played all our favourite disco music from the 70s and 80s. This was solely to get our guests up on the dance floor and dance the night away, which they did.

As we were leaving our house to attend the party by taxi, Julie turned to me and said, "Don't be doing a speech tonight!"

"Why?" I asked.

"I don't think it's necessary," she answered.

At this point I didn't have the courage to admit I had already written one. We arrived at the Golf Club and bought a couple of drinks at the bar. The room was decorated with silver balloons, silver wedding banners and silver streamers thanks to Julie's efforts earlier in the day. It did look good! The evening started as most parties do. We welcomed guests as they arrived, thanked them for coming, gratefully accepted any cards and presents handed to us and guided them towards the bar.

After we had welcomed our invited guests and they were mingling and finding seats, it was time to announce that the food was being served. This was my chance! I had arranged with the bar staff and assisted by the DJ to have an unused empty beer crate hiding behind the decks. I retrieved the crate, placed it on the dance floor, took the mic and announced I had a few words to say. I called up Julie, Olivia and Alfie to join me. Because I was stood on a crate, I was for the first time in our relationship taller than Julie. I made a couple of jokes about how I could see the crown of her head for the first time and how precarious it must be walking about at this height. With Julie's words about not giving a speech ringing through my mind, I delivered the following words with a mild apprehension.

Ladies and Gentlemen, can I have your attention please? I would just like to say a few words.

About 27 years ago I asked my best friend to marry me... he said no, so I asked Julie.

We were married 25 ago; it was the best day of my life which doesn't go down too well with Olivia. To be fair we have had a blast and enjoyed every minute of marriage.

When you tell people you have been married for 25 years there is always someone who says, "If you had committed murder on that day, you would be out by now!"

THE WORLD ACCORDING TO ANDY CARTER

Well I'm really glad I didn't murder anyone cos the last 30 years, 25 of which married, have been fantastic.

In a quote from one of Julie's favourite films 'Rita, Sue and Bob Too'

'We have done some things'.

For anyone of you who are lucky enough to remember my speech at the wedding you may recall I threw out a till roll with a list of thank-yous on it. Well, tonight is list part two, 25 years after the first. Take note, newlyweds!

Married 9136 days which means

9136 nights as well

This equals 219,264 hours

Due to work shifts we have spent approximately 4568 nights apart, which means we have had approximately 4568 days together.

So technically you are here under false pretences as we have only in real terms been together 12 and a half years – not 25.

We have had:
- 2 Children
- 2 Houses
- 1 Garage
- 0 Fall outs
- 1 Retirement
- 12 Cars
- Been on over 30 Holidays
- Sex, more than twice but less than 9136 times
- 3 Knee operations

- 1 Vasectomy
- Seen the dentist over 60 times
- And eaten out more times than is possibly good for you
- Countries visited include Australia, Finland, Fuerteventura, Ireland, Lanzarote, Malaysia and Spain.
- And all that helps with being married for this long.

> *I would like to thank you all for coming and helping us celebrate our Silver Wedding. All of you mean a great deal to Julie and me.*
>
> *Thanks go to Mike Tempest-Mitchell for helping arrange things with the golf club.*
> *Thanks to Woodhall Hills for the use of their facilities.*
> *Thanks to Yorkshire Hog Roast for cooking the pig.*
> *Thanks to Daniel the DJ for supplying the music.*
> *But most of all thank you to Julie for being my wife. I have loved every minute.*
> *Love you! xx then I kissed her.*

That was that, or so we thought. Alfie then surprised everyone, he looked up at me on the crate and spoke:

"Can I say something?"

This came totally out of the blue. Normally a shy eight-year-old, wanting to stand on a crate, with a microphone and address a couple of hundred people? Wow! You could have knocked me down with a feather. He was only stood on the crate for a few minutes and because of the spontaneity of events we have no recording of Alfie's words. From memory he mentioned how grateful he was that Mum and Dad taught him to follow his dreams, tell him he can achieve anything in this life if he works hard and he loves us very much. Well as you can appreciate, he stole the show, he got a standing ovation with cheers and whoops. Meanwhile Julie and I stood there gobsmacked, bursting with pride and an odd tear shed. I pulled myself together and announced the food was served.

As guests were migrating to the food area outside, Mick, who was my best man at the wedding, strode over to me with some purpose. He was holding out a few sheets of A4 paper stating, "Here, you may as well have this because after yours and Alfie's performance this needs to be binned!"

I was shocked: he had written a speech which Julie and I had no knowledge of. When he had witnessed mine but especially Alfie's attempt, he had suddenly lost all confidence, got stage fright, anxiety and possibly a cold sweat about delivering the speech he had written. We tried to persuade him to read it out, but he was adamant he wouldn't. We were both disappointed he would not perform it but possibly the time had passed. It was a great party with all our guests dancing and drinking well into the late hours. After the party, on arrival at home we read what Mick had written down. To read another person's impression of us was very humbling. Oh, how we did wish he had done it. So here it is the speech which was never delivered.

Good evening, ladies and gentlemen. On behalf of the bride and groom I would like to welcome you here tonight to celebrate their 25th Wedding Anniversary. For those who weren't at the wedding, I was the best man.

Well – 25 years!

There are many jokes that can and have been told as you are aware! But we all know that for these two none of it has been sentence-like!

THE WORLD ACCORDING TO ANDY CARTER

Sorry to bore you at this time but for those of you who don't know, I have known Andy since he was eight years old and yes Julie wasn't even born then!!

Growing up living next door to him was interesting! We became good friends with a shared interest in Rick Wakeman, beer and girls. As we got older, we started cubs then proceeded through scouts into venture scouts.

One day I was approached by the local guide troop who had a couple of girls who needed to complete their service badge, and could they come and help?

The first week Michelle and Julie turned up and changed Andy's life! After that there was lots of weekends away with the kids (in inverted commas)! and scout meetings held in the scout hut on a Friday night with Chinese takeaway.

One Sunday after arriving back from cub camp where Andy had been Chief Catering Officer he turned to Julie and proclaimed as he got out of the car:

"One day, young lady, I am going to marry you!"

Well, ladies and gentlemen ... he did!
And here we are 25 years later.
On paper back then a stranger couple you couldn't find:
Julie,
Young, good looking, a whole life to look forward to modelling, jet setting around the world etc
Andy,
Well? Enough said really, at least he had hair then!!
In reality: two people totally in love with each other from top to bottom. In fact, I would probably suggest he could love Julie even more than Bradford City.

Between them they have managed to achieve so much. Their holidays are legendary, not only to Australia which they both love but to Lanzarote. We went their for a week as a four and it seems it was on that holiday Olivia was conceived. Fortunately, I don't think I was there when Alfie was conceived… phew! Two great kids who do their parents proud. Having said that, Olivia has just turned 14 so that could all change between now and when she is 16.

Finally: their friendship and love.

Given their working relationship over the last 27 years many marriages would have been tested, but for Julie only seeing Andy a couple of days a week seems to have worked. Andy refers to Julie as his best mate as well as his wife and mother of his children. All in all, a formula which has worked!

Ladies and Gentlemen: 25 years of marriage under any circumstances is an achievement, 25 years of marriage when you only see each other a couple of days a week deserves a medal, but 25 years of marriage to Andy deserves a sainthood!

With that, ladies and gentlemen, can I ask you to stand and raise your glasses in a toast to the bride and groom.

The Toast:

Andy and St Julie of Carter.

That was that the speech which never was delivered, due to embarrassment, stage fright and Alfie's few words which stole the show. We both wish Mick had found something within to make the speech and perhaps if we'd seen the contents earlier, we would have persuaded him. It never happened and perhaps was meant to be that way. I like to think it was a chance missed.

Speech? What speech?

DRUG SMUGGLER...ME?

Every passenger on every flight into Australia is handed an Incoming Passenger Card (IPC) which informs the authorities who you are and is an effective legal record of a person's entry into the country. On this card is a list of items you should declare on your arrival. These include medication, illegal pornography – why anyone would declare something that is already illegal is beyond fathom – weapons, over two and a half litres of alcohol, currency exceeding $10000, animal products, seeds, grains, wood items and any footwear or attire which may contain soil from an alien nation. You must also declare if you have been around freshwater, farms or farm animals in the previous 30 days before arrival. The list is more extensive than this, its purpose is to allow the Australians to protect their land from unwanted micro-organisms which may get into the food chain or crops. On the plane videos are shown on the importance of completing the IPC and stresses if you are in doubt, you should declare what you have rather than not declare and face a hefty fine or expulsion.

That is what I did: I declared my daily medication which consisted of five tablets a day for a month's visit and two wooden plaques which were intended Christmas presents. We landed at Perth airport and disembarked with passport and IPC in hand and commenced the long walk/ mini hike to passport control. This was completed pleasantly quickly as we were among the first off the plane and it was all done digitally. Then down a flight of stairs into the baggage reclamation hall. As we left the stairs, we were met by two security guards adorned in high visibility vests asking if we had declared anything on the IPC.

"Yes," I said, "I have two wooden plaques which are Christmas presents, and my medication for a month."

"How big are the wooden plaques?" he enquired.

"About six inches by nine inches," I answered, thinking he may want to see them.

"Did you buy them, or have you made them yourself?"

"I bought them in a Christmas market in Leeds, England, and they are still sealed in cellophane."

At this point he nodded, stamped the IPC and allowed me to continue towards the carousel to collect my case. That I thought was that... oh, no! It was half past one in the morning, at the end of an extremely long period of travel, about 30 hours, and all I wanted to do was get my case, meet my sister and get to her house as quickly as possible.

This unbeknown to me was where the fun started. After waiting 15 minutes for my case to appear on the carousel I lifted it off and headed for the exit. Before we could leave the airport we had to navigate Border Control. This process seemed to be more official as the officers were dressed in proper smart uniforms, not a high visibility jacket in sight. Olivia and I lined up in the queue of about ten people as we patiently waited for the guard to check our stamped IPC. As we arrived at the front, I was guided toward a female officer who took a quick glance at my card and said, "Please go this way," and ushered me in a direction completely opposite to all the other passengers, including Olivia. I was eventually met by a tall, menacing-appearing guard who held my IPC in his hand and said,

"You have declared medication?"

"Yes," I concurred.

Now in all my visits to Australia I have always declared medication and the only time it has been questioned was when a guard asked if it was for personal use, which I confirmed, and that was good enough. Never in my previous visits was this a problem. In fact, when the female guard sent me to the other tall guard, whose name according to his ID badge was Ali, I presumed he wanted to check the two pieces of wood. Oh no, now for the most bizarre question, Ali asked,

"Do you have a prescription for it?"

"Er no!" I answered with a tone of voice which may have implied his lack of knowledge. "In England, the doctor writes you a prescription, which you take to the pharmacist who then dispenses your tablets and keeps the prescription." Funnily enough the same happens in Australia so I found out later, due to local knowledge.

On hearing my answer Ali then asked, "Well do you have them in a box with your name and address on it?"

"No, I removed the boxes as part of the space saving within my suitcase."

All this time Ali stood at the other side of the counter with an expression stating 'don't mess with me, boy, and certainly don't try any ice breaking jokes', the whole situation was very intimidating, his manner and behaviour made me feel quite nervous and anxious. Have I done something wrong without knowing it? Am I going to be fined or worse arrested for something I was oblivious of, after all Olivia had ticked the same box on her IPC and sailed through, why was I being made an example of? All questions I was asking myself, not helped by this daunting Border Control Guard, Ali. Am I to be considered a drug smuggler or even a baron? Questions I didn't have answers to.

Ali then said, "Lift your case on to the counter and we better have a look."

"Yes, Sir!" I said trying my best not to annoy him any further. Up my case went on to the counter as instructed, I opened it and we both gazed into it. I knew exactly where my tablets were as I had put them all in a centre pouch of the case, so I leaned across and opened the zip, extracted a few of the tablet sheets.

"This one is metformin, I take that twice a day, this one is empagliflozin, I take in the morning, and this one..." as I held up the third sheet...

"I can't remember its name, but I also take this in the morning, and this one is a statin which I take in the evening."

I handed the sheets to Ali, and he examined them very closely. As if underlining a point, he stated in a slightly condescending manner, "You should have a prescription for these... stay there!"

I did as I was told and watched him walk to a counter in front of an office where he was discussing my tablets with an obviously more senior, elderly female colleague.

After what seemed an age but was more like two or three minutes, he turned and started to stroll slowly back towards me. In this time my imagination and wild thoughts were churning and buzzing within my mind: Me, a drug smuggler, that will be something to tell them in the White Bear on my return. As Ali arrived back to join me, he was still pondering through the sheets of tablets. I said in a nervy, timid voice,

"You are starting to worry me now."

"Worry you!" he queried.

"You've been watching too many 'Nothing to Declare' programmes." The only slight piece of humour exercised throughout the whole encounter.

"There is no need to worry, you just need a prescription." Well, that isn't going to happen cos I ain't got one, you idiot, I thought to myself. There was a pause which I suspect was more for effect then he came out with the most bizarre statement of them all, he said,

"I am not going to confiscate them from you this time as I can see you are only here for a month and that you are carrying about a month's supply, but next time you should carry a prescription or at least a box with your name on it, thank you for your time, off you go." Without further ado I placed the sheets of tablets back in my case, closed it and continued out of the Customs Hall, to meet with Elaine, Jan and Olivia who had been instructed or ordered to leave the room, were waiting for me… Phew!!

In conclusion, I have thought about this incident more than once and I can't find any reason for the Border Force to stop me. Everybody suggests in jest that I must look a bit shifty or dodgy, but that doesn't explain the truth, it's just a light-hearted assumption. Why did the Border Force stop me, when Olivia had ticked the same box on the IPC? Judging by the average age of the passengers on the flight, there must have been dozens carrying medication. My father takes all his drugs and tablets, a hell of a lot more than me, in a tupperware box and has never been stopped. So why did Ali make such a fuss about a prescription? The most alarming part for me through the whole episode was when he stated, 'I won't be confiscating them this time!' now I wasn't too sure of his pharmaceutical expertise but why would he threaten to confiscate medical drugs? For all he knew these tablets could quite easily be life preserving which needed to be taken daily, yet he suggested he had the power to withdraw them from you, baffling. Ali told me not to worry, but I did, I walked out of the customs hall quite sheepishly felling like I'd been accused of attempted drug smuggling, but why did they stop me? What was their reason, and what was their need to check? Alas I will never know!

A Drug Smuggler?... Not Me!

GOLF

I have a love-hate relationship with this crazy game. I find it a game which is great when you play well but very frustrating when you don't. Confidence is the key for me, standing on a tee with friends or other golfers watching you is chest expanding when the ball flies from your club to an area of the fairway you are happy with. Alternatively, when the ball bobbles off the tee peg, gets twenty yards off the tee in any direction or is launched too far left or right, the emotion is one of embarrassment, anger and deflation. You will receive some very nice comments of encouragement and sympathy, but you know behind your back, or under the breath onlookers are in stiches of laughter, merriment and delight in your failure. When you have completed a round of 18 holes all the bad shots are forgotten, but the two or three great shots, even good bad shots are remembered and are the reason you return for further punishment. The strive to do more great shots is intoxicating. A great shot in every round is inevitable when a 200-yard drive is worth exactly the same score as a two-inch putt. Hitting a straight, not necessarily long drive, chip to within a few feet of the hole or sinking a long putt, the goal is to return to the course and try and repeat the good shots on a more consistent basis.

THE WORLD ACCORDING TO ANDY CARTER

My golfing journey started in the late 1970s. I was a venture Scout at the time and was endeavouring to complete my Queen's Scout Award. As part of the award, I had to take up a new sport and show a significant improvement over a 12-month period. Consequently, I picked golf. I purchased a cheap set of clubs with a carry bag and started to play with two friends at the municipal (open to the public) course at Gotts Park in Leeds. The first round I ever played my card was marked at 145 shots. On the same weekend 12 months later I played a round, and my card was marked at 96 shots – a significant improvement I would say. This resulted in that part of my Queen's Scout Award being passed.

I would play each Saturday with my friend Martin and his brother-in-law. To beat the crowds, we would be stood on the first tee at dawn. In summer this could be as early as four o'clock in the morning. There was always the same fourball there every week with the same idea. We would play a round then pay when we'd finished around eight o'clock. We would chip in a pound each with the winner taking all. I never won the pot and Martin rarely won, so it was like taking sweets off a kid for the more senior brother-in-law, I might as well have thrown my pound down the drain. As stated before, the good shots, few and far between as they were, ensured we repeated the same process the following Saturday. The only slight negative to this weekly arrangement was when we were socialising at nine o'clock that Saturday evening it felt like it was two o'clock the following morning because we had been awake for so long.

This is how I played for a long time at Gotts Park pay and play, but as I lost touch with Martin the regularity dwindled. Occasionally I would have a round with a fellow scout leader friend, but never did I play on a regular basis. Golf is a game that requires practice and regular play, the more you swing a club the better or more consistent you get. Consequently, my lack of play meant my game suffered, never getting better, just slightly worse. I always had a set of clubs in the back of the garage so if the call came, I could pull them out and go play. The time difference between rounds got wider and wider until eventually when I played, I'd developed a twist in my grip and swing. Metal woods had entered the market and because of this twist the impact on the ball would dent the top of the club head. I therefore stuck to wooden woods which camouflaged this habit, that is I couldn't dent a solid wooden club head. I was once invited to the driving range with my good friend Mike Tempest-Mitchell. Now this guy loved golf, the only thing he loved more was his family and I'm sure that was debatable. Any chance of a round of golf and he was there. Religiously every Saturday he would grace the first tee and any other day of the week he could fit in. Off we went to the driving range, Mike to practise, me to kill an hour of time with a mate. By this time the twist in my swing hurt my hands and I wore holes in leather golf gloves, golf became a chore and not an enjoyment. Mike stood in his bay watching me try and hit a golf ball. He then asked if he could examine my relic wooden clubs. On inspection he insisted the clubs had a slight bend in them, no wonder I couldn't hit the ball. I couldn't see the bend myself but kept quiet and accepted his assessment. Then he made one of the biggest mistakes of his whole golfing career. He handed me his big metal driver and said,

"Hit this one, you need to use a proper club."

"No," I replied, "jif I use your pristine, magnificent driver, I will put a dent in it here," as I pointed to the crown of the club.

"Don't be daft, you need a decent club, here have a go!"

"No!" I repeated, "I'll damage it!"

He wouldn't accept my argument and insisted, "You can't damage this club, it's built like a tank."

I refused his suggestion several times more, and each time he insisted it would be alright. Now for my mistake, I accepted the challenge, more to shut him up than anything else, praying inside his club would survive its pending ordeal. I set the ball on the tee peg, held the club, which I could tell was quality, and swung as hard as I dare. To be fair the ball went some distance and as Mike followed it in his sight line he said,

"See, that went far, I told you, you just needed a proper club."

As he was looking down the range I was looking at the club head and remarked, "See, I told you I'd put a dent in the club." And sure enough I has damaged this beast of a top of the range metal headed driver.

Mike was gutted, I was embarrassed.

"Was the club expensive?" I asked.

"Only £135," he said with a bemused, slightly angry resigned tone.

"Sorry," I sheepishly replied, but the damage was done, and sorry came nowhere near making it better.

The rest of the session had a solemn, quiet atmosphere around it. This incident has been mentioned a couple of times since, but it's largely been forgotten as the years have rolled by. Was it Mike's fault? He insisted I had a go. Or was it my fault? Accepting the challenge knowing what the outcome would likely be. It didn't affect Mike's thirst for the game as he went on to be captain of his club and still plays on a regular basis to this day. The damaged club has long since been discarded.

    As I have said, golf for me is a game built on confidence. The final nail in the coffin for my game was when I attended a golf day to Filey with Phoenix Park Rugby Club. Fifty of us went on a coach and had a day of golf. One round in the morning followed by lunch and another round in the afternoon, culminating in dinner and presentations. Of course, by now my game and confidence was rock bottom, the twist, the pain in my hands and the inability to hit the ball off the tee was as bad as ever, but I gave it a go. On the tee I was hoping to be the last out, so everyone had gone down the course, but no, there was more than half watching. The ball went nowhere, embarrassing, but off we went me and my three colleagues. I did enjoy the whole day very much. Luckily for me as bad as my driving and long game was, my short game, chipping and putting, were on fire. I think this stems from being on family holidays, as a young boy we always went putting or later pitch and putt which gave me a good foundation. In the afternoon we played a competition called a Texas Scramble, which brought my miniscule talent for chipping and putting to the fore. At the presentation dinner that evening our Texas Scramble Foursome won the competition, the only golf triumph in my whole life. The following Saturday we were playing rugby at our home ground and as I walked into the changing room, I heard a member of my team describing in minute detail with disbelief, disdain and ridicule 'Lofty's golf swing'. I was devastated, that small confidence and interest for the game evaporated in that single moment. To know and hear people laughing about you behind your back is morale sapping! I made the conscious decision that afternoon I would pack in golf for at least 20 years and then if I decide to play again, I will go for lessons before hitting another ball. The break from golf was nearer 30 years rather than the 20 suggested. I sold my clubs and bag and never thought about playing in all that time. Mike never tried to persuade me even though we attended many functions at the golf club, but then again why should he? He was quite aware of the damage I could do!

So why, I hear you ask, am I playing golf again after 30 years? The answer is quite simple: I went for lessons. Julie had decided she would like to play golf, encouraged by our friend Jill, who is a very keen golfer. Julie joined Woodhall Hills Golf Club and enjoyed her few rounds with Jill and other lady members. She even went on a golf club ladies' trip to Portugal and played a championship course, the first time she'd played a full 18 holes. Olivia and Alfie also got the bug and the three of them would go off to the driving range with sets of borrowed, given and made-up sets of clubs. Now the attraction of this was, how good would it be if all four of us could play golf every Sunday or school holiday as a family, what a good day out! I had found a half decent set of clubs and bag at a charity shop for a fiver for my use. One day the four of us set off to the driving range for an afternoon's entertainment. Although I'd had a 30-year break from this frustrating game, nothing had changed. I couldn't hit the ball, my hands hurt, and the £2 driver, another charity shop purchase, was getting destroyed with dents on the top. After ten or 20 balls of this purgatory I had lost interest. Do I go back to no golf or do what I said all those years ago and get some lessons? The latter was decided, so Alfie and I booked a course of five one-hour lessons to see what could be done. Within ten minutes of my first lesson the professional had got me hitting a ball straight, brilliant! On completion of the course of lessons, I had regained confidence to have a go at golf again.

On hearing this Mike was or seemed delighted and he didn't let go. "Come to Woodhall Hills," he would say. "We could play every week."

This became a bit of a dilemma as my friends who I go to The White Bear with most Sunday nights are all members of Baildon Golf Club, in fact at one point I would be sat with, Mr Last Year's Captain, Mr Captain, Mr Vice Captain, and Mr Forty Year Member, all who wanted me to join them. The decision became quite simple, Mike took me to Woodhall three or four times, the Baildon tribe didn't, Woodhall is situated on the way home from work, Baildon is eight miles beyond home, and less important, in my eyes Woodhall is the prettier course. I joined Woodhall on their cheapest membership and spent the whole summer playing golf with Mike. I loved it, I caught the bug. It was no less frustrating, but Mike was sympathetic and very patient with me, which was appreciated. I now have an official handicap which is reducing and gives the game more of a purpose. The good shots are becoming more frequent which is building that confidence, yet there are days when I could quite easily pack it all in. Mike's weekly golfing partner sadly passed away and his widow told Mike she didn't know what to do with his clubs. She didn't want to keep them, yet she didn't want to sell them, she just wanted them to go to somebody who might love them as much her husband did. Mike said to her, "I know just the man." So I now own a set of Ping golf clubs with bag and trolley and I love them, perhaps as much as he did.

People say, 'Golf is a good walk spoilt' whereas in my opinion 'Golf is a good walk with a purpose'. Golf is a great social sport, it keeps you fit, you meet up with the same friends every week and of course there is the 19th (the bar) where friends and competitors discuss, analyse, and dissect each shot of the round just completed. When you play golf well or hit the perfect shot, there is no greater feeling. Perhaps I should have had lessons rather than a 30-year break. Then again, I have worked in the Fire Service all that time, had a family to raise and watched my passion Bradford City on a Saturday, so I don't think I had the time. I have always said, when you and your partner work shifts and have a family, you can only afford one interest. Sorry, golf, my interest was Bradford City.

DREAM HOUSE

During the late seventies as a group of friends we had developed quite a regular weekly routine. At that time our choice of nightly hostelry was the now demolished White Cross in Pudsey. The pub was situated across the car park from the 1st Pudsey Scout group headquarters, where I was involved as an assistant cub leader and helped the scout leader Kevin when I could. All the friendship group would work during the week and end up attending scout meetings on a Friday night. After each scout meeting, we would all walk across the car park and into the pub to start the weekend. Friday night was like a mini school reunion, the place was packed with weekend revellers, all stood in their own little groups, the majority of which were our age and people we had recently attended school with. It was so crowded you had to plan your trips to the bar or toilets as it was not easy pushing your way through the hordes, passing groups of ex school friends who wanted to chat about what you were doing now the school life was over and we were integrated members of the adult world. Friday night soon became my favourite night of the week, culminating in a few pints of Tetley's Dark Mild and on to the local Chinese takeaway for shrimp curry and fried rice. It was quite an art transferring rice into curry and curry into rice a bit at a time ending up with two trays of equally mixed sustenance to consume. All this was done while sitting in the car parked on the main road, laughing and joking with not a care in the world, they were good times!

Saturday nights were slightly different but followed a theme. The 'Pudsey Crawl' became a regular weekly event, with the group of friends, mostly with scouting connections, meeting at a set time in the first of the several pubs we would frequent that evening. We would commence at the Black Bull, proceed to the Junction, then visit the Butcher's Arms, The Park, and The Golden Lion. Depending on our chosen route, we would either enter the Royal or the King's Arms before concluding our exploration of Pudsey pubs at the esteemed favourite White Cross. When last orders were called and signalled by the bar's bell, we would buy our final pint, finish it, and head to the Kashmir curry house on Leeds Road in Bradford for Shami Kebab and Vegetable Vindaloo with three chapattis. It was compulsory to order a Vindaloo by all the attendees, because if you had anything with less spice you were considered a sub-standard individual, peer pressure at its finest. We would return to the scout hut at 1:00 am, crash on the floor in our sleeping bags, and sleep off the effects of the night's indulgences.

During this period, Kevin, who was regarded as the figurehead of the alliance, informed us that his parents were moving house away from Pudsey to a village called Idle situated on the northeast side of Bradford, six miles away. Disappointment was the immediate reaction to this information as it appeared the leader of our social group was to move away. To ease the depression, Kevin assured us nothing would change as he would drive across to

Pudsey, leave his car at the scout hut and drive home the following morning, having slept off the effect of any alcohol. Additionally, if necessary, he was prepared to walk the six miles when required, which he did on numerous occasions. A feature of the White Cross was a huge fish tank situated in the far corner from the bar. It was approximately 6x4x3 and housed many different species of tropical fish of all shapes and sizes. On one occasion, while we were sat beside the aquarium and looking thoughtfully into our half drained, partially consumed pints of Tetley's finest lubricant, Kevin put forward a plan for our consideration.

"My parents are going caravaning next weekend so why don't you all come over to Idle, we could do the Idle crawl rather than the Pudsey crawl and then you could all crash out on the through lounge floor in your sleeping bags."

After a slight pause for thought, this proposal was met with nods of agreement as it would be something different to the usual Saturday night shenanigans but would have no reduction in the copious amount of alcohol usually consumed.

The night in question was a cold damp November Saturday when the participating personnel started to arrive at Kevin's relatively new home on Westfield Lane in Idle. The attendees were arriving in the darkness of the early, late autumn evening with an excited anticipation of the new pub crawl adventure which awaited. When all 12 of us had arrived and arranged our sleeping bags preparing for the anticipated drunken slumber later that evening, we set off towards the first pub on the planned route, The White Bear. As the crawl proceeded the air was cold and the ground was damp due to that day's rainfall, but the sky was clear, and the stars twinkled, making it an exceptionally pleasant evening.

We were all in our early twenties, young, carefree and just in for a good time. From The White Bear we crossed the road to The New Inn for the second pint of our evening's expedition, then down the steep hill and into The Oddfellows where a pianist was playing tunes on the piano. As we ordered our drinks and sat down, he turned to us and asked if we had any requests, to which I asked,

"Can you play the theme tune for the snooker programme Pot Black; I think it's called 'Black and White Rag'."

"Yes, I can do that," he said. "However, I have a question for you: would you prefer me to play it correctly or in the style of Les Dawson?"

We knew exactly what he meant because Les Dawson was a comedian famous for playing tunes on the piano, off key and with wrong notes, but keeping the tune recognisable. This was too good an opportunity to miss, so in unison we replied:

"Les Dawson style."

He played this piece of off-key music, which led to laughter and amusement among the group, as well as admiration for the talent being displayed before us. When the pianist had finished impressing us with his very amateur-sounding rendition of 'Black and White Rag', he turned round and announced,

"Just to prove I can play it properly, here is the correct version with all the notes back in the right place and order."

He resumed, playing the tune exactly as it should be, just like the intro of the familiar snooker-themed programme. From The Oddfellows we descended the hill into the village to the Black Swan then on to The Alexandra. The beer and drinks were flowing well and the star-twinkling sky and crisp, sharp winters night make the walk between hostelries quite spectacular and exhilarating. The group engaged in animated and cheerful conversation, as each member relished this novel Saturday night experience. After leaving the Alex we missed out the Albion and headed to the Dog and Gun; this was a favourite of mine as it sold Timothy Taylor's Landlord which I preferred to the usual Tetley's Bitter, then down to the George and Dragon, before the long slog up the hill, over the canal bridge back toward Idle. Halfway was The George which was to be the final hostelry of the eight, so we called in, as it would have been rude not to, and consumed the mandatory pint followed by one for the road before resuming the rest of the journey back to the village. As was the tradition with the Pudsey crawl, this beer-fuelled marathon needed to be concluded with a very nice, very spicy and very hot curry. By the time we arrived back in the village, due to the long climb and different speeds of walking, our group had split into two or three spaced out smaller groups. Five or six of us entered the Khyber restaurant, and a couple more rejoined us as we ate, bringing most of the group back together.

After finishing our curry, we left the restaurant with running noses, sweaty brows and watering eyes due to the intense spice and heat of the vindaloo and proceeded on a steady half mile walk up to the summit of the hill, eventually arriving at the house located on Westfield Lane. The bravado, banter and alcohol induced volume was in full flow as we staggered towards the destination, ready for the anticipated slumber in sleeping bags laid out on the lounge floor. Upon arrival, one member of the group indicated his intention to return home that evening on his recently purchased moped, as he preferred not to stay overnight. He was probably well over the legal alcohol limit, but it was his decision and the rest of us were in no fit state or could be bothered to persuade him otherwise, so off he went. Twenty minutes later the remaining three members of the party entered the front door of the house; one was completely naked except for his underpants on his head and was wet through, which raised eyebrows as it wasn't and didn't look like raining when we had arrived, the other two were holding what appeared to be a pile of clothes.

"He's only been in the canal for a swim!" one of them stated with joviality in his voice.

"What? In this cold weather, it's bloody freezing," I said with astonishment.

"Oh, it wasn't that bad," replied the inventor of cold-water swimming. Well perhaps not the inventor, but it certainly wasn't an accepted pastime in the 1980s.

"In fact, it was quite invigorating, refreshing and sobering," he continued.

Kevin was not pleased; in fact, he hit the roof! And anger spewed from his lips.

"You've walked from the canal stark bollock naked?" he shouted.

"Well not exactly, I had my underpants on," justified the wet and naked individual, with a sort of unconvincing smile in his voice.

Kevin proceeded with loud irritation. "On your head or round your bollocks?" he demanded.

"Oh, round my head!" was the reply as the humour dissipated from his voice.

"Well thanks a lot, thanks a bloody lot! I live here, and you have just walked over a mile stark bollock naked, a fact which any of my neighbours could quite easily have witnessed and decided to call the police, thank you very much!"

By now the mood was quite sombre and subdued as the rest of the group, who up until this point had appreciated the funny side of this daring stunt and had been laughing with great gusto, realised that the host of the evening was not very pleased and could possibly evict us all. As apologies were beginning to be given by the now waist-covered, underpants-clad perpetrator, the phone rang. Kevin's eyes stood out on stalks, 0100hrs and the phone rings, who could this be? Who's ringing at this time in the morning, was it the perceived disgruntled neighbours or the police? Surely no one else would be ringing at this time. The dilemma for Kevin was, does he answer it, or let it ring giving the illusion no one was in? There was a pause as the decision was being taken, should he, or shouldn't he? He did. He picked up the receiver and the line went instantly dead, on hearing the phone answered the caller had instantly hung up! Not the best result, who was it, who had rung his house phone number at that time of night? The only thing this achieved was to fuel Kevin's already incensed anger.

"See, that's probably a neighbour, seeing if we are in and are now in the process of calling the cops!" he shouted. "All because you, idiot, walked a mile stark naked, well thanks again, we must live round here! I'm off up to bed, let's hope for your sake we don't get a knock on the door!"

This incident, as funny as it may have seemed, did knock the edge off what had been a fantastic evening of laughter, drinking and eating. The fact that one of us had seemingly upset our host was embarrassingly realised as we all decided to follow suit and retire to our laid out sleeping bags. There was the odd comment of joviality as we were falling asleep in the dark, referring to the last final hilarious act of the evening, all designed to try and get some humour back into the proceedings, but fatigue took over and the ten of us quickly entered the land of nod with snoring the only sounds to be heard.

The following morning soon arrived, sleeping bags started to rustle with movement as the bodies in the room were stirring and realising the hangovers had kicked in. Groans and moans were expelled, with comments of 'I'm never drinking again' and 'oh my head!' were the sounds breaking the dawn silence. Birds could be heard from outside and the odd motor vehicle passed as we reached for cigarettes and embarked on journeys to the toilet and back. Julie, who had been sleeping next to her friend under the dining room table, emerged and informed everyone she was about to open the curtains. She threw them open and gasped loudly, the sight which had invaded her eyes took her breath away.

"Wow!" she exclaimed. "Wow look at this!" She motioned for me to rise and witness what she was seeing.

"What?" I enquired, as I moved to gaze out of the patio door window.

"That! Look at it!"

"Look at what?" I was confused. I had been to Kevin's house on Westfield Lane on numerous occasions, but this was Julie's first visit, and this was the first time she had been there in daylight.

"The view! The View, look it's fantastic, it's panoramic, Bingley and Saltaire to the left, Baildon and the moor straight in front and Guisley and Otley to the right, it's Brilliant! And look at this massive garden, it seems to go on forever. Amazing, I could live here!" That was the moment, that was the epiphany, it was entrenched in her mind, from then on, that one day she could and would like to live in the house on Westfield Lane. She gazed at the stunning scenery for what seemed like hours, identifying landmarks and pointing out places of interest to anyone who would listen. She loved it, she couldn't get enough, not just the view but the size and potential of the large garden. As Kevin came downstairs to rejoin us, he continued to complain about the previous evening's incident, though his anger had faded with time. Coffee and paracetamol were being consumed, sleeping bags were folded away as the phone rang, still not convinced this could just be an innocent call, Kevin gingerly picked up the receiver. "Hello."

"Hi, it's me," was the response from the other end. "Did you get my call last night?"

"What call?" Kevin enquired.

"I phoned you up to let you know I had got home ok."

"Oh, it was you, why did you hang up, because we had no clue it was you?"

"Oh sorry! I didn't think." Whether the guy who left early on his moped the previous night ever found out the commotion and anger he had helped to cause after his departure is questionable, but after that whenever he wanted to let anyone know he had arrived home safe he would speak to them or do what was the more usual three rings before hanging up. On this news and realisation Kevin's wrath dissipated and he eventually saw the funny side of the prank of the naked man with underpants on his head, but somehow, he still wasn't happy about the perceived position it had put him in.

From that morning onwards the house on Westfield Lane was Julie's dream house, every time we went to see Kevin or his parents as we returned home Julie would state, 'I could live there'. This wish or dream lasted 40 years until the sad day arrived when Kevin's mother passed away, and after a couple of years his father followed, it became apparent the house on Westfield Lane would have to be sold so amazingly the first thing Kevin did, remembering Julie's admiration for the property, was ring us and ask,

"Is Julie still interested in my mum and dad's house?"

"Yes, I am," replied Julie excitedly.

"Well, it's yours if you want it."

Once valuations and calculations were done, it was clear we could afford to leave Sorrin Close after 29 years to move to Julie's dream house. We were happy at Sorrin Close and would never have left if it wasn't for the fact Westfield Lane became available. I like to tell people with my tongue in cheek, 'I have given the girl of my dreams her dream' – gushy, I know, but it sounds good!

TWO HOURS FROM ANYWHERE

Olivia has graduated from Aberystwyth University with a 2:2 in Marine and Freshwater Biology which makes her sound like a scientist, don't you think? We are absolutely thrilled to bits with this result as she was expecting a third, so after four years of ups and downs we are so proud of her achievement, surpassing all expectations. There is a story behind this success which began when Olivia was 14 years old, she has always had a very special love for animals, especially dogs, and one of her biggest frustrations has been her mum is allergic to dogs, and I don't by any means share Olivia's passion. I can appreciate other people's lovely dog, but I certainly don't want one myself, I'm not keen.

Olivia's love for animals led to her wanting to be a vet, a dream she had since she was very young. So, in pursuit of this dream she started to do work experience as extra-curricular activities all geared towards the requirements to enter Vet School at a university. She started off as an unpaid volunteer at Bradford Cat Rescue, this work gave her a valuable grounding for dealing with and looking after poorly, abandoned cats. She then progressed to actually getting paid for weekend work at a kennels and cattery in Burley in Wharfedale, once again gaining valuable experiences. In this period, she also helped a sheep farmer with lambing. Shipley vets also provided work experience while she was in year 11. Her GCSE results were very good and kept her on track to achieve her goal.

Then two months into her A levels we were told by her school that they were pulling her out of chemistry, Julie and I had been called in to see a team of Olivia's teachers to be told this and we left the meeting believing we had been fed a load of bullshit. We couldn't understand how a student who had achieved an 'A' in her Chemistry GCSE was suddenly told, six weeks into the 'A' level process, she was incapable of achieving chemistry. Was it the fact the school needed a certain pass rate to be able to advertise their 'A' level results on a banner outside and needed to drop the also-rans, or was it other detrimental reasons? They tried to explain it was due to changes in the curriculum which students were finding hard to understand, to which Julie enquired if it was down to their teachers and teaching being competent instructing the new chemistry subject? Well, it all went down from that point really, never question a teacher's ability because they rapidly shut up shop and brought the meeting to a close, recommending Olivia studied for the new BTec course, which was new to the school, instantly ending Olivia's dream. No chemistry 'A' level, no vet school and we had already attended the open days at the vet schools in Bristol and Edinburgh universities. Also, at this time she was still working at the cattery and kennels, helping the cat rescue and volunteering on an evening at an equine vet near Keighley.

So, what next? After some thought Olivia suggested she may like to study Marine Biology. Julie wasn't happy about this, stating she was not in favour of Olivia going to university and spending three years studying for a 'nothing degree'. If Olivia thought she was just going to study dolphins in the warmer seas of the world, well she was very much mistaken. After this conversation and debate as the dust was settling, I suggested to Olivia she ought to tell the people at the equine vets she was no longer able to achieve becoming a vet. When she told the senior vet at the practice she would not be attending anymore, without prompt or cue he said,

"Not to worry, if I was your age and had my time again, I would not be a vet, I would study Marine Biology."

I wasn't there but I can well imagine Olivia's slight smirk and chest expanding as she replied, "My mum says Marine Biology is a waste of a degree."

"Nonsense! How many times on the ten o'clock news do you see reports about how our oceans, seas and creatures in them are struggling? When you graduate in four- or five-years' time there will be jobs ten a penny for Marine Biologists."

Well, Olivia couldn't get home quick enough to tell her mum how wrong she was about a Marine Biology degree. That was that, a decision was made, and marine biology was not quite the new dream but certainly was the new goal.

Universities discussed were Aberystwyth, Liverpool, Essex in Colchester, Hull and Plymouth. As parents we were not happy with Colchester as it is an army garrison full of squaddies. We went to Liverpool's open day, but it wasn't that impressive to be honest. When Olivia had completed her mock A levels the results were good but not quite good enough to start a university course, so we needed to find a university which offered a course in marine biology but also did a foundation course. The preferred choice, Aberystwyth, did not according to Olivia offer this option which was unfortunate as we had booked a night in a hotel so all four of us could attend the open day. Luckily, we could cancel with no fee to pay so that was knocked on the head. Essex University did offer the foundation option, so Olivia applied and was offered a place. This was bittersweet as Aberystwyth was the dream but with no foundation course seemed to be out of the question, or so we thought. Julie asked Olivia to ring Aberystwyth to enquire if they did a foundation course or some other option which would enable her to enrol. Typically, as a 17-year-old Olivia knew best and was adamant they wouldn't and didn't do a foundation. This led to the odd highly charged discussion and debate between mother and daughter.

Born from frustration on the day before Aberystwyth University open day Julie took the bull between the horns and phoned the admissions department to enquire about the possibility of Olivia applying and doing a foundation. To all our surprise they confirmed the foundation year was a new addition to the Marine and Freshwater Biology course, and we should, if possible, attend the open day the following day! The first I knew about this was when Julie rung me as I was busy minding my own business delivering teeth round the dentists of East and South Yorkshire.

The phone rang.

"Hello, love," I said as her identification was displayed on the car's hands-free setting.

"Hi, are you doing anything this weekend?" she asked.

"No, I don't think so," I replied after a few seconds of thought.

"What are you doing after work today?" she enquired.

"Nothing I can think of."

"Good! We are going to Aberystwyth."

"Aber... where?" I questioned with a bemused voice.

"Aberystwyth! I've been in touch with the university, and they are providing a foundation course and highly recommend we attend the open day tomorrow, so I've booked us into the Airhaven Guest House. We need to set off straight after you finish work and Olivia and Alfie finish school." That was that, totally out of the blue we were going to Aberystwyth on the West Coast of Wales.

Having endured an extremely long five hour drive we arrived at the Airhaven Guest House where we were welcomed by our hosts Janice and Windsor.

"Welcome to Airhaven, may I ask where you have come from?" Janice asked.

"Bradford, West Yorkshire," Julie confirmed.

"Ah well, you know what they say about Aberystwyth, don't you?" Windsor asked in a very strong Welsh brogue.

"No," I said, slightly baffled by the question.

"It's two hours from anywhere."

We were tired after the long journey and just wanted to get settled in, and his comment was slightly confusing, so I nodded and smiled politely in acknowledgement, never suspecting I would hear the phrase again.

The following morning arrived, the date of the open day, we'd had a good night's sleep and been given a hearty full Welsh breakfast cooked by Windsor who continued with his buoyant Welsh charm. We packed the car, said our goodbyes and headed for the university. On arrival we were met by masses of student volunteers, all acting as stewards, pointing which way to go, answering questions and being general guides round the campus. We found the car park and was directed to the building where registration was taking place. There were lots of branded freebies, water bottles, pens, pencils, erasers, keyrings and other products. Having informed the officials in the large hall which subject Olivia wished to study, we were ushered on to the Biology Department. We were introduced to the lecturer who had given the introductory address and when he asked Olivia where she was from, she replied, Bradford, West Yorkshire. Now being a product of a slow thing from slow land I never twigged on the next part of the conversation.

"Ah, you know what they say about Aberystwyth, don't you?"

I knew I'd heard this before but didn't quite cotton on.

"No!" Olivia replied.

"It's two hours from anywhere!"

Bugger! I knew I'd heard it and was slightly disappointed I'd missed the punchline. We were given a guided tour round the Biology Campus and shown different experiments and procedures carried out within the Department, all of which was very interesting, and Olivia seemed very impressed and enthusiastic about the possibility of studying there.

In the afternoon, following some lunch, Olivia had an appointment to meet with the admissions officer. Olivia was introduced to her, and she asked, "Where does Olivia come from?"

"Bradford, West Yorkshire," I said, anticipating what I knew was coming.

"Ah," she said. "Well you know what they say about Aberystwyth, don't you?"

Quick as a flash I was in, I knew I had the right answer, so with a smirk and knowing smile I answered, "Yes! It's two hours from anywhere."

Then without batting an eyelid she retorted, "Yes! Including Dublin."

To which we all laughed at in unison. It wasn't the answer I'd anticipated, wow what did she mean? Over the next four years the answer became very apparent. Drive to Chester then it's two hours to Aber, drive to Wrexham then it's two hours, get to Shrewsbury then it's two hours, get to Cardiff or Swansea then it's two hours, and presumably because of the lady's last answer get to Dublin then it's two hours to Aberystwyth; I presume some sort of ferry is involved on this last example.

That was the beginning of the Aberystwyth saga, the start of Olivia's university experience. She was invited back to the Biology Department's own open day in the following March and then in September; a whole year later, we moved Olivia into her halls of residence, the first of four different accommodations while she was studying there. On Fresher's week she joined the rugby team and in her first year won the Fresher of the Year award and has been Social Secretary, Captain, and President of Aberystwyth University Women's Rugby. She joined the Surfing Club, surfed and swam in the Irish Sea, she's had parties, and bonfires on the beach, attended numerous Rugby Club Socials, where the aim seems to be to get really drunk. She has held two jobs as well as endured the Covid epidemic and met a Welsh-speaking, rugby-playing farmer who works in engineering, and obviously due to her degree result must have done some studying. We have always been very proud of Olivia, but seeing her develop into adult life, watching her deal with ups, downs and challenges in the way she does fills my chest with much admiration, love and pride. As she starts on her life after education, always remember,

'Aberystwyth? It's two hours from anywhere!'

HOW MUCH?

A debate was had today about the value of money and how it seems to have changed in my lifetime. What I am about to say can only apply to my generation. Previous generations will try to impress, or counter argue how little money was worth when they were young compared to newer generations who will slightly disbelieve and wonder how cheap commodities were worth in my youth.

For the first ten years of my life, I lived with pounds, shillings and pence. The counting of this currency didn't mean too much to me as I had no conception or understanding of the value of money. I would receive the odd penny, threepence piece (discontinued in 1973) or sixpence from grandparents to buy some sweets, but I never understood how money worked. Half pennies, pennies, three pence, sixpence, shillings, half crowns, crowns and notes were all in use. In February 1971 the country brought in what was called decimalisation; as a nine-year-old I remember there being quite a fuss made of the fact, a sixpence piece would be worth two and a half pence, and a shilling (twelve pennies) would be valued at five pence. For me and I suspect my generation, decimalisation was good. I could understand one hundred pennies equalling a pound rather than two hundred and forty pennies, or twenty shillings also equalling one pound.

One practicality for me of this new system was the fact I could attend Cub Scouts on a Thursday evening with a sixpence piece in my pocket equivalent to two and a half new pence. This small silver coin would cover the cost of one penny for subs, half pence for a drink of juice and a biscuit at break, and the remaining penny for a bag of chips with scraps on from the fish and chip shop to consume as we walked home. When I started attending Pudsey Grammar School with a couple of friends, we were allowed to catch the bus from the bottom of Owlcotes Road to the end of Cemetery Road. This journey cost two pence, so if we walked the one point one miles, I was able to save the fare and buy sweets. As I got older, commodities did tend to increase in price, but once again even in my teens I never understood the concept or value of money. I don't think this materialises until you actually start earning money. I had a paper round employed by the local newsagent which paid one pound 25 per week and I also became a petrol pump attendant on a Tuesday and Thursday night for three hours at a rate of fifty pence an hour. These payments mostly seemed to replace the financial gain from adults, but added to pocket money, saved bus fare and birthday money. My first realisation of how much something cost was when I wanted to buy my first ever seven-inch single vinyl record. The record was 'Won't Somebody Dance with Me' by Lynsey de Paul in 1973. Fairbank and Harding is a music shop in Pudsey which sold the latest chart-topping singles. I went there with Mum to buy the disc. I was astounded to find it cost 49 pence, it seemed so expensive at the time, so much so I thought mum would resist my pleas and refuse to spend so much money on a record, but my nattering wore her down, she relented and bought me it. Wow! All that money for a single record, an LP was about £1.99 which to me was extortion. Today you can pay 25, 30 even 40 pounds for the same remixed vinyl LP.

I left Pudsey Grammar School in 1978 to enrol at Airedale and Wharfedale College. Between leaving school and starting college I got a summer job at a firm called Nortec Plastics in Farsley. This was a small extrusion plastics company which produced plastic bin lids, paint trays, and butter tub lids amongst other plastic products. I sat next to an extrusion machine as it spat out these plastic objects which I would trim and pack them all day, but it put money in my pocket, 28 pounds a week over an eight-week period. On leaving college I started full time employment at Leeds University. In the three weeks between leaving college and joining the University I was encouraged to draw the dole. This was the unemployment benefit at the time worth £23 per week. I was not happy about this because of the social stigma of being 'on the dole', but as pointed out to me it was a benefit; I was entitled to so why not draw it? At Leeds University my annual salary was in the region of eighteen hundred pounds a year, which more than doubled when I joined the fire service; it was then I realised how poorly I had been paid while working at the University. We were at training school when we received our first pay slip. I was looking at mine and remarked on how good the pay was. One of the other recruits heard my comment and asked,

"Do you think so? I've taken a pay cut to be a fireman."

"Why did you leave your last job for less money?" I enquired.

"For job security and the pension," was his reply.

That was the realisation my salary had nearly doubled yet others had taken pay cuts.

Going back a bit to the year 1978, my group of friends were all sat round a table at The White Cross pub in Pudsey. At that time this was our favourite watering hole. The government had just published the annual budget and had announced to our astonishment the chancellor had put one penny duty onto a pint of beer. We were disgusted; our delightful pint of Tetley Bitter was now 29 pence as opposed to 28 pence. This was cheek and an insult as we sat in stunned silence staring into the pints on beer mats on the round table. Then I came up with a profound statement.

"This is bloody outrageous, I'll tell you something, if this stuff ever gets to 50 pence a pint" (never in a million years believing it would) "then I'll be packing it in!" as I lifted my pint to my lips for another drink, and the rest of the group mumbled and nodded in agreement. Along with most of my friends I was a smoker, a packet of 20 cigarettes cost in the region of 40 pence depending on brand. Unlike the £16 plus they cost today. When I gave up smoking on 01/09/1985 I was smoking 40 cigarettes a day. At today's prices this habit would be costing me £32 per day or £224 a week! ...Scary!!! In 1982 I went to see the Rolling Stones in concert at Roundhay Park, a ticket cost £10 which seemed extortionate then, but compared to concert prices today of £100 or more, it now appears to be quite the bargain.

Julie and I bought our first house on Grange Avenue, Thornbury, Bradford in 1988 for £33,000. Not long after the purchase the mortgage rate reached 15%. Our repayments were about £400 per month which was a large chunk of money when the average working wage was £10,000 per year. Times were hard but I believe it's all relative. My Station Officer in the fire service bought his house in the late sixties and at the time was paying a mortgage of £16 per month and he was struggling to pay his monthly fee. Today the young adults can easily be charged £1800 a month on a £330,000 mortgage when the average earnings are at £34,500 per annum. I know and understand it is hard to get onto the property ladder in today's society, but it always has been. People out in society are pleading with the government to help today's first-time buyers with mortgage repayments. Why?! We were struggling with a rate of 15% and we had to budget and deal with it. We got no state assistance. I remember a fireman colleague complaining he was about to take out a mortgage of £250,000 as he was purchasing a farmhouse; he said,

"I know the house is beautiful but to have a mortgage of a quarter of a million quid is terrifying."

Julie and I had just taken out a mortgage for £89,000 on our three bedroomed detached house in Idle, and that seemed bad enough. In today's market £250,000 is classed as a relatively standard mortgage for an average property.

One final thought to end on which amuses me is the fact that the famously named 'Penny Bubbly' now retails at approximately ten pence each. Of what I have written in this piece I cannot guarantee how precise the numbers discussed were at the time, but they are as accurate as I remember them with no exaggeration. Finally, I wonder if in the future people being worth one million pounds plus will become normal as the rates and cost of living increases due to time in years. Perhaps by then a loaf of bread will cost £20. A sobering thought, I think!

BLOODY USELESS

My **family and friends know my DIY skills are poor if non-existent.** I often joke that in our house, DIY stands for 'Don't Involve Yourself'. This humorous saying is repeated to hopefully mask my embarrassment and discomfort in my inability to carry out even the simplest of household maintenance and other semi-skilled tasks. Many people are surprised when they observe how remedial my competence is at carrying out the simplest assignment. Even the elementary things like screwing a screw into a wall I can get wrong. Putting up pictures can be the most time consuming and exasperating chore for me when others seem to easily put two level holes in a wall, screw in two screws and as if by magic hang two or three pictures which are equidistant and level, but mine can be all over the place. When Olivia did gymnastics, she asked if I could install a chin up bar to the inside door surround of the pantry. Foolishly I agreed – how hard could this be? So off we went to Argos, purchased the previously identified chin up bar and I began to fix it in position. I got out my inexpensive drill, my spirit level, cheap screwdriver and endeavoured to fit the bar. Using the level to ensure the bar was horizontally straight, I set to, to install it, and I am convinced to this day I had done it right until we stood back, examined my handiwork only to realise it had somehow developed a good 15-degree slope. No way! How did that happen? I contacted a skilled friend who promptly came over, resolved the issue, and ensured the bar was level. However, two redundant screw holes remained in the painted wood due to my mistake.

As a teenager I was not really interested in anything DIY and was never taught the techniques on how to do things correctly. When a project was on the go at home I would be playing or watching rugby, scouting or in a pub somewhere. My father, who was a trained electrician, was also very good with wood. He once spent a couple of weekends building homemade fitted wardrobes and bed in my sister's small bedroom, which made great use of the limited space. He worked Monday to Friday 9-to-5 so time to carry out his projects on a weekend was at a premium and the last thing he needed was to be distracted by trying to teach me, the not very enthusiastic teenage son. As a keen photographer he constructed a worktop to fit over the bath so he could use the bathroom as a dark room to develop and print his own photographs. I left the house one morning having used the bathroom facilities only to find on my return it had metamorphosized into a fully working lightproof dark room complete with blackouts at the window, bench for his enlarger and chemical trays, light excluders round the door and a lightshade made from a treacle tin with an orange filter. My parents would do all their own decorating, filling holes, sanding, painting and hanging wallpaper. I would leave them to it as I would often find somewhere else to be, making sure I was out of the way you may say. Occasionally I would be told to keep a day free so I could help do some sanding and painting, but eventually they realised it would be easier just to get on with it themselves, as my inferior standard fell way short of their expectations. When Julie and I bought our first house we decided to paint the walls and gloss the woodwork, with Julie examining my attempt at glossing – she banned me from painting anything in any house ever again, which has stuck to this day. It is embarrassing and guilt consuming not being able or allowed to help paint your own home. But I don't possess the motivation, patience, concentration levels or ambition to carry out these sorts of jobs; it's a lot easier to pay a professional to do it for you, and this usually results in the job being done properly and to a timescale rather than achieving a make-do amateur standard, which could take several weeks to complete.

Most firefighters have a second job due to the spare time the shift pattern allows, to help pay bills and enjoy extra family holidays. These can be jobs using skills learnt in previous jobs, self-taught skills or just labouring. A firefighter needed to apply to the brigade for permission to do these extracurricular jobs and had to prove they held the necessary insurances and had a good sickness record. This was to dissuade firefighters being on sick leave because of something they had done while not doing their 'proper job'. It was pointed out more than once that some had small businesses and could not afford to be on the sick, but nevertheless these were the rules. Some colleagues would vocally complain, what's it to do with them what I do in my spare time? But from my point of view the brigade were just looking after their own interests. The shift pattern was two days, two nights, four days off, so once permission was obtained, employees were permitted to engage in secondary employment, provided it did not occur on the day before a nightshift. These periods were designated for rest to ensure that employees received a full eight hours of rest time before returning to work that evening. This was a bit irrational for me because of this rule a firefighter who did accountancy or photography as a second job, were not allowed to sit at a table to carry out related tasks between their night shift, yet if the same firefighter played amateur sport such as Rugby, Football or Cricket, this was overlooked, and indeed promoted, perhaps it was assumed all secondary employment is physically challenging yet playing sport is accepted because fitness levels were being maintained.

In 1988, when I joined Blue watch at Bradford fire station, my sub officer asked me during my first tea break,

"What can you do for the shift?"

Not understanding the question I asked, "What do you mean?"

"Well, are you a plumber, a sparky, a joiner, a builder or painter and decorator?"

Slightly embarrassed by having to admit I couldn't do any of the skills mentioned, I sheepishly replied, "I could print you a tee shirt or two." Referring to my previous job in Dying, Finishing and Printing at Leeds University.

The sigh of disappointment was quite overwhelming as he realised I hadn't a practical skill to boast about, and it was never mentioned again.

But one of the leading firefighters heard this and responded, "Don't worry, when you're out of probation you can come window cleaning with me!"

I wasn't to know at the time, but that statement moulded my secondary employment history as a firefighter. On the day I qualified from my two years' probation I was not asked,

I was told, I would start window cleaning, an unskilled labouring job with the leading firefighter the following day. I worked on the windows with him for four years before investing in my own round which I did for 11 years, until it eventually broke me, so I sold my round, and as recommended by another colleague, started delivering cars up and down the country. Yet again another job which required very little practical skill and was not weather dependent.

Often, on the morning of a new shift, I would overhear two firefighters discussing their latest building project being carried out on the previous days off. I would stand there, bemused by their conversation, and due to my lack of understanding I could not form a mental picture in my brain of anything they were talking about, they may as well be explaining each scenario in a foreign language. Occasionally I would ask the odd question in relation, just to indicate a slight interest, but never really understood any answer given. This could be frustrating, but when you had never been given the training or be interested in doing this sort of skilled work, is it any wonder I was bewildered? Steels, spacers, dots and dabs, skimming, where a few technical terms I remember, even if I had heard of them before carrying out the process needed to complete such a task was way beyond my knowledge. It was decided by the Fire Service authorities we would as crews fit smoke detectors free of charge in properties which had been involved in a fire, or didn't have this essential piece of equipment, and we as firefighters would be expected to fit them. When told this I went cold with a shudder – they want me to screw screws into somebody's house ceiling when I hadn't a clue how to do it properly? We weren't given any training as it was just assumed everyone knew how to do the task correctly. The task consisted of using bradawls, plugs and screwdrivers. I wasn't comfortable with this prospect of making holes in members of the public's cherished houses, so I shied away when possible. On one occasion one of my fire fighter colleagues watched me struggle to fit a smoke alarm in a property we had visited, in my mind I was willing him to take over, but he didn't, and when I had just about made an acceptable job of it we returned to the fire engine for him to say to the rest of the crew,

"I now understand why Andy asks me to do all his home joinery tasks because having seen him try fit that smoke detector he hasn't got a clue."

The little confidence I had was now well and truly shattered but the embarrassment I felt turns my stomach today. A middle-aged man who can't do the simplest task like fit a smoke detector. Now there's a story!

I have realised over the years with the few miniscule DIY tasks I have attempted to complete that having the correct tools for the job is essential. This, it appears, makes a task so much easier than using cheap tools with a make-do-and-mend attitude. Affording the right equipment when you do as few of these jobs as I do can be unjustified. Paying top price for a tool you will only need once, or not for a few years is not recommended. Therefore, seek out an individual with the appropriate equipment or hire a professional tradesperson to complete the task for you. Why can't I hammer a nail into wood without it bending, or screw a screw into a wall without it ending up misaligned? Why can't I gloss wood with a smooth finish or change a tap washer? Why don't I have the concentration, stamina and motivation needed to carry out long monotonous labouring jobs? In fact, why am I bloody useless at any of these tasks? The answer is quite simple, I have neither had the instruction, the interest or motivation to complete the above, as mentioned as a teenager there was always somewhere better to be when DIY was being carried out. I feel I have always lacked self-confidence at the prospect of trying out any little house maintenance project. Fear of making a balls-up of any task can be quite oppressive, the nervousness and trepidation I feel before even attempting to start can be overwhelming, but this is all down to lack of training and know-how of where and how to start. I sometimes wonder if I had left school and got a job in the building industry or trained as a plumber, electrician or carpenter the three houses I have lived in may have appeared very different. This fact is something not to dwell on as I didn't leave school to join any of these trades so speculating on what I may have been like with these skills is slightly futile.

I handle most household tasks, aiming to contribute and maintain a high standard. I can wire a plug, I enjoy gardening after instruction and discussion with Julie, I would never do anything without her knowledge as she is quite the expert in this field. Mowing the lawn, digging, even planting seeds are all tasks I can do for myself but once again after two or three hours I lose motivation and interest to finish properly. I can do the laundry, iron, cook and clean, tasks I can find therapeutic when I realise what needs doing; to be honest, I can look after myself, which stems from my time in the scout association where cooking, keeping a clean and tidy campsite and looking after equipment were essential skills, but of course in these cases I had a kind of informal training by achieving badges and awards for achieving the criteria. Cleaning is a chore I can do, which I try to carry out with pride, my secret is to not take on too big a job in one go. Clean one maybe two rooms at a time rather than try and do the whole house in one go. I put my ear buds in, get lost in the music I am listening to, usually loud heavy rock, and hit the task with vigour and enthusiasm. I take pride in my standards; however, for confirmation of whether others share this view, you would need to ask them directly.

In conclusion, why are my DIY skills so remedial and substandard? The main contributory factors are, none or minimal training, very little interest and motivation, and not possessing the correct tools for the job. The few tasks mentioned which I am quite competent in are jobs which I have been taught how to do, these jobs never needed any skill just graft, knowhow and endeavour. Throughout my career as a firefighter, I consistently held a secondary job which helped to finance the hiring of professionals for the completion of necessary skilled projects in my homes. Revealing my inability to perform simple tasks to colleagues and acquaintances is distressing and embarrassing, but this is what I am.

Bloody Useless!!

MY OPINION OF ME

This subject may be difficult to write about, my opinion of me... mmm thought provoking. To write about what you think of yourself compared to how others perceive you could be like chalk and cheese. To do it properly I will be self-critical, perhaps slightly too much, but when the only person who is with yourself 24/seven is you, this subject should be easy. So here goes, let's see what I come up with; it could be long.

Granny May said my best characteristic was my inability to hold malice. I am unable to bear a grudge although there have been a few times over my years I have tried. I feel hate is a very strong word and on the few occasions I have been wronged I have never hated anybody. An example of this was in 1997, Bradford City had been promoted the previous season and the rise in football standard was something they were struggling with. To be fair in the March they really did look doomed to being relegated back to where they came from. I am naturally a positive person and believe it's not over till it's over. In sport a team or individual may be losing by quite a margin with a few minutes remaining, I still sometimes foolishly think the win is still a possibility. Unfortunately, 99% of the time the inevitable happens. A great example was when Devon Loch was leading the

Grand National in 1956. He was leading by five lengths with 40 yards to go when inexplicably he jumped in the air and landed on his barrel (stomach) allowing E.S.B. to run past him and win the race. Over the years there have been many similar examples. Prior to a union meeting at around the same time as Bradford City's struggles, firefighters were gathering in the mess room waiting for the start when a colleague asked me if I thought City would stay up this season. Being the great optimist I am I admitted I thought it was unlikely but could see them surviving, adding it's not over till it's over. Regrettably, a rather bombastic, self-opinionated firefighter heard my comments and in a loud, aggressive and confrontational voice told me in no uncertain terms I was talking rubbish that I knew nothing, and City were already down.

"No, they're not!" I meekly replied with a hushed voice. "It's not over yet, they can still survive."

"Don't talk shit," he shouted.

By this time the room of 50 or so firefighters were silenced on hearing the raised voice as their attention was diverted to where I was standing.

He continued loudly, "They haven't got a prayer of staying up, they are already down and anyone who believes anything different just has not got a clue what they are on about! You, my friend, are talking total bollocks!"

At this point there was a collective sharp intake of breath from the watching audience as they anticipated my reply.

"I just think they have a chance of..." I was cut short.

"Rubbish absolute garbage!"

I was shouted down. I felt about six inches tall, I felt embarrassed at the rumpus he had caused, I felt self-conscious

THE WORLD ACCORDING TO ANDY CARTER

as all the room was looking at me and at that moment, I wanted the floor to open and me to disappear. As if to ease the tension the chairman called the meeting to order.

All meeting I couldn't concentrate, the conflict was on my mind, I was churning inside. I was unable to settle. How was it possible for this guy to butt into a conversation he was not involved in and embarrass me in front of the fire station personnel. At the conclusion of the meeting, I stood up and left immediately, call it running away but the mental scarring was too much to cope with. Over the next couple of months when we met at the change of shift, I was never rude to the individual but just acknowledged him with a nod and hello. As it turned out Bradford City needed to win the last two home games of the season to stay in the division and they did. I enjoyed a small piece of satisfaction from this, call it karma. I didn't know what I was talking about…eh? The day came in late May when we both crossed on the landing.

"Morning, Andy," he said while passing.

"Morning," I replied, not particularly wanting to start a conversation. He walked a few steps down the stairs as I was ascending when I heard him stop, he turned and asked,

"Andy, have I upset you at all?"

"No," I lied, "what makes you think that?"

"It's just that we used to have good conversation whereas recently you have just given me one-word responses!" he stated.

He'd got me! My body language and persona had given me away so there was no point denying it.

"Well yes in fact you did" I said "At that union meeting in March when you told me, in front of everyone I was talking total bollocks when in fact City stayed up didn't they? You made me feel very belittled, embarrassed and self-conscious."

He was extremely apologetic and full of remorse saying he didn't realise he'd had that effect. I accepted his apology and understanding of my hurt feelings. From then on in it was all back to normal, friends, colleagues, and fellow City fans once again. I tried my damnedest to hold malice but failed miserably, life is far too short.

I certainly lack self-confidence; I can't decide whether I'm indecisive or not. I get the impression my public image suggests I am a very confident person but the need to be told I am doing or did well is confirmation I crave for. When I left Training School the Sub Officer wrote in my final report I 'lacked self-confidence'. Then at my end of course interview with two very senior officers they were surprised and disputed this fact having witnessed me refereeing a football match between the recruits and instructors two weeks prior.

Trustworthiness is a characteristic I think I possess; this is partly due to the fear of being caught out. The amount of CCTV, mobile phones and internet means I dare not be dishonest in case the evidence proves I am. This could also be down to the self-confidence issues. When we moved into our house on Sorrin Close, we were living on a building site for the first two years. We wanted a small bund wall building in the garden, so we were using cement left each evening by the builders. Every morning a cement mixer would arrive on site to deliver that day's bulk mortar for the site bricklayers to use. Any cement left over at the end of the day would be left overnight and then disposed of. The evening in question I got my wheelbarrow and gathered the abandoned cement so the guy building my wall could use it the following evening, I covered it in plastic sheeting to keep it fresh and never thought anything of it; of course, in real terms this was an act of stealing. The following morning, I was leaving home for work and stopped to talk to one of the builders who had over the months become a friend.

"Oh, Andy!" he said. "We've got a right problem this morning."

"Oh no," I remarked, "nothing serious I hope."

"Not really, but it's a problem, this morning's delivery of cement is running late, and someone has cleared us out of what was left over yesterday. So, the brickies are here but there's nothing for them to do!"

"How long before the delivery arrives?" I asked guiltily.

"Not sure, could be anytime now or this afternoon, but we are stuck as there is no cement to use."

I drove off to work having said goodbye feeling very uncomfortable with myself, what should I do? Here's where my indecision problem kicked in. Should I confess, let the builders have back what I'd pinched or just say nothing hoping they wouldn't discover the pile of contraband in my back garden? I wrestled with this dilemma while driving for over a mile until I reached a roundabout, travelled all the way round it and came back home to confess my misdemeanour. The builders were unnervingly relaxed about my confession and were surprisingly grateful for the cement I gave back. Perhaps honesty really does pay.

I can't deal with confrontation, it really does affect me, even a mild wrong word can be on my mind for hours, if not days. Because of this mentality I never wanted promotion in the fire service I just wanted to be a good firefighter and drive fire engines. One of my Station Officers openly stated 'I don't do confrontation' but surely if you are in a management role it demands confrontation and instruction. Fallouts between staff members, misbehaving staff, rule breaking staff and staff sickness has all to be dealt with on a personal basis. Surly this means as a manager you may upset one or two colleagues. This fact is something I would not be comfortable with; I would not be able to control my emotions. I much prefer to do as I'm told rather than instruct a colleague to carry out a task they may be uneasy with. My character demands 'work issues stay at work; home issues stay at home'. I firmly believe manners and consideration should be a given. Whether you're a pauper or a billionaire, manners and consideration cost you nothing. Respect for other people should be shown by everyone. A great example of inconsideration is the car driver who parks the car across, outside or diagonally in a marked bay. Because this is what I believe, I try to be a considerate person, whether driving, holding doors open, standing aside to let people through with a polite or positive comment. I consider myself to be a happy person, trying to see good in any bad situation. If a situation or problem is 98% negative it means, there is at least 2% positive to focus on. I always seek the silver lining. I will always compliment people to make their day feel better and if someone in any environment wears a name badge, I will refer to them by name – from experience I find it makes all the difference. I try to treat people as I would like to be treated.

I lose concentration quite easily; because of this I was never a good studier or reviser. Exams, as pointed out previously, are not a forte. Newspaper headlines will attract my attention to read the article below, but halfway to three quarters of the way through I lose concentration and interest and move on. In my young adult days this would happen when reading novels, I'd read a book, get three quarters of the way through, lose interest, put the book down, forget about it and never read the end. This characteristic is a hindrance, with physical repetitive work, digging, gardening, shifting snow, car cleaning and DIY are all chores I start with enthusiasm only to get bored and never properly finish. Perhaps this is laziness, but I think it's more down to not being able to hold concentration. DIY has never interested me; it's never floated my boat as I have never been taught the skills or had an interest to learn. I often joke that 'in our house DIY means Don't Involve Yourself, when really, it's due to lack of knowledge, skill and confidence. Screwing a screw in a wall is a problem for me.

I am aware I have a reputation of being a bit of a tight arse where money is concerned, which is not something I enjoy. People in general seem to be very willing to spend other people's money but like to hold on to their own with rigidly controlled purse strings, people want a piece of the pie but rarely want to contribute themselves. Nobody knows the details of friends or colleague's financial affairs, are people tight or are they just being frugal and thrifty as they look after their personal income? If you go out for drinks with the intention of just buying your own, it always seems to be the case you get dragged into rounds be them large or small, and if you resist to comply with your original plan, it enhances the charade of being miserly. In my early twenties being a single man when my money situation was not plentiful, I was invited out for a trip to a pub for drinks with two couples. The two gentlemen bought a round of five drinks each then it was my turn. I tried to point out I thought this was a bit unfair, as the ladies were not expected to buy drinks, yet I was expected to buy theirs. My point of view spoilt the evening and upset me, it put a sour atmosphere on proceedings; I was only trying to be fair, but it wasn't interpreted that way by the others. If you don't go out you are accused of being miserable, if you go out and just want to buy your own drinks you're deemed tight, and if you go out and throw money round like confetti people take advantage. Why is it when individuals receive a windfall, a lottery win, a large bet comes in or even inheritance, others seem to think they are entitled to benefit from those persons' gains? Why can't people just be happy for the beneficiary and let them enjoy their fortune?

    I believe in justice and making people responsible and face the consequences for their own actions. If an individual is foolish enough to glue themselves to the road, I say leave them there, put cones round them and allow others to carry on with their daily lives. The glued will soon find a way of releasing themselves when they realise their intended disruption is having no effect. I had to accept the fact I received a speeding fine travelling at 34 mph in a 30 zone. As unfair as it seemed, having been trained to drive 11-ton fire engines safely at breakneck speed, I had broken the rules and had to accept and suffer the consequences of that misdemeanour, being a result of my own action.

    I can be my own best friend; I do enjoy my own company and my own space. Having said that I cannot imagine a life without Julie who is the love of my life. What I mean is I do talk to myself a lot, both out loud and within, perhaps this helps with lengthening my short concentration span. As a child I had a special little friend known as Binker, named after the character in A.A. Milne's poem of the same name. I spent a lot of time talking to Binker (myself) specifically when lying in bed as a young boy while trying to get to sleep. I have been described in the past as a 'Jolly chap' which is fine by me; it's certainly a better description than small, fat and ugly. Jolly is a persona I try and live up to, it's a lot better being happy and joyful than being sad and miserable. I do like to be funny, always trying to see the lighter side of things. Occasionally my sense of humour and jocularity has been inappropriate, trying to get a laugh when misreading the situation. This fortunately is a rare miscalculation in my maturer years. There is no better feeling than seeing someone beaming with a great smile or even belly laughing at something you have said or done. The rush of endorphins gives great pleasure, being a successful stand-up comedian must be one of the best jobs in the world, perhaps second only to firefighting. I always try to be positive; every cloud has a silver lining, and I always look for it. I believe things in life happen for a reason which all adds to the path we follow, you cannot, and I try not regret things, decisions throughout my life have led me to this point in time writing this piece. There have been times with hindsight I may have chosen a different route, but who's to say that journey, that decision may have led to abject misery, a life I do not lead. You can only make a life decision on the knowledge and experiences you have at that moment in time. Hindsight is not in my opinion a wonderful thing, it's futile, you can't go back and change things, but you can learn from encounters of the past. We can only look forward and make the most of seemingly bad or uncomfortable situations using our knowledge and judgement at that point.

Having said all that, I am a worrier, the smallest of problems can weigh on my mind, even though I can appear to be very laid back and calm, my insides can be churning and occasionally it will show through, often my best friend Julie is the only person who will detect this. Like anyone I do like to be liked and although it's rare I can lose my temper. Anger is a strange one for me as when I'm angry I tend to lose all vocabulary, all that comes out of my raised voice is cursing and swearing which is something I am embarrassed by, especially when I state I dislike confrontation. Perhaps because of this I am very rarely angry, maybe it's better described as annoyed. I can get frustrated in certain circumstances which will end with me unavoidably saying some sarcastic or demeaning quip about the situation which is an aspect that frustrates me. Tardiness and lateness are things I despise, I believe it's the height of rudeness to be late for appointments or time slots. I prefer to be two hours early rather than two minutes late. Obviously, there are times due to unforeseen circumstances I will be late – in these rare cases a phone call or message explaining the situation is the right thing to do. Knowledge, or should we call it trivia, is something I like to gain. I have had my moments of success in quiz games and generally feel I know a lot of useless information.

Patience is a virtue, and I consider myself a patient person. Perhaps patience splices in with the appearance of being laid back. I don't know the answer to this, that's for others to comment for or against. I wouldn't describe myself as opinionated, but I do have opinions, just like other people.

I may not necessarily have the right opinion, but it's mine and I try to respect other points of view, I feel this makes me open minded. I rarely spend hours arguing opinions; if someone insists their judgement is right, why argue for an hour just to end up still disagreeing. I believe the best method to stop an argument is to agree verbally with your fellow debater. This does not mean you comply inside, but it does abruptly stop a waste of time spending an hour or so ruminating, only to end up some time later with the same conflicting viewpoint. I am an emotional guy; I find it very difficult to hide my feelings. You could say I wear my heart on my sleeve. Whether I'm sad, happy, angry (seldom), joyous, depressed, jealous, annoyed, frustrated or mindful, you will be able to detect how I feel by my body language and the way I respond to situations. Is this a good or bad thing? I don't know, it's just the way I function. I am a family man, a loving son, husband and father. I try to see the good in everyone and every situation, but because of this I sometimes naively take people at their word which on occasions can lead to me being betrayed, disappointed and deceived.

It would be a very interesting exercise for somebody who knows me well to write a similar piece describing their opinion of me before reading this narrative. All I have written is what I feel to be an honest account, which has been quite a humbling challenge. I am a believer in right from wrong, in fairness, politeness, consideration, humour, discipline, respect, honesty and like to think I am a popular human being. If I am right or wrong that is for the reader to decide. I understand I cannot be liked by everyone, which I accept. There is much more to my character and makeup than I have covered, all with stories and examples proving a point, but if I did a complete synopsis, it would fill a book of encyclopaedic proportions. This I appreciate, we all have intricated, elaborate, individual and complex personalities and what I have described are the backbone of mine. All this is:

"My opinion of me"!

DEATH

This I find a strange subject to discuss as most people don't want to talk about it. Many seem to believe if it's mentioned or talked about you are tempting fate and the whole procedure will miraculously be brought forward. I have never heard it said he or she died because they were talking about death last week.

I consider myself fortunate that I haven't lost a close loved one to death and I've lived 63 years so far. I have never experienced sitting in a long black limousine following a hearse. I have of course been to many funerals and shed tears, but never as I say for a close relative. When someone who you see regularly, live with or plays a major part in your life dies, I think the grief is harder than when someone you have a close connection with, but you don't see very often, dies. It's the living with, and the missing of an individual that leaves a void in your daily life which hurts the most. Like out of sight, out of mind makes it slightly easier because it's sad they've gone but not a lot different to the relationship which does not involve daily or weekly contact.

After dealing with death more than once in my firefighting career it is not something you get used to, but you just deal with it. I remember going to a Road Traffic Collision (RTC) early in my career, it was a particularly bad incident where four out of five young males lost their lives in one vehicle. As a team we just dealt with the carnage alongside the ambulance staff, we did what we had to do. As the victims were being transported to the hospital, I stood in the middle of the closed dual carriageway, thinking of those young men. How less than an hour before the incident they were all probably chatting, laughing and as alive as you and I. Talking about upcoming plans, holidays, or nights out, not knowing they would not be with us within the hour. That is the side of death I struggled with for a long time, the realisation that life can end within the next hour is quite a sobering reality. We all get up in the morning feeling invincible, not ever contemplating it could be our last day in this life, but it happens every day, the fire service taught me that. It is important to enjoy life and make the most of it. While embracing the present, it is also prudent to prepare for the future by setting aside resources for tomorrow. I've always said my plan is to be one million pounds in debt the night before I die, the only problem with this philosophy is getting the timing right and of course leaving the debt to your loved ones left behind.

I think a lot of people turn to faith or religion to cope with the prospect of death. An elderly member of one church congregation I attended wondered,

"Looking at the average age of everyone here, how many attend church as some sort of insurance policy?"

I also believe you should look after number one, ie yourself, as self-preservation. To illustrate this point, I often use the analogy: "If an armed individual entered this room and stated, 'I have only one bullet, and it is intended for one of you two,' my opinion is this, as much as I care about

THE WORLD ACCORDING TO ANDY CARTER

you, I am sorry, but it has to be you." Most individuals I have communicated this to have understood and accepted the point I am attempting to make. In fact, the vast majority indicate that, from their perspective, it would be me receiving the bullet. That is until I said it to a devout Christian friend who I am very fond of. Her answer to the gunman scenario would be opposite to mine and she would willingly take the bullet so I would survive. Why? I asked. Her answer floored me; 'Because I know where I'm going and it's a far better place!' Wow! To have a faith like that I find astounding, it shook me. I think faith is a personal thing which can be very private and confidential. A Christian believer and an atheist were discussing whether there was life after death. The atheist believed that death is like before birth: nothingness. To which the Christian said,

"If I'm wrong when death happens, what have I lost? But if you're wrong, you are in trouble."

Mmm, now there's a thought, or even insurance.

It is inevitable that there is a date in the future when my demise will happen, Dad has taught me 'not to worry about something you have no control over'. It will happen; I can't do anything about it so why worry? Using his wise words death does not scare or faze me, in fact because of what is happening in the world at present, wars, unrest, pandemics, cost of living crisis, and people generally being unsafe and unkind, you could be forgiven for thinking death could be some sort of relief. I must stress I do not advocate this theory and will not be trying to end my life prematurely, because like most other people I possess a self-preservation system within, meaning I will do almost anything to survive.

Suicide, I feel, is the saddest thing anyone can do, to find yourself in a mental state where death is the best option must be awful, the desperate state people who commit suicide are in I think is unfathomable. I cannot empathize with the mindset that perceives death as the only solution in any situation. I believe a lot of attempted suicides are a cry for help, and some suicide is a plea for help gone wrong, meaning the victim doesn't really intend to end it all. I believe I wouldn't have the courage to carry out suicide, but we never know when we would end up in the mental state required to contemplate such an action. No matter how bad life seems to be, there are too many good things and good people to leave prematurely. I do think though, that those people in constant pain, those whose quality of life has been changed through injury or disease, should have the right to decide whether to end their life prematurely and with dignity if they so wish. It's their life and they should be allowed to do with it as they wish, not having some do-gooder telling them they should live a life with their unbearable pain. We put animals out of their pain for humanitarian reasons, it's the kindest thing to do, yet insist on keeping humans surviving and suffering for so called moral reasons.

Society has itself to blame for the suicide rates rising, the young people of today seem to be taught that if they have a bad day, or things in their life don't turn out as planned or even somebody disagrees with an opinion or action their mental health could be an issue. This involves interpreting small problems as large problems. In my youth we were taught to 'grow a pair', man or woman up, deal with it and move on. Please don't get me wrong, there are people who have dreadful mental health issues and are in need of professional help who should not be disparaged, but having a bad day at work or school, arriving home feeling low or under a cloud is not in my opinion a major mental health issue, yet one of the most common questions asked these days seems to be 'how's your mood?'.

So, what would I like at my funeral? Good question! What an individual wants and what an individual gets can be two complete opposites. At the end of the day how can you put in a complaint if the family you leave behind don't carry out your wishes? Should funerals benefit the deceased or help loved ones cope, with the passing? When I first met Julie, she was adamant about being buried and taken to the cemetery by two black horses with plumes, in a glass horse-drawn carriage. "Over my dead body!" I said to which she replied, "No, Andy, over mine!" She has since changed her mind, and now would like to be cremated. Playing the devil's advocate, I may choose to bury her and have the horses, assuming I don't go first!

At my aunt's funeral, I asked the director to arrange my funeral. Later, at a colleague's funeral, I asked the celebrant, another former firefighter who I know well, to preside over my service. First problem, both said they would willingly oblige but what date did I have in mind? A question I could not answer. Additionally, it is possible that I may outlive the proposed officials, which presents another minor obstacle.

My only stipulation I have for my funeral is that when I am transported to the crematorium on my 'last trip' I request wholeheartedly and without jest that the hearse is driven at road speed or even faster. I DO NOT want it travelling at 20 mile an hour holding up all the traffic. As a driver I have spent too many hours stuck behind a funeral cortege in queues of traffic because everybody believes the deceased's last journey should be long and slow…well not mine thank you, let the public get on with their daily lives without me, in a box, holding them up.

Now for the music, which for me is quite simple, I would like four songs. I wish to be brought into the crematorium to the tune, "Everybody Hurts" by R.E.M., along with two hymns "Abide with Me" and "How Great Thou Art". If I'm only allowed one song, it would be Abide with Me. To sum up my character and the happiness life has brought me, I would like everyone to walk out to the tune 'If You're Happy and You Know It Clap Your Hands'. I understand guests may be shocked at this last choice but it's all me. I have always aimed to be happy, trying each day to wear a smile. We sang this song at every campfire we led while being a scout leader, and I hope attendees leave the funeral with a wry smile and perhaps a chuckle, recalling the good times we shared. This I would prefer than people leaving in floods of tears, aren't I a presumptuous git? It may be hard for my loved ones as my demise will be the end of me, but I would like my jollity and efforts in life to be celebrated and not mourned.

Lastly, I would like to leave a sum of money behind the bar at the wake so everyone can have a drink on me and raise a glass saying,

"To Andy! It's about bloody time we got a drink out of the old bugger!" Some people I know will suggest they have been waiting all my life to get a drink out of me! I would like my ashes sprinkled in the penalty box at the Kop end at Valley Parade Football Stadium. Whether all that I have requested will be fulfilled depends on those I leave behind. I may not be present, but it is possible that I will be observing.

THE WORLD ACCORDING TO ANDY CARTER

From a purely self-indulgent point of view, I hope the end of life is like the film 'Ghost' where the character played by Patrick Swayze is still around in spirit for a week after his death before he is taken off to the spirit world. Just to be able to see who turns up at your funeral and hear what is said about you could be quite self-gratifying.

Having expressed my thoughts, I understand that the passing of anyone is a solemn event. There is no return from it, at least not yet. Therefore, it is important to make the most of the one life we have, as it is not a rehearsal. You don't have to fill every minute for the sake of it as long as you're happy. Just be sure the day before your life ends you can say,

"Well! That's bin a gud 'un!"

ERIC AND THE BOTTLE

T he phone rang, it was Eric.
"Hi Andy, it's Eric, would it be possible to do some shopping for me?"

"Yes," I replied. "Have you got a list?"

"I have, could you get me a bottle of Campari, Kevin likes it, four tins of Hobgoblin Red, two bottles of Sainsbury's lemonade, a two-litre bottle of coke, two bottles of tonic water and half a dozen eggs?"

"Not a problem," I said, writing it down, "I'll be with you sometime this afternoon." It was a lovely day, so I decided to walk the two-and-a-half-mile round trip, to Sainsbury's, buy the goods, then walk home via Eric's. Because the list was full of liquid products, including the eggs, I decided to take a small rucksack so I could put it on my back rather than struggle with two or three heavy carrier bags clinking, clanking and banging round my legs all the way to Westfield Lane.

I located the items, put them through self-scan, where a lady verified my age due to the alcohol, put them in the rucksack, paid and headed for the exit. As I left the store along with numerous other shoppers, the whole place was hit by a deafening crescendo of sirens, bells and flashing lights. The shoplifting alarm had been actuated. Everybody paused with perplexed faces, looked towards the security guard who strolled over wearing a frown and looked in the first shopper's bag. As he was doing this, everybody else continued through the doors with no apparent guilt. I just kept walking with purpose; totally oblivious it was me that was the cause.

Eric was pleased to see me when I arrived and invited me in, I emptied the contents of the rucksack onto the kitchen worktop. Quite quickly it became apparent there was a problem. The Campari bottle still had its security cap firmly slotted over the bottle top and neck. This security device is best described as a thick clear plastic sheath which fit very snuggly on the top of the bottle.

"Oh no!" I exclaimed. "I forgot to get the security tab removed."

"I'm sure between us we can sort it out," said Eric. "I've got a Dremel."

At this point he produced what can best be described as a dentist drill with a small circular saw, about the diameter of an old sixpence on the end. For the next 40 minutes it was like a scene from a Laurel and Hardy film. Taking turns, one holding the bottle while the other attacked the plastic top with the Dremel, which was comparable to sanding wood with a dishcloth. A 90-year-old engineer and a 60-year-old with no practical knowhow attempting to remove this simple but awkward security cap. At this point I realised it was me responsible for the bells and sirens activating at the supermarket. It was me who was the shoplifter, although I had paid for the items, it was me who should have been arrested and marched away which Eric thought was highly amusing, suggesting a prison term all for a bottle of Campari and a four-pack of Hobgoblin would not have looked good on my CV.

Dremel, screwdrivers, even pliers were used with ponderous progress. Eventually the cap succumbed to the results of our labour by being prised off with a screwdriver. Unfortunately, the bottle also had enough of our attempt and cracked due to the unprecedented forces being applied to it as leverage for the screwdriver.

"At last," I shouted.

"That took some doing," said Eric with a calm tone.

"Yes, it was quite secure, but it still didn't prevent me leaving the supermarket with it in my rucksack."

At this point we both burst into fits of laughter, realising the trouble a simple oversight could cause. Still laughing I said my goodbyes and with a wave set off to walk over the fields, home.

www.ingramcontent.com/pod-product-compliance
Lightning Source LLC
Chambersburg PA
CBHW071300110426
42743CB00042B/1121